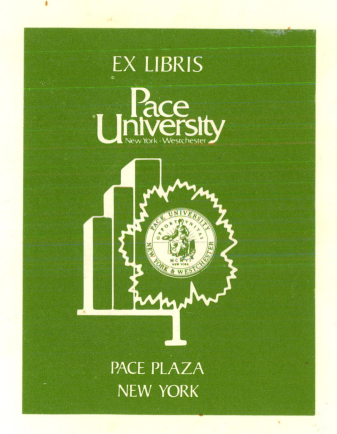

KAZANTZAKIS and the Linguistic

Revolution in Greek Literature

PRINCETON ESSAYS
IN EUROPEAN AND
COMPARATIVE LITERATURE

ADVISORY COMMITTEE
Robert Fagles
Claudio Guillen
Simon Karlinsky
Theodore Ziolkowski

KAZANTZAKIS and the Linguistic

Revolution in Greek Literature / by Peter Bien

Princeton University Press / Princeton, New Jersey

Copyright © 1972 by Princeton University Press
ALL RIGHTS RESERVED
L.C.C.: 79-154991
I.S.B.N.: 0-691-06206-4

*Publication of this book has been aided by the
Research Fund of Dartmouth College
and by the Whitney Darrow Publication
Reserve Fund of Princeton University Press*

This book has been composed in Linotype Granjon

Printed in the United States of America
by Princeton University Press, Princeton, N.J.

To Christos Alexiou

DEMOTICIST AND HUMANIST

Prefatory Note

The source materials, indicated in footnotes, are identified only by the author's name or an abbreviated title. For full data, see the Bibliography.

In transliterating Greek words, I have not followed a particular system or mystique, but have simply tried to make the English equivalent sound more or less like the Greek, except where the resulting confusion would seem to outweigh the gains. The letter "i" must always be pronounced "ee" as in *machine*.

An abbreviated version of this monograph was delivered at the 1969 symposium of the Modern Greek Studies Association, and at the University of Birmingham (England) in connection with its ambitious program in neohellenic studies.

The manuscript was read in whole or part by Evro Layton, Costas Proussis, Christos and Margaret Alexiou, Constantine Trypanis, Helen Kazantzakis, I. Th. Kakridis, and Alfred Vincent. For their effort and for the many suggestions they offered, I give sincere thanks. I would also like to thank Pandelis Prevelakis, who first suggested the need for a study of Kazantzakis' demoticism, and the librarians of the University of Salonika, the National Library in Athens, Woodbrooke College (Birmingham), the University of Birmingham, Harvard University, and Dartmouth College. Leave-time for research and writing was made possible by grants from the Danforth Foundation and Dartmouth College.

I am indebted to the following for permission to use copyrighted material: Helen Kazantzakis, Richard Clogg, and the Institute of Neohellenic Studies at the University of Salonika.

Woodbrooke
December 1970

Contents

KAZANTZAKIS and the Linguistic

Revolution in Greek Literature

Prologue

In choosing as my subject the demoticism of Kazantzakis, I
hope to present this Greek writer in a much broader way than
he is usually seen. Most people in the English-speaking world
know Kazantzakis only from his novels, which represent just
the last sixteen years of his fifty-one-year career, and they know
the novels only in translation. Even Greeks and others who
read his books in the original may be unaware of Kazantzakis'
earlier career and in particular of the role that the language
question played in that career. My object therefore is really
twofold: (1) to give a sense of Kazantzakis' zealous involvement with demotic over the entire length of his active professional life, and (2) to provide the necessary background so

that we may comprehend why demoticism arose and what forms it took.

If we study Kazantzakis apart from demoticism we severely limit our understanding not only of him but of the general conditions of Greek literary life. Linguistic problems have been intimately connected with literary ones in Greece, and with political life as well; indeed "the foreign investigator of modern Greek literature will most likely be astonished at the insistence with which the language question manifests itself at every turn of Greece's intellectual life."[1] It is vital for us to realize that the problem of language obsessed Kazantzakis from the very start and that this obsession was one of the few constants stretching unchanged throughout all the other permutations of his career. Since he is a prime example of the three-way tie uniting politics, language, and literature, a study of his role in the linguistic revolution provides a convenient entry into the general atmosphere of his times in Greece, in which all of the writers of his period were forced to work. It will also teach us basic things about his own achievements.

How strange, then, that Kazantzakis said next to nothing about his demoticism in his autobiography, *Report to Greco*. But this silence does not mean that he became indifferent to this aspect of his "struggle"; on the contrary, there is ample evidence elsewhere to show his continuing obsession with the language question. What it does mean is that it behooves us to fill in this gap and to offer a counterbalance to the many studies that see Kazantzakis only in terms of his supposedly nihilistic philosophy, his politics, metaphysics, or prophetic zeal. My own feeling is that Kazantzakis, like all true artists, was driven by an addiction to language. He himself would no doubt claim that his search for God was the single most basic incentive for his career; I would make bold to say (along with

1. Hourmouzios, p. 1,444.

D. H. Lawrence): "Never trust the artist. Trust the tale."[2]
The totality of Kazantzakis' work seems to have as its common
denominator—perhaps even more than the search for God,
even more than political or humanitarian zeal—a determination to mobilize the twenty-four recalcitrant letters of the
Greek alphabet and make them express his complicated soul.

The addiction was not to language in general, but specifically to demotic Greek. We can appreciate this all the better
if we remember that a writer who works in and loves Greek
does not find himself in the same situation as a writer who
works in and loves English. In the latter case, a successful author is assured a huge readership in the original, and most
likely eventual translation into other major tongues. Conrad
and Nabokov are examples. But a Greek who writes in and
loves Greek assures himself of a readership of two or three
thousand if he is lucky, and is destined in almost all instances to remain completely unknown outside his own country. Kazantzakis was consummate in French and could have
adopted this major foreign tongue—as did the Greek poet
known as Moréas—if he had so desired; indeed, he had every
reason to wish to abandon Greece and the Greek language, not
only after the Civil War in 1946, but as far back as 1920, when
the fall of Venizelos nullified all of his linguistic efforts up
to that time, initiated in him an abiding hatred of "official
Greeks," and encouraged him to try to make a career for himself in western Europe (though he never wished to leave
Greece for good).

In addition, we must remember that Kazantzakis had ambitions to become world famous. All these factors would have
justified an abandonment of the Greek language, and indeed
Kazantzakis did write several books directly in French, as we
shall see. His entire being as a literary man, however, was de-

2. Lawrence, p. 2.

pendent on Greek—on the whole of Greek culture and civilization, it is true, but most basically on the language itself as an
expressive medium. The result is that even at the times of his
most intense scorn for everything Greek, demotic remained an
obsession which controlled him.

Throughout most of his career Kazantzakis cultivated a
pose that denigrated these purely linguistic and artistic factors.
But it is hard to maintain a pose continually; sometimes an
unsuspected remark or provocation will call forth the poseur's
own very deep need to be sincere. Kazantzakis, who had equally strong needs for posing and for sincerity, continually gave
himself away. At the very end of his career, for example, he
replied to a friend's letter: "You write that of all my toil, that
which remains is my labor in the demotic language. I believe
you are right. Theories are transient; the only things that resist time are poetry and linguistic perfection."[3]

This was in 1957. A few years before, in the period after
the Civil War when the self-exiled Kazantzakis found himself persecuted as a communist, traitor, and anti-Christ, he
was provoked into hitting back, much as poor Mr. Bloom is
finally provoked by the ultra-nationalistic Citizen at the end of
Joyce's Cyclops episode. Kazantzakis proudly shouted: "I am
reviled as an EAM-Bulgarian and an unethical traitor. Immortal Greeks: I have sacrificed my entire life for the spirit of
Greece; I have labored passionately in the Greek language and
the Greek tradition. My conscience is clear. . . ."[4] Still earlier,
in a tone more sarcastic and plaintive than bluntly pugnacious,
he wrote to Börge Knös: "And so, here I sit, exiled in the paradise of Antipolis, laboring on the Modern Greek language and
spirit to the best of my ability. For forty years now, I've been
doing nothing else—with no reward except tremendous perse-

3. Synadinou, p. 224.   4. Dimos Irakleiou, p. 31.

cution by the official Greeks."[5] In these moments of extreme provocation, Kazantzakis spoke not of God, or philosophy or politics, but of the artistic drive within him: his involvement with the Greek language.

Actually, Kazantzakis attested to his love of demotic all through his career, despite his public pose of disinterest in purely artistic factors. On occasion he seemed defensive about his relation to language, as though his mother tongue were a kind of trap—"If only I didn't love our demotic tongue so much, if only I could avoid returning to Greece"[6]—but generally he spoke in fully positive terms, especially in the years preceding 1920, and then again from the early 1940's until his death. His various statements about demotic record not only his aesthetic enjoyment of the language, but the sense of urgency and exhilaration of one who wages a holy crusade. In *Journey to the Morea* he tells this characteristic anecdote about a visit he once made to Sparta with the poet Sikelianos:

. . . A curious flower upon a fence had caught our eye; we stopped to pluck it. Children clustered around us.

"What do you call this flower?" we asked.

No one knew. Then a dark-haired little boy jumped up: "Auntie Lenio will know!" he said.

"Run and call her!" we told him.

The little boy ran off toward the town, and we waited, holding the flower. We admired it, sniffed it, but were impatient; we longed for the word. And then, in a short while, the boy returned.

"Auntie Lenio," he said, "died the other day."

Our hearts constricted. We sensed that a word had perished; perished, and now no one could place it in a verse

5. *Biography*, p. 485. 6. Prevelakis, p. 103.

and render it immortal. We were terrified. Never had death seemed to us so irrevocable. And we left the flower spread out on the fence, like a corpse.[7]

In an interview in which he recounted the same anecdote, Kazantzakis then added: "I adore demotic. . . . For forty years I have toured the villages, gathering words. Κρυφοπαχιά: what a lovely word—the woman who has flesh where it is needed."[8] Or μεράστρα, meaning whore, because like the μεράστρι, the Morning Star, she returns home in the wee hours. Kazantzakis then expressed his joy at having translated Homer into demotic, that is, in having been able to find demotic equivalents for every Homeric word. Elsewhere, he said that he persisted in thinking of his translation of the *Iliad* as a "literary monument that will glorify our demotic tongue," and he confessed his joy "at seeing the wealth, harmony, and plasticity of our demotic language. I don't think that I've ever felt a greater sensual pleasure. What a language, what sweetness and power!"[9]

What I would like to do in this study is to document Kazantzakis' long involvement with demotic, to show its permutations, and to reveal how it both hindered and fostered his development as an artist. I wish at the same time to put forth a thesis, as follows:

7. Kazantzakis, *Journey to the Morea*, pp. 89–90. The story is true in the spirit though not in the letter since Kazantzakis began collecting several years before he met Sikelianos. His first wife, Galateia, describes his interest in the tiniest villages of Crete, and his desire to record peasant speech as early as the summer of 1911. Though Galateia's book is an autobiographical novel, not a biography, I think we can accept such details as reasonably accurate. See Kazantzaki, Galateia, p. 146.
8. Yialourakis, p. 161. Cf. *Biography*, p. 18.
9. *Biography*, pp. 519, 514.

1. In the years roughly 1910–1920 Kazantzakis' demoticism existed in a suitable context, but his crusade took more of a political and pedagogical character than a literary one. This period ended in 1920 because it was then that Kazantzakis became severely disillusioned with Greece and began to see himself as a European, cosmopolitan writer.

2. In the years roughly 1920–1940, Kazantzakis continued his demoticism; indeed, language was often his sole link with a Greece that he otherwise disdained. This disdain was augmented because various of his projects on behalf of demotic were frustrated entirely or partially and because the texts that he did manage to publish in an "uncorrected" language were subjected to abuse. All this made him more intransigent than ever, and determined him to apply his exacerbated linguistic zeal to the *Odyssey*, turning it into a paradigm for spelling reform and a repository for thousands of words that might otherwise have been lost. But in its subject matter and ideology the *Odyssey* is very far from what might be called the demotic spirit; indeed some would say that the poem has nothing to do with Greek reality, except in its externals. In other words, Kazantzakis' demoticism—though now manifesting itself in literature and not in pedagogical reform or in politics—still had not found a proper literary context.

3. In the years 1940-1957, years in which Kazantzakis renewed his love of Greece, he provided better literary contexts for his crusading demoticism in (a) his translation of Homer's *Iliad*, and (b) the novels, which attempt to deal with everyday Greek life in a language congruent with the new subject-matter he had found.

I hope to document this thesis by tracing Kazantzakis' linguistic allegiance step by step in terms of specific works and activities. But first I need to present some essential background, for we must view Kazantzakis' relationship to demotic in a

full and proper context. After formulating the language question itself in a brief, generalized way, I shall speak of it in
relation to the European humanist tradition embraced and invoked by Greeks on all sides of the controversy, and shall then
attempt to clarify the various factions among the Greeks themselves, bringing us from roughly 1800 to 1906, when Kazantzakis settled in Athens and began his literary career.

This background material, in Part One, which in effect will
form a tiny and perhaps eccentric history of the language question, may be skimmed or skipped by those already familiar
with the situation, or who find themselves depressed by philological minutiae. Such readers should realize, however, that
my chief purpose in this section is to introduce the many
figures associated directly or indirectly with Kazantzakis. They
may find their curiosity about various people aroused when
they encounter them in the material dealing with Kazantzakis
himself, in which case they may then wish to orient themselves by referring to the index and using the section that follows as a ready-reference. My history is "eccentric" because it
necessarily dwells perhaps disproportionately on those who
affected Kazantzakis directly and whom he himself invoked.
Thus, for example, Dragoumis receives more attention than
Palamas or Solomos, whereas in a general history of the subject the emphasis would be reversed. For those desiring other
surveys there is a more than ample literature.[10]

10. On the language question in particular, the development of
Greek in general, and problems of bilingualism, see: Atkinson;
Bachtin; Browning; Costas; Ferguson; Glinos; Householder; Kordatos, *Istoria*; Megas; Semenov; Thomson, Triantafyllidis; Vlastos,
Greek Bilingualism; Weinreich. A bibliography of books and articles by both demoticists and *katharevousianoi* is in Triantafyllidis,
Eisagogi, pp. 611–44. This monumental book is perhaps the single
most useful volume for those wishing a complete survey with extensive documentation and illustration.

PART ONE

The Historical Background

The Language Question

THE LANGUAGE QUESTION

What was, and is, the language question? It can be formulated most simply as follows: What shall be the language of the Greek state? The question became pressing during the Greek Enlightenment, which preceded and helped foment the War of Independence of 1821, as we shall see in some detail when we discuss the work of the chief representative of the Enlightenment, Adamantios Korais. It may seem self-evident that the language of any new state should be the one that its people speak. But the situation in Greece was, and is, immensely complicated by history, in particular (a) the glorious achievements of the ancient Greeks, achievements that were invoked in order to prod the modern Greeks to free themselves from the Turks; (b) the especial place occupied in the Greek past and present by the *koine* Greek of the first centuries after Christ, since this was the language of the New Testament; (c) the preservation of "official" Byzantine Greek as the medium for the documents of the Orthodox Church; (d) the feeling among some that as the spoken tongue of the uneducated masses of Greeks developed, it was "barbarized" because it assimilated Turkish, Italian, and other foreign words, and underwent grammatical and syntactical changes; (e) the fact that this contemporary spoken idiom—demotic—seemed not to have an extensive written literary tradition to bolster it; (f) the problem of demotic's regional variations, which were sometimes so serious that people from various parts of Greece could not understand each other. This list could doubtlessly be extended, but in the interests of simplicity let us say that the options open to the new Greek state fell into two main categories: some form of "purified" language and some form of demotic.

THE HELLENISTIC AND BYZANTINE LEGACY

We must realize that the problem of Greek bilingualism goes back at least to hellenistic times and was thus something inherited and not invented by the founding fathers of the new state. Alexander's conquests and Greek commercial leadership spread Attic Greek throughout Syria, Persia, and the eastern Mediterranean, where it became the medium not only for business transactions but for education, poetry, philosophy, governmental decrees, and even Jewish scripture.[1] Under these circumstances it was only natural that classical Attic should have undergone considerable changes in vocabulary, syntax, and inflexion. By the time the Old Testament was translated for the Greek-speaking Jews of Alexandria (Septuagint version, begun in the third century B.C.), *koine*—that is, "common"—Greek had established itself; it was to remain the chief international tongue for six hundred years, until the fourth century A.D. Though basically Attic, hellenistic *koine* admitted elements from other dialects and such other languages as Syrian, Hebrew, Aramaic, Latin; lost the difference between long and short vowels; found ways of normalizing irregular declensions; abandoned the dual; weakened the dative; tended to be more analytical in structure; gave new meanings to old words ($\pi\alpha\iota\delta\epsilon\acute{u}\omega$, for example, came to signify "to chastise" alongside its original meaning, "to educate children"); replaced certain classical words with their diminutives ($o\mathring{v}\varsigma$ with $\mathring{\omega}\tau\acute{\iota}o\nu$); and so forth.[2]

This *koine*, the spoken language of the common people throughout the empire of Alexander and his successors, survives not only in the Septuagint Bible but in the bills of sale, letters, school exercises, etc., found in Egyptian papyri[3] of the period, and of course in the New Testament. However, it was not the accepted medium for writing, since a bilingualism—or really a trilingualism—developed during the early Roman

1. The historical survey that follows is drawn from Kordatos, *Istoria*, pp. 11–26; Triantafyllidis, *Stathmoi* and *Eisagogi*; Browning.

2. For a full catalogue of changes, see Triantafyllidis, *Eisagogi*, pp. 10–14; Browning, pp. 31–49.

3. For texts, see Triantafyllidis, *Eisagogi*, pp. 183–95. Each sample is accompanied by an analysis of the linguistic changes from Attic.

period, especially among the educated Greeks and Greek-speaking people living in Rome itself. These people came in touch with the classical tradition by means of literature, orators, and philosophy, whereas the masses throughout the Greek-speaking areas no longer went to theatres or academies, and lost touch with the tradition. The educated deplored the ways in which popular *koine* had been depleted of classical vocabulary, especially in the abstractions necessary for philosophical discourse. Thus by the first century A.D. we find an Atticizing movement gathering momentum, with Dionysius of Halicarnassus the earliest leader and Phrynichus of Bithynia the theoretician. By Phrynichus' time (ca. A.D. 200) it is clear that Atticism had become formalistic, with every departure from the classical language considered barbaric. Phrynichus censured ὀπωροπώλης (fruit-dealer) for example, as fitting only for "people of the marketplace"; the educated must say ὀπωρώνης. He condemned ψύλλος (flea) as barbarous because, for the ancients, this insect was feminine: ψύλλα.[4] We shall meet this same kind of formalism again when we come to Kontos' *Linguistic Observations* seventeen centuries later.

That a true diglossia had developed is evident not only from the disparity between Atticistic texts and the New Testament, but from the testimony of the philosopher Sextus Empiricus, who tells us that the purists spoke Attic among themselves and employed it for their lectures, but were forced to use the *koine* when addressing the common people.[5] To their servants they said πανάριον ("bread-basket," from Latin *panarium*), to each other ἀρτοφόριον.

Atticism, however, had no effect on the spoken tongue in

---

4. *Eclogae nominum et verborum Atticorum*, §181, 308. See Rutherford. Numerous citations are in Triantafyllidis, *Eisagogi*, pp. 17, 405–18.

5. *Adversus Mathematicos*, sec. I, par. 234.

general. Moreover, its excesses were resisted by many writers, who employed an "educated" *koine* that retained Attic characteristics but was not a dead language. Thus we have the triglossia mentioned earlier: (a) Atticism, (b) the educated *koine* of writers like Plutarch, Galen, and Marcus Aurelius, and (c) the popular *koine* used in most of the New Testament. When Paul went to the marketplace, we should remember, he discoursed not only with the Epicurean and Stoic philosophers but with casual passers-by (διελέγετο . . . ἐν τῇ ἀγορᾷ . . . πρὸς τοὺς παρατυγχάνοντας); we know that he aspired to proclaim God's truth without a high-flown display of words or wisdom (οὐ καθ' ὑπεροχὴν λόγου ἢ σοφίας καταγγέλων).[6] Groups (a) and (b) fought each other, the Atticists attacking Plutarch and being satirized for their pedantries by Galen and even by the Atticistic Lucian.[7] Although Atticism was strong, affecting even its opponents, it could not survive the inexorable eclipse of pagan culture by Christianity, an eclipse that involved the burning of libraries and that became total in 529 with Justinian's decree closing the heathen philosophic academies.

Meanwhile, however, the Church had begun to favor the educated *koine* with its Attic elements. There are hints of this tendency in the New Testament itself. Luke, though certainly not an Atticizer, employs language more traditional than Mark's. His vocabulary is richer, he clings to the dative (some-

6. Acts 17:17; I Cor. 2:1. The language of the New Testament is analyzed in Triantafyllidis, *Eisagogi*, pp. 19–20 and 411–18, where he shows how it departed from the prescriptions of Phrynichus. Also Browning, p. 53.

7. Kordatos, *Istoria*, p. 14. Plutarch defended himself in *Peri tou akouein*, IX, 42 c-e. Galen, VI, 633.4K; XIV, 624.17K; VIII, 581–88K. See Browning, p. 51. See Lucian's *Lexiphanes*, 21–25, and his *Rhetorum praeceptor*, 14–28. Triantafyllidis, *Stathmoi*, p. 318, cites the *Pseudosophista*.

times using it erroneously),[8] and he likes to substitute Greek words[9] for Mark's foreign ones (e.g. ἑκατοντάρχης instead of κεντυρίων, Latin centurion). The non-Pauline Epistle to the Hebrews, a theological dissertation, employs complicated syntax and broad vocabulary, as students struggling with New Testament Greek learn to their dismay. In general, however, the New Testament was composed in the contemporary spoken idiom, as were the Apocrypha and the writings of the earliest Fathers. But from the second century onward, Christian apologists embraced the learned type of *koine*. This was natural, since they were attempting to make their religion comprehensible to those schooled in Greek philosophy and since they wished to counteract the charge that Christians were illiterate.[10] It is essential to realize that these learned churchmen became the channel through which bilingualism was perpetuated. We have seen that the Atticists spoke one language among themselves and another to their servants. Similarly, so the story goes, John Chrysostom once had to halt one of his sermons and continue in the vernacular because a simple woman in the congregation complained that he was incomprehensible.[11] The Church, at the very moment when it was defeating paganism, paradoxically carried forward the bilingualism of its pagan enemies who had despised the New Testament as unsophisticated and semi-literate.

Thus by the early Byzantine period Atticism proper had run

8. Luke 4:1. Cf. Mark 1:12, Matt. 4:1. Cited by Browning, p. 42.

9. Luke 7:6; Mark 15:39, 44 ff. Browning, p. 46, gives other examples.

10. Triantafyllidis, *Eisagogi*, pp. 418–22, gives citations from Origen, Chrysostom, Basil, etc., in Migne, *Patrologia Graeca*, vol. 78: 1,080, 1,124, 1,500; vol. 83: 784, 946; vol. 32: 1,084; vol. 61: 25, 27a; vol. 62: 485; vol. 11: 776. Browning, p. 54, invokes Clement of Alexandria (3rd century).

11. Browning, p. 55.

its course and the educated *koine* had become the official instrument of religion. During the thousand years of the Eastern
Empire this educated *koine* became an artificially preserved
written language used for documents of church and state, no
longer resembling the spoken tongue even of the educated
classes. The popular speech of the masses—preserved, as we
shall see, in Ptohoprodromos and elsewhere—was scorned. To
complicate things still further, a new movement to employ
Attic gathered increasing force, especially after classical studies were resumed in the ninth century; this movement became dominant under the Comnenoi and the Palaiologoi
(eleventh to fifteenth centuries). Perhaps the most extreme
representative of the new Atticism was Anna Comneni, ἡ "τὸ
ἑλληνίζειν ἐς ἄκρον ἐσπουδακυῖα,"[12] as she characterized her-
self. At a time when some people, at least, were talking like
this:

    Ἀνάθεμαν τὰ γράμματα, Χριστέ, καὶ ὅπου τὰ θέλει!
    ἀνάθεμαν καὶ τὸν καιρὸν καὶ ἐκείνην τὴν ἡμέραν
    καθ' ἣν μὲ παρεδώκασιν εἰς τὸ διδασκαλεῖον,
    πρὸς τὸ νὰ μάθω γράμματα, τάχα νὰ ζῶ ἀπ' ἐκεῖνα!
                         (Ptohoprodromos)[13]

Anna Comneni in her *Alexiás* was writing like this:

    . . . βοησάντων δὲ πάντων τὸ "ὁ θεὸς μεθ' ἡμῶν" ὅλους
    ῥυτῆρας κατ' αὐτοῦ τοῦ Κουρπαγᾶ ἐνέδωκεν ἐπί τινος
    λόφου ἱσταμένου, εὐθὺς οὖν τοὺς κατὰ πρόσωπον αὐτῶν
    ὑπαντιάσαντας τοῖς δόρασι βαλόντες κατὰ γῆς ἔρριψαν.[14]

By the fall of Constantinople in 1453 we thus have triglossia

12. Triantafyllidis, *Eisagogi*, pp. 42, 219–20.
13. Cited in Triantafyllidis, *Eisagogi*, p. 206, from Hesseling-
Pernot, eds., *Poèmes prodromiques*, ιν, p. 72.
14. Cited in Triantafyllidis, *Eisagogi*, p. 220, from Bk. xi, ch.
6. The work dates from the start of the 12th century.

once more—Atticistic, official ecclesiastic, and various spoken dialects (for the popular *koine* of the hellenistic, Roman, and early Byzantine periods had lost its unity as the Empire itself devolved into half-independent states in poor contact with one another).[15] After the fall of Constantinople, Atticism was weakened; yet it continued to find adherents among the surviving aristocracy, the Phanariots. (Consider, for example, Alexander Mavrogordatos' impeccably Atticistic letters to his sons, exhorting them to shun the degenerate Greek of the marketplace: Τοῖς παισὶν εὖ πράττειν. Ἕως πότε τῇ χύδην, ὦ ποθεινότατοι, καὶ ἀγοραίᾳ διαλέκτῳ λεσχηνεύοντες οὐ παύεσθε;)[16] The Church clung to its fossilized idiom for official documents and of course recited the Gospel in the original language, which, though "uneducated" when first used, had by this time become still another artificially preserved tongue that had to be studied to be understood. The speech of the people continued to go the way of regionalism, while at the same time clearly remaining one language.[17] Following the liberation from the Ottomans, Peloponnesian Greek became the favored idiom in the capital at Nauplion and eventually in Athens after the government was transferred there in 1834. This triglossia was the complicated legacy that history gave to the fathers of the new Greek state. The warriors who fought in the Revolution were largely illiterate; they spoke the color-

15. Triantafyllidis, *Eisagogi*, pp. 37–38. A great factor in this diversification was the Fourth Crusade, which resulted in many Greek-speaking provinces coming under Venetian rule.

16. Cited in Triantafyllidis, *Eisagogi*, p. 317. Mavrogordatos' dates are 1636?–1709. Pages 309–23 give other examples of archaizing during the *tourkokratia*.

17. This has been a subject of debate. Those who wished to impose an artificial *koine* on the new state naturally tended to deny the existence of a pan-hellenic demotic and to emphasize regional differences.

ful demotic that comes down to us in the memoirs of Kolokotronis and Makriyannis and in the ballads. The theoreticians were educated men as often as not filled with visions of the golden age of Hellas resurrected. The Church saw the revolt as a contest between Christianity and the infidel Turk. Linguistically, therefore, all three elements of the historical triglossia had "claims" on the new state.

The options open, as noted before, were some form of purified language or some form of demotic. In the first half century of the state's existence—as in the period of Enlightenment directly preceding the Revolution—the controversy centered primarily on what form or degree of purification should be effected. Some, as we shall see, wished the new Hellenes to write and even speak the language of their glorious ancestors of the classical age; the Church naturally fought to strengthen and preserve the written Greek of Byzantine times; certain scholars, notably Korais, advocated a "corrected" and purified demotic. In the period from roughly 1880 to the present, the controversy has centered on whether or not any form of purification is justified. The struggle has thus been between demotic and *katharevousa* (the name eventually given to Korais' compromise-language, which was adopted as the official idiom of the new state). But just as the purists split into various factions, so did the demoticists. Some, like Psiharis (and Kazantzakis), went out with notebook in hand to record the speech of illiterate peasants, feeling that here they would find "pure" demotic and that this should be the model for the written language; others favored the demotic of more educated speakers. Some, again like Psiharis and Kazantzakis, insisted that the regional differences in Greece were minimal, that written demotic should therefore be drawn from all the various areas of the country and be pan-hellenic. Others campaigned for Athenian demotic as a standard.

These remarks should give an initial idea of the problem, even though I have necessarily omitted the nuances and have presented the various alignments in an over-schematized manner. I trust that at least some of the nuances will emerge as we continue.

RELATION OF THE LANGUAGE QUESTION TO EUROPEAN HUMANISM

What I should like to do now is to view the language question against the backdrop of European humanism. In doing this we shall see one of the strangest and saddest facts about the controversy, namely, that people on opposite sides often shared basic assumptions, their differences being in secondary matters. The most basic assumption that they all shared was expressed by Psiharis in his famous dictum: "Language and fatherland are the same."[18] This dictum, in turn, was a fundamental axiom of the Western humanism out of which emerged not only the radical demoticist Psiharis, but also his opponent Korais and even the most extreme of the reactionary classicists.

By humanism I mean the refusal to see society as part of God's plan; the humanist views society in an empirical, finite, and anthropocentric manner that turns the "earthly kingdom" into a purely natural and secular commonwealth. The precise way in which this view developed in Italy, beginning in the thirteenth century, and was transmitted to Constantinople in the sixteenth and seventeenth and thence to Greek intellectuals everywhere, is succinctly traced by Campbell and Sherrard in their book *Modern Greece* and need not occupy us here.[19] We must realize, simply, that educated Greeks of the late eighteenth and early nineteenth centuries came into inevitable contact with these humanistic ideals of secular liberalism not

18. Psiharis, p. 34.
19. Campbell and Sherrard, pp. 37–40.

only in Constantinople, Chios, and other centers of education in the East, but also in those cities of the West, particularly Paris, where many of these Greeks were furthering their education or pursuing their careers. We must realize as well that this humanism was naturally thought by the Greeks to derive from ancient Hellas, since from the thirteenth century onward the discovery or rediscovery of Greek texts stimulated the secularization and liberalization of thought. In this opinion the Greeks were of course supported by Western classicists and philhellenes.

When neither man nor society is viewed as part of a divine plan, new ways of defining each must be found. The way that became paramount for the Greek Enlightenment, and indeed for subsequent periods of Greek intellectual life down to our own day, was linguistic. For Psiharis, language and fatherland are one; for Korais: "Just as it is true concerning each individual person that 'a man's character is known by his speech,' so, in the same way, the character of an entire nation is known by its language."[20] In the realm of political thought, the criterion of language became the chief way of identifying a nation or people. For Korais and others of the Greek Enlightenment, the modern Greeks were blood-descendants of the ancient Hellenes because they still spoke the Hellenic language. In this, Korais was subscribing to the dictum of his friend Friedrich von Schlegel, "Quot linguae, tot gentes,"[21] and to Herder's claim that nationalities are indestructible natural phenomena whose characteristics are transmitted through the very essence of nationality: language.[22]

But in the background was also the fact that other nations

20. Korais, *Epistoli*, p. 52.
21. Chaconas, p. 49. Also cited in Sherrard, p. 181. The Latin is: "There are as many tongues as races."
22. Chaconas, p. 13.

had defined themselves, and developed a flourishing and creative culture, only when they had begun to write the language
by which their true character could be known. The obvious
examples were Italy in Dante's time and France in the time of
the Pléiade, but there were other examples as well. In all
such cases, the definition of language and of character seemed
to go hand-in-hand, and the change seemed to be away from
a religious conception and toward a humanist (and thus Hellenic) one. In short, European nationalism involved a weak-
ening of the ecumenical language, Latin, and a corresponding
strengthening of the various vernaculars.

This basic equation between nationality and language—an
equation closely identified with Western humanism—was what
all the various Greek linguistic factions shared as a fundamental assumption. Their differences, as I have suggested, lay in
secondary matters. Who, for example, were the Greeks? If
they were blood-descendants of the ancient Hellenes, deflected
from the continuation of Hellenic greatness simply by the acci-
dents of history, then the only language by which their character could be known was ancient Greek. If they were an entirely new breed, both biologically and culturally, and if that
breed had developed its own virtues, then the only language
by which their character could be known was the demotic of
the villages. If they were new and unique, but at the same
time the inheritors and destined preservers of ancient Hellas,
then the only language by which their character could be
known was some mixture of ancient Hellenic with contemporary demotic.

INVOCATIONS OF THE PAST

No matter what the view, the proponents saw themselves within the humanistic tradition in the ways I have indicated, and
felt free to invoke examples from the past. The archaizers in-

voked the hegemony of the Attic dialect as a precondition of the Golden Age, and concluded that modern Greeks must write and even speak Attic. Psiharis invoked the same period, but came to an opposite conclusion. Demosthenes, he argued, used common words and spoke the language of the people. Φανταστῆτε τὸ Δημοστένη νὰ μιλᾷ καθαρέβουσα! ("Can you even imagine Demosthenes speaking katharevousa!")[23] The conclusion, of course, was that modern Greeks should speak demotic. Psiharis reinforced this conclusion by reminding the modern Greeks that the revered ancient language had itself undergone changes. The archaizers admired Homer as much as Plato, and yet "Plato did not speak the same language that Homer spoke, nor that spoken by Menander afterwards."[24] By analogy, the development of modern Greek—its right to alter the forms found in Byzantine Greek and the koine— should be honored.

Korais is a particularly good example of the indiscriminate invoking of the ancients, for as a compromiser he cited them in support of both aspects of his program: demotic's "correction" on the one hand, and its retention on the other. His major energies went toward awakening in the modern Greeks an appreciation of their heritage and with this a desire to adjust their vulgar tongue until it came more in accord with ancient forms. Toward this end he advocated as "the first task in the regulation of the language . . . the purging of truly foreign nouns."[25] But in the same breath he warned that this should be done neither indiscriminately nor completely, "since not even the ancients managed to free their beautiful language from many Arabic, Hebrew, Persian, and even Indian words." Elsewhere, he argued that time alters languages—just as his opponent Psiharis was to argue half a century later—and he

23. Psiharis, p. 207.   24. *Ibid.*, p. 212.
25. Korais, *Atakta*, vol. iv, p. η´.

invoked as witness "the practice of all the enlightened nations" [i.e., of the humanistically advanced nations such as France] which periodically revise their translations, adapting them to the nation's prevailing idiom."[26] (He was justifying his own sample translation of the New Testament into *katharevousa*.) Still more strongly, he asserted: "All one need do is observe the progress of the human spirit in other countries in order to understand that nations can be called enlightened only when they perfect their language. The Italians, French, and English began truly to free themselves from barbarism only when their educated men, at first few, undertook to write in the common idiom."[27]

Psiharis had a different conception of what perfecting one's language meant, but he too cited the Italians and French for living their own life, casting off the Latin past, and honoring their own tongues, whereupon ideas, art, and scholarship followed.[28] He singled out Dante, who "gathered words and variants from various dialects in order to establish a common tongue," and Malherbe, who went to the marketplace to discover correct usage: "Quand un lui demandoit son avis de quelque mot françois, il renvoyoit ordinairement aux crocheteurs du port au Foin, et disoit que c'étoient ses maîtres pour le langage."[29]

Of all the liberalizing and humanizing heroes of the past, Dante was probably the most frequently cited. Solomos invoked him as a champion of the vulgar tongue;[30] Kazantzakis

26. *Ibid.*, vol. III, p. ζ'.
27. Korais, *Epistoli*, pp. 41–42.
28. Psiharis, pp. 61–62.
29. Psiharis, p. 27, citing *Oeuvres de Malherbe* (Paris, 1862), I, lxxix.
30. In his "Dialogue," pp. 16–17. The epigraph is from *Purgatory*, xxvi, 121–23:

A voce più ch' al ver drizzan li volti;

consciously tried to follow in the great Florentine's footsteps. But the period of the Pléiade in France was not overlooked. The demoticist Manolis Triantafyllidis wondered in 1914 whether a book such as Joachim du Bellay's *Défense et illustration de la langue française* (1549) was needed in Greece, citing in particular du Bellay's belief that the French language is not barbarous and is capable of formulating high philosophical ideas.[31] He came to the happy conclusion that the need probably no longer existed, since du Bellay's points had been stated so often in Greece in recent years. I would add here that the situation in France in the sixteenth century was not precisely identical with that in Greece in the nineteenth and twentieth, yet the spirit of du Bellay's endeavor was the same: to honor the vernacular without overlooking its deficiencies, and to try to enrich it.

Of particular interest to us in this consideration of the humanistic assumptions of all the figures we are touching is the fact that du Bellay, like his subsequent counterparts in Greece, felt free to invoke the ancients at the very time he was struggling to escape their deadening influence. In a sense, therefore, he remained under their influence, since he used their own example to show that an artificially imposed literary idiom is deleterious. He speaks, for example, of those Roman "purists" who thought Latin barbarous and thus wished all dignified

---

   e così ferman sua opinione,
   prima ch'arte o ragion per lor s'ascolti.

(To rumor rather than to truth they turn their faces, and thus do fix their opinion ere art or reason is listened to by them.)

See under Solomos, in *Bibliography*. A brilliant paper on the relationship between Solomos and Dante was delivered by Mr. Zissimos Lorenzatos at the 1969 symposium of the Modern Greek Studies Association and is printed in *Modern Greek Writers*.

31. *Apology*, p. 173.

writing to be in Greek. But the "demoticists" prevailed and the Romans enriched and cultivated their own common speech, whereupon their culture flourished. We return to the assumptions of Psiharis and Korais, both of whom invoked and honored the humanistic, liberalizing tradition and especially its fountainhead, the ancient Greeks themselves, in order to prove paradoxically that the ancient Greeks must no longer dominate the moderns.

Du Bellay, Dante, Malherbe, Demosthenes, the Romans—to this list of prototypes, the eclectic polymath Kazantzakis added Luther for his efforts on behalf of a pan-German vernacular and Lomonosov for similar efforts in Russia.[32] Turning to Spain, Kazantzakis sensed his own kinship with the sixteenth-century demoticist Louis de Leon, who was imprisoned for five years for preaching that the people must learn to write in their own language rather than in Latin.[33] Kazantzakis' affinity with de Leon arose not only from philological agreement but also from a shared sense of mission. De Leon was consoled in his imprisonment, Kazantzakis assures us, by the realization that he was witnessing for the truth just as did the persecuted Christians of the early Church. Martyrdom was the price, and also the opportunity, offered by the demotic-humanist struggle.

Kazantzakis' especial affection for Dante can be explained by a feeling of kinship in this regard as well as by philological concern. Dante was exiled and persecuted for his beliefs (though not for his linguistic beliefs); he was a lone, bitter voice crying in the wilderness against the stupidities and perfidies of mankind. Kazantzakis often felt himself in the same position, and was consoled at these times by the memory of Dante. At one point in 1932, for example, when he suspected that he had been double-crossed by a supposed friend in a

32. Kazantzakis, *Syllogos*, p. 12.
33. Kazantzakis, *Spain*, pp. 48–49.

matter connected with his struggles for demotic, he commented: "I often shudder when I see the villainy of even the choicest people. In my whole life I have not encountered even three honorable, pure, sincere men. *Ma non ragioniam di loro . . . Guarda e passa*! How right was that great, proud, distressed man, the Florentine exile!"[34]

In his terzina on Dante,[35] Kazantzakis imagines the Florentine running out to Tuscan villages to collect words, and he imbues him with the same enthusiasm and joy that he himself (inspired by Psiharis) felt when he discovered upon the lips of the people a word which he could then preserve by incorporating it into his writings:

$$. . . \tau\rho o\upsilon\lambda\hat\omega\sigma\alpha$$
$$\tau'\alpha\dot\upsilon\tau\iota\acute\alpha,\ \tau\grave\alpha\ \lambda\acute o\gamma\iota\alpha\ \tau o\hat\upsilon\ \lambda\alpha o\hat\upsilon\ \nu\grave\alpha\ \pi\acute\alpha\rho\epsilon\iota.$$
$$\dot\lq H\ \delta\rho o\sigma\epsilon\rho\grave\eta\ \lambda\alpha\lambda\iota\grave\alpha\ \kappa\iota\ \dot\eta\ \pi\lambda o\acute\upsilon\sigma\iota\alpha\ \gamma\lambda\hat\omega\sigma\sigma\alpha$$
$$\pi\hat\omega\varsigma\ \pi\epsilon\rho\epsilon\chi\acute\alpha\epsilon\iota\ \tau\grave\alpha\ \sigma\pi\lambda\acute\alpha\chi\nu\alpha\ \kappa\alpha\grave\iota\ \tau\grave\alpha\ \phi\rho\alpha\acute\iota\nu\epsilon\iota!$$

. . . cupped his
ears to catch the people's words.
How the refreshing talk and rich language
inundate and delight his bowels!

One of Kazantzakis' cherished projects was the translation of the entire *Divine Comedy* into demotic Greek. This he accomplished in 1932.[36] After his version was published there was the expected controversy over the supposedly radical demotic he had favored.[37] He was accused specifically of employing

34. Prevelakis, p. 296. The passage from Dante, slightly misquoted, is from *Inferno*, iii, 51, and means: "Let us not speak of them, but look and pass."

35. Kazantzakis, *Tertzines*, pp. 101–102.

36. There were subsequent revisions. The terzina on Dante was written in the same year, in honor of the poet Kazantzakis had just translated. See Prevelakis, p. 127.

37. Kazantzakis, *Dante*.

unknown, incomprehensible terms, regionalisms from Crete, and even of coining words arbitrarily.[38] His reply to these charges affords a fine example of the way in which he and the other Greek demoticists (his argument here is hardly original) considered themselves disciples of earlier linguistic reformers in other lands, Dante in particular:

"The rare word, that which has not yet been sufficiently employed in the written language (and not that which is no longer in use, for I employ no such words) lends to the translation the savory substance which certainly, in Dante's time, was possessed by the still-virgin Italian which was scorned by the learned and unused by writers. Our demotic tongue is in a period analogous to that of the Italian demotic of Dante's time. What Dante did, we ought to do also. He said: 'Sixteen great linguistic idioms exist in Italy. The poet must collect words, phrases, and syntactical patterns from all these regional dialects, make a selection, and use them, in this way composing the living, pan-italic, written language.' This is what he said. But since he was a Florentine, he involuntarily emphasized the Florentine idiom most of all; for no one can create—and not only create, but weep, sympathize, rage, love; that is, stir up his soul from the depths—without having recourse to his maternal tongue.

"In translating Dante, I attempted the same task. From the whole of Greece I collected all the linguistical and syntactical material I could, and I made a selection. But since it is my lot to be a Cretan—thank God!—I often unconsciously emphasized our Cretan idiom. I say 'Thank God!' precisely because it seems to me that our Cretan language approximates the strict, resonant, manly language of Dante.

"In the *Divine Comedy*, all the demotic words which seemed

38. Alexiou, L. For other critiques, see Katsimbalis, items 902–908.

rare and unknown became commonplace and well-worn in time, losing the striking nuance of rareness that they possessed when they were first written. I hope that the same will one day happen in our demotic, and that all the words and expressions in my translation that now provoke astonishment will have by then become pan-hellenic, and that only a minimum will remain rare."[39]

I wish to conclude this treatment of the European, humanistic background to Greece's language question by citing and discussing briefly one additional figure, Baldassare Castiglione, whose book *Il Cortegiano* (begun 1508, published 1528) makes fascinating reading for anyone interested in the problems we have been confronting.[40] Though Castiglione was not invoked by any of the Greeks, so far as I know, he seems to me to bring together a great number of the attitudes and arguments we meet among the various factions in Greece, and thus to hammer home the truth that the diverse partisans all had a common home in the Western humanist tradition.[41]

Of particular interest is the fact that in Castiglione's time the demoticism of Dante had congealed into a new *katharevousa* that was ironically playing the same role as the earlier Latin it had sought to displace. Castiglione makes his characters discuss whether good writers should imitate Dante, Petrarch, and Boccaccio, thus employing the often archaic terms of "classic" Tuscan, or whether they should eschew "many old

39. Reprinted in Alexiou, E., pp. 319–24. The reply is called "Letter to Lefteris Alexiou" and is dated Aegina, April 10, 1937. It appeared in *To Kastro* (Irakleion), June 1937, pp. 3–10.

40. Castiglione, pp. 72, 76, 79. (Book 1, sections 29–40.) In the last paragraph I have retained the word "conceits" from the Hoby translation of 1561.

41. Vlastos cites Castiglione in his *Greek Bilingualism* (pp. 25–27) but seems ignorant of *The Courtier*. For him, strangely, Castiglione exemplifies "the mentality of the purist."

Tuscan words," and employ "words in current usage in Tuscany and elsewhere in Italy." In the course of this discussion they touch upon the questions of regionalism, of inevitable linguistic change, of correctness versus comprehensibility; and—as we might have expected—they invoke the ancients each time they wish to justify a position. They observe, for example, that the linguistic arteriosclerosis then evident in Italian can be observed in all languages, including Latin and ancient Greek, where "orators and poets gradually abandoned many of the words employed by their predecessors: for Antonius, Crassus, Hortensius, and Cicero rejected many of Cato's words, and Virgil many of those used by Ennius; and others followed suit." And if Petrarch and Boccaccio themselves were still alive, they too would never speak or write those of their own words that had since fallen out of use. One of the speakers then presents ancient precedent for the development of a common tongue from all the various dialects of Italian, a language "universal, rich and varied, like a delightful garden full of all kinds of flowers and fruits":

"This phenomenon would be nothing new, since from each of the four languages on which they could draw, the Greeks selected whatever words, expressions and figures of speech they wished, and constructed a new so-called common language. . . .

"Among Latin writers . . . Titus Livius was not rejected, even though one critic said that he found traces of Paduan in his work; nor was Virgil, on the grounds that he did not speak the Latin of Rome. . . .

"But we, being far more strict than the ancients, impose on ourselves certain outrageous new laws. . . . For although the function of our own language, as of all the others, is to express well and clearly the conceits of the mind, we take delight in being obscure . . . and . . . employ . . . words that are not understood even by noble and educated men, let alone the common people."

Their conclusion is very sensible. We ought indeed to be selective in the words and syntactical patterns we use, but to select because such terms or figures, even if they abuse the rules of grammar, give "grace and brightness to an oration" and bring "a life and a sweetness" to our ears. Current usage and aesthetic delight become the two rules of thumb.

I cite all these precedents, perhaps somewhat laboriously, because I wish to place Kazantzakis and his fellow demoticists indisputably in a great humanist tradition embracing not only Dante's Italy but other "enlightened" countries of the West, and thus to point up the immense irony whereby the spirit of the demoticists' attempt to suppress *katharevousa* was really not impossibly far from the spirit of Korais and the other more enlightened eighteenth-century humanists who developed *katharevousa* in the first place. In both camps, the object was to enrich the existing vernacular so that it might fulfill its office of expressing well and clearly the conceits of the mind. The differences between the eighteenth-century humanists and the demoticists who later opposed them lay, as I have tried to emphasize, in secondary rather than primary assumptions.

Kazantzakis and the others, unlike their predecessors, realized that a language cannot be degenerate, it can only be in need of lexical enrichment; that usage should determine grammatical laws rather than vice versa; and that the imaginative wealth of the contemporary speaker is a much more meaningful form of dignity than the wealth of speakers dead for two thousand years. Dante, Castiglione, and du Bellay would have seen Kazantzakis and the others as behaving like humanists— indeed like ancient Greeks or Romans—precisely because they wanted modern Greek to be liberated from the deadening influence of antiquated vocabulary and syntax. But, unfortunately, the self-styled defenders of the humanistic heritage, chiefly the professors of Athens University, were too arteriosclerotic in their humanism to be able to see beyond the means to the end. Even when they pressed for the complete Atticization of Greek, they still unknowingly shared with their opponents the humanistic assumption that men and societies are defined by their languages. Psiharis' hated dictum embraced even them.

Failure by many in each of the camps to recognize and stress this common humanistic ground resulted in increasing polarization. Some of the demoticists, as we shall see, linked demoticism to an anti-humanistic nationalism based on an irrational Nietzschean adoration of the Folk; others linked their linguistic crusade with a Marxist adoration of the working class. Though certain figures tried to keep the crusade apolitical, they were in a minority.[42] The outcome, of course, has been the complete tangling of the language question with inflammatory politics, with consequences extremely deleterious for the nation whose progress all factions had hoped to encourage.

42. E.g., Delmouzos. See Sotiriou, pp. 49–52. The Marxist view insists that the language question never *became* political; that it was political from the start, since Korais' language was allegedly a way in which the bourgeois class could assert itself over the peasantry.

Korais

The Situation Leading to Korais

I should like now to dwell upon what was happening among the Greeks themselves, thereby bringing us up to 1906, when Kazantzakis began his career, and introducing us in a more particularized fashion, by means of concrete examples, to the people and issues that formed the inevitable background to that career as far as the language question was concerned.

The period with which we are primarily involved is the whole of the nineteenth century and the end of the eighteenth, although there were some notable demoticist precursors much farther back than that. I cannot, of course, hope to give even a remotely complete account of this vexed subject; for this I refer the reader to the relevant primary works and to the considerable body of secondary material that has already appeared. I shall confine myself to certain basic figures, some of whom I have already introduced, and to basic linguistic examples. Beyond this, I shall dwell perhaps arbitrarily on certain other figures chiefly because they touched Kazantzakis' career in one way or another.

I have already given a brief description of the legacy of bilingualism operating in the late eighteenth century, when the liberal/humanistic movement began to prepare the War of Independence. The Greek peasants, largely illiterate, had been speaking their demotic, singing their wonderful folksongs, and reciting their epics for centuries, but all this was a tradition almost exclusively oral, and in any case these were not the people involved, despite their great hopes for land-reform. Those stimulating the movement for independence were chiefly:

(1) The clergy. They joined not primarily because they were infected with the hellenism of the Enlightenment, but because they wished orthodoxy to be delivered finally from the infidels. Linguistically, as I have already indicated, they considered themselves the preservers of New Testament and Byzantine Greek.

(2) The Phanariots. These were the cosmopolitan, educated, and wealthy group whose ancestors during the centuries of Turkish domination had clustered around the palace of the Orthodox Patriarch, in the Phanar section of Constantinople. They served as the Patriarchate's civil administrators, and

were eventually employed in a similar capacity by the Ottomans as well, throughout the Empire, filling such offices as
dragoman of the Sublime Porte and of the Fleet, prince of
Moldavia, Wallachia, etc. Like the clergy, they saw themselves as a nucleus of continuity between the Byzantine glories
and the reestablished free Greek state of their dreams. But,
unlike the clergy, they were open to secular thinking, and indeed it was this group that became most receptive to the humanistic hellenism deriving from the West. Equating freedom with ancient Hellas, they campaigned for a revival of
classical culture. Since part of their humanism was a belief
in language's definitive role, as discussed earlier, they naturally
tended to advocate various degrees of Atticization of Modern
Greek, although there were some notable exceptions to this
trend.[1]

(3) The merchant-bourgeoisie class.[2] This class had developed over the centuries in centers such as Venice, London,
Paris, Manchester, Leghorn, Vienna, and Marseilles. In contact with enlightened Western thought, and receptive to it because of their own rationalistic values, the members of this
class saw the movement as a chance to oppose vested interests inside Greece. Linguistically they made notable financial
and intellectual contributions to Korais' program for a compromise-language.

The situation in the late eighteenth and early nineteenth
century, then, involved a demotic language almost exclusively
oral, and a written language in forms including Atticistic,

1. For example, Dimitrakis Fotiadis Katartzis, of Phanariot background, active in Greek intellectual circles in Bucharest. In 1782 he
spoke for demotic, calling it the force needed to civilize the Greeks.
He was laughed at for his pains. His ideas came from his study
of the relation between Latin and French. See *Apology*, p. 47.

2. See Campbell and Sherrard, p. 40.

koine, Byzantine, and the various "educated" compromises between the contemporary spoken idiom and these past traditions. No one of the compromises had achieved fixity or become the accepted written language.[3]

EXAMPLES OF WRITTEN DEMOTIC IN CRETE AND THE IONIAN ISLANDS[4]

Before going ahead to see how this situation found a temporary resolution in the compromises of Korais, we must recognize certain qualifications. I have stated that the demotic language, although possessing its own poetic tradition in the form of folksong and epic, was almost exclusively oral. Historical conditions, however, made possible some notable examples of written demotic. Except for some isolated pockets, mainland Greece remained under continuous Turkish rule for almost four hundred years.[5] But Crete did not. After being allotted to Boniface of Montferrat as a result of the Fourth Crusade in 1204, Crete was purchased from him by the Venetians, who held it until 1669, exerting a profound influence on its culture. We should remember that the new humanism that began to develop in Italy in the thirteenth century became intimately associated with Venice when the Venetian state occupied Padua in the early fifteenth century, and thus gained control over the university there, which was the center of the new trends.[6] Cretans began to establish printing presses and other commercial enterprises in Venice in the fifteenth and sixteenth centuries; the schools operating in Crete were staffed to a

3. *Apology,* p. 46.
4. See Kornaros, Hortatsis, *Voskopoula,* Marshall.
5. The Peloponnesus was captured by Venice in 1687 but won back by Turkey in 1715.
6. Campbell and Sherrard, p. 39.

great extent by teachers educated at Padua. In short, the two cultures mingled in such a way that Crete saw a diminution of Byzantine influences and an augmentation of Western ones. This in turn stimulated a flowering of poetry and drama in the late sixteenth and early seventeenth centuries, toward the end of Venetian rule. The works produced, the best known of which is Kornaros' epic romance *Erotokritos*,[7] were modeled to greater or lesser degree on Italian, French, or Latin prototypes, but were written—this is what is important for us—in demotic, offering conclusive proof of the ability of the spoken language to express well and clearly the conceits of the mind.

The products of the seventeenth-century literary flowering in Crete were not direct factors of any significance in the linguistic situation we have been describing, but their indirect influence in the future was immense. To see this influence we must turn to another region that, like Crete, was brought into contact with the West because of historical circumstances, but that, unlike Crete, escaped Turkish rule almost entirely. This was the group of islands in the Ionian Sea off Greece's west coast: Corfu, Levkas, Ithaca, Cephalonia, and Zante. Though the dates vary in each case, most of these Ionian islands were under continuous Venetian rule for three hundred years.[8] Naturally they were affected by Venetian culture, as was

7. This poem has had a curious, amphisbaenic history. On the one hand, it entered the folk culture and has been passed down by illiterate bards; on the other, it was made "respectable" by being paraphrased in *katharevousa* by the Phanariot D. Fotinos, 1818, who did not neglect to atticize some of the characters. Thus the counsellor Phronístas becomes Sophocles!

8. Exact dates of Venetian rule: Corfu 1206–1214, 1386–1797; Levkas 1502–1503, 1684–1797; Ithaca and Cephalonia 1483–1485, 1500–1797; Zante 1482, 1485–1797. The Turks had annexed all but Corfu in 1479.

Crete, but they also developed and preserved their demotic tradition. One stimulus for this was undoubtedly the fact that when Crete fell in 1669, refugees came to settle in the Ionians, bringing with them *Erotokritos*, Hortatsis' blood-and-guts tragedy *Erophile*, the idyll *Voskopoula*, and other works of their own florescence. The situation in the Ionians was to be of crucial importance for the subsequent course of the language question in Greece because it was these islands that produced Dionysios Solomos, the "national poet" and inspirer of a whole school of other Ionian poets who chose demotic as their medium.

Solomos was born in Zante in 1798 and later lived in Corfu. Though Venetian rule had ended in all the islands the year before his birth, he was at first Italianate in culture. Educated in Venice and at the University of Padua, he began writing verse in Italian. But—so the story goes—one night in Zante he heard an old illiterate ballad-singer in the streets, and was so enchanted that he awoke to his true vocation as a Greek poet using demotic, the language of the people. In the interests of neat historical transmission, it would be nice to think that this ballad-singer was a descendant of the Cretan refugees.[9] In any case, we know that *Voskopoula*, at the very least, was known directly by Solomos. This poem, first published in 1627, enjoyed such popularity that large sections of it were incorporated in the demotic ballads. Solomos invoked it in his lovely *Dialogue* in defense of demotic, written sometime between 1823 and 1825.[10] Here, the Poet assures his adversary the Pedant (a disciple of Korais) that even the thrice-learned poet Christopoulos uses words which "are the same as those I find written in *Voskopoula*, a poem of which no woman is ignorant, and which is two hundred years old."

9. See Campbell and Sherrard, p. 221.
10. *Dialogue*, p. 22.

OTHER SURVIVING TEXTS

It is clear that the Cretan texts had begun to permeate Greek culture not only indirectly but directly as well. This process was of course to continue. Seferis, for example, was haunted by the *Erotokritos*, and Kazantzakis presumably ransacked it for words as he did all other surviving texts.[11] Nor were these the only demotic works to survive. There were the oral ballads, first collected by Fauriel and later, as we shall see, by N. G. Politis; there was the Byzantine epic *Digenis Akritas*, the sixteenth-century Cypriot love-poetry published by Legrand in 1881, Machairas' Chronicles (Cyprus, mid-fifteenth century), a *Chronicle of the Morea* dating from the previous century, etc. The twelfth-century poems attributed to Ptohoprodromos were published and analyzed by Korais in an effort to prove to the extreme Atticists that modern Greek was truly a descendant of ancient, and thus needed only to be corrected, not suppressed entirely. As he wrote in 1828, he studied Ptohoprodromos in order to teach himself "how our common tongue differs from the common tongue spoken almost seven hundred years ago; to investigate what it gained and what it lost during this dark interval, and in what ways we may increase the gains and reduce the losses."[12] This same Ptohoprodromos was spread out on Kazantzakis' desk along with the *Chroniko*

11. See: Fauriel, Politis, Digenes Akrites, Legrand, Siapkaras, Machairas, *Chronicle of the Morea*. All the surviving manuscripts of *Digenes Akrites* are in the learned language, but one of them has many demotic characteristics. Some scholars assume that the poem was composed in demotic and then "corrected" in the 300–400 years between its composition and the earliest extant copy. Others feel that it was of a learned character from the start. Bibliography in Dimaras, pp. 504, 506. See the well-known essay in Seferis' *Dokimes*, pp. 207–49.

12. Korais, *Atakta*, 1, p. ε'. In addition to Ptohoprodromos, he invokes all the poets of the 16th, 17th, and 18th centuries. See Korais, *Syllogi*, p. 152.

tou Moreos, Digenis Akritas, and Machairas while he was attempting to pour all the resources of demotic into his translation of Homer's *Iliad.*[13]

Korais

Having examined the above qualifications to the general situation prevailing at the end of the eighteenth and beginning of the nineteenth century, we should be prepared to appreciate the full range of pressures and possibilities that offered themselves to Adamantios Korais when this remarkable man determined to give Greece the single unified and unifying language it needed if it was ever to become a true nation-state. We should also be prepared to appreciate the degree to which compromise—at least at this point in history—had become the unavoidable path. It is to Korais' credit, however, and a measure of his extraordinary energy, that compromise tended to be viewed by him not as a concession, but instead as the appropriate and proper linguistic solution for his people. He argues generally from strength, not weakness.

We should realize from the outset that if Korais' *katharevousa* developed into a curse for the Greeks, it was not so much his fault as that of his supposed followers, in whose hands his principle of correction underwent such a stretching that it elicited "an unbridled purification backwards in the direction of ancient Greek, completely at odds with the basis of his original teaching."[14] Later Atticizers such as P. Soutsos opposed him in principle as well as practice. All told, as the demoticists themselves have been only too happy to declare, it is grotesque for Korais to be invoked as "the father and defender of today's official language."[15]

13. Kakridis, p. 117.
14. *Apology*, p. 56.
15. *Ibid.*

I do not mean to overlook what we, having the advantage of hindsight, would now call the linguistic superstitions of Korais, or the extraordinary contradictions in the pronouncements of this man who considered logical rationality his god. Nevertheless, it is encouraging to see how truly demoticist Korais could sound. Whole sections might be lifted out of his writings and placed in a demoticist manifesto (provided that his corrected language was first uncorrected). Even with all the superstitions and contradictions, his allegiance to the contemporary language is encouraging because it reminds us once more that the very developer of *katharevousa* shared with the demoticists the basic assumptions I have tried so repeatedly to emphasize: language and fatherland are one, what is needed is a unified, truly national language consonant with the character of the Greek people. On occasions, Korais carried this chain of reasoning to its logical conclusion. (I cite this passage in Greek so that we may also see the language he used.)

Καθὼς ἔχει προσώπου χαρακτῆρα διάφορον εἷς ἀπὸ τὸν ἄλλον, ὡσαύτως φυσικὰ καὶ λόγου χαρακτῆρα διάφορον πρέπει νὰ ἔχῃ. Ἀλλ' ὁ χαρακτὴρ οὗτος δὲν ἐμπορεῖ νὰ φανῇ τοιοῦτος, ὁποῖος εἶναι, πάρεξ ὅταν γράφῃ τις εἰς τὴν φυσικὴν αὐτοῦ διάλεκτον, ἤγουν εἰς ἐκείνην, τὴν ὁποίαν ἐθήλασε μὲ τὸ γάλα, καὶ λαλεῖ καθ' ἡμέραν, ἢ τοὐλάχιστον λαλεῖ συνεχέστερον παρὰ τὰς ἐπικτήτους ἄλλας γλώσσας.

. . .

Ἡμεῖς ἔχομεν χρείαν μεγάλην νὰ γράφωμεν εἰς τὴν γλῶσσαν, εἰς τὴν ὁποίαν καὶ νοοῦμεν, ἐὰν θέλωμεν καὶ τὰ νοήματα τῆς ψυχῆς ἡμῶν νὰ κανονίσωμεν, καὶ τὴν γλῶσσαν ἱκανὴν νὰ τὰ ἐκφράζῃ νὰ καταστήσωμεν.[16]

(Just as one person differs from another in personal

16. Korais, *Epistoli*, pp. 43–44; p. 41.

character, so he naturally must differ as well in linguistic character. But this character cannot manifest itself as it truly is except when a person writes in his natural language —that is, in the language which he suckled with his mother's milk and which he speaks every day or at least more regularly than other, acquired languages. . . .

As for us, if we wish to bring order to the conceptions of our mind and to render the language capable of expressing those conceptions, we have a great obligation to write in the language in which we think.)

It is here, I should add, that Korais invoked the example of the Italians, French, and English, as we saw previously. (His sentiments were impeccable; the contradiction came in the way he expressed them, for his own language was very far indeed from that which "he suckled with his mother's milk"!)

To these arguments, Korais added others. His linguistic position, we should remember, arose more from political considerations than from the psychological and ethical ones implicit in the passage I have just cited. A great admirer of that most logical consequence of rational enlightenment, the French Revolution, which he had witnessed at first hand, Korais defined enlightenment as resistance against feudal or monarchical rule. These democratic sympathies he extended to the language question. Each language, he wrote, belongs to a whole people, not to certain overlords. "All the members of a nation share this property with democratic . . . equality. No one . . . has . . . the right to say to the nation: 'I want you to speak like this, to write like this.'"[17] Here we see in an early manifestation, and from a source that the uninformed might consider strange, the identification of demoticism with populism stressed in the twentieth century by *katharevousa*'s

17. *Ibid.*, p. 49.

opponents. Indeed, as we continue with Korais' ideas, we build up a repertoire of practically all the issues and arguments so heatedly debated a century later by Kazantzakis' generation.

Immediately after claiming language as a people's shared democratic possession, Korais added that not even the strongest tyrant can change a language by force. "Only time," he said, "has the power to alter the dialects of nations, just as it alters nations themselves."[18] What is important here is Korais' recognition of the natural alteration of languages, a fact central to the demoticists' position later on, and one that they wrongly accused Korais of denying. Korais not only recognized this alteration, he honored it. We have already seen how he invoked "the enlightened nations" for periodically revising, for example, their translations of the Bible, adapting them to the nation's prevailing idiom. "What charmed the ear of people living a century or two ago," he argued in connection with his own sample rendering of the New Testament, "cannot also please those living today."[19] Elsewhere he stated most emphatically: "We write not for the ancestors who have been dead for centuries, but for our fellow Greeks of today."[20]

Despite the contradictions implicit in his program of correcting the language, it is clear that Korais honored demotic in and for itself. "The contemporary spoken idiom is neither barbaric nor Hellenic, but the new language of a new nation, the daughter and heir of an old tongue that is abundantly rich—ancient Greek."[21] This attitude made him search the Ptohoprodromian poems and other surviving texts for words that contemporary demotic might revivify.[22] It also made him

18. *Ibid.*, p. 50.   19. Korais, *Atakta*, iii, p. ζ´.
20. *Ibid.*, iv, p. η´.   21. *Ibid.*
22. *Ibid.*, ii, p. ιε´.

dream of a demotic dictionary, and include in his *Grammar of the Common Hellenic (Greek) Language* certain peculiarly demotic forms, such as the expressive diminutives, even though the grammar as a whole corrects demotic severely.[23] The scheme for a demotic dictionary holds especial interest for us since Korais' unfulfilled dreams in this regard devolved upon so many future Greek intellectuals, Kazantzakis included, and alas are still not perfectly fulfilled. The rationale for the dictionary was a comprehensive one. Part was Korais' hope that a full knowledge of existing though perhaps forgotten demotic words would make recourse to ancient terms unnecessary.[24] Not only were many usable items buried in older demotic texts, but many words which had survived in one region were unknown in other regions.[25] A dictionary would serve as a bridge over these temporal and spatial gaps, thus helping to create a new *koine* which would be unified and pan-hellenic.

But Korais, it must be acknowledged, was prey here to the superstition that if a word is to be truly Greek it must be of Greek provenance. Thus another part of his rationale for the dictionary was the hope that these resurrected words connected somehow with the Greek past would free his new nation from reliance upon loan-words from Turkish, Italian, or other barbarian sources. He valued demotic in and for itself, but he saw it primarily as heir—in a literal, narrow sense— to the ancient tradition. (Compare Kazantzakis a century later, who asserted that a word is Greek, no matter what its origin, if it is alive on the lips of the Greek people.)[26] This

23. Korais, *Ton meta thanaton*, Vol. VI, p. 65. Yannis Vilaras was another who drew attention to demotic's unique powers of augmentation. *Apology*, p. 54.
24. Korais, *Syllogi*, p. 244.   25. *Ibid.*, p. 342.
26. Kazantzakis, *To glossikon*, p. 7.

narrowness explains a final part of Korais' rationale for the proposed dictionary, which he felt would aid people both to comprehend ancient Greek more exactly and to purify demotic.[27] Taken in sum, the scheme for the dictionary, it seems to me, attests to Korais' sincere interest in the contemporary language. If nothing else, his mania for collecting words established a precedent which infected future generations and greatly benefited the demotic cause.

It is also worth noting that Korais combined this mania with his liberal anti-clericalism in a delightful way, since he proposed to finance scholarly expeditions to remote villages by means of collections taken up in church, and especially by soliciting monies that would otherwise have gone to monasteries![28] In effect he was offering his linguistic program as the gospel of a new form of salvation, and was calling for a new self-sacrificing disciple, prepared like the monks of old to witness for the truth. This quasi-religious zeal, tacit and inchoate in Korais, became vocal and fully formed by the time we reach Kazantzakis.

Korais not only dreamed of a dictionary, he compiled one, though never by touring the villages with notebook in hand.[29] Some sample entries will demonstrate his aims, which were to convince his readers that the word in question was acceptably Hellenic despite its form, and to hint that the form could often be made more "authentically" Hellenic with very minimal alterations:

ΦΩΝΑΖΩ. Εἶναι ἀπὸ τὸ Φωνάω, εἰς τὸ ὁποῖον προσθέσαντες τὸ ζ, ἐσχηματίσαμεν τὸ Φωνάζω κατὰ τὸν τύπον τοῦ Κραυγάζω. Τοιούτων διπλῶν σχηματισμῶν, διὰ τοῦ αω καὶ αζω, δὲν λείπουν παραδείγματα οὐδ᾽ εἰς αὐτοὺς

27. Korais, *Syllogi*, p. 341.   28. Chaconas, p. 68.
29. See Korais, *Atakta*, Vols. ii, iv, v, and *Syllogi*.

τοὺς παλαιούς· ἐπειδὴ ἔλεγαν Ἀγαπάω καὶ Ἀγαπάζω, Ἀτιμάω καὶ Ἀτιμάζω . . .

ΑΡΓΟΣΤΟΛΩ, συνώνυμον τοῦ κοινοῦ Ἀργοπορῶ, τοῦ παλαιοῦ Βραδύνω. Λείπει ἡ λέξις ἀπὸ τὰ Λεξικά, καὶ ὅμως ἡ χρῆσις αὐτῆς εἶναι κοινή, καὶ ἡ σύνθεσις εὐφραδεστάτη, ἀπὸ τὸ Ἀργῶς καὶ τὸ Στέλλομαι, τὸ ὁποῖον ἐσήμαινεν εἰς τοὺς παλαιοὺς καὶ τὸ Πορεύομαι.

ΑΛΩΠΟΥ ἤ ΑΛΕΠΟΥ εἶναι τῶν παλαιῶν ἡ Ἀλώπηξ. . . . Πρέπει νὰ γράφεται Ἀλωποῦ, καὶ ὄχι Ἀλεποῦ· διότι παράγεται ἀπὸ τοῦ Ἀλωπώ, τοῦ ὁποίου τὸ τελευταῖον ω ἐτρέψαμεν εἰς ου δίφθογγον, καθὼς καὶ ἀπὸ τὸ Μιμὼ ἐσχηματίσθη πρῶτον τὸ Μιμοῦ, ἔπειτα τὸ χυδαιέστερον Μαϊμοῦ. . . . Τοῦ Ἀλωπώ, ἤ Ἀλωποῦ, τὸ πληθυντικὸν πρέπει φυσικὰ νὰ ἦναι, Ἀλωποὶ (κατὰ τὸ Λητοὶ) ἤγουν Ἀλώπεκες (χυδ. Ἀλωποῦδες).Here he cites a second century A.D. cleric: Οὗτοι γὰρ εἰσὶ Θῶες, Ἀλωποί. . . .

ΑΦΙΝΩ. Korais presents this as an irregular verb, a synonym of Ἐῶ. That it is actually the ancient Greek Ἀφίημι, compounded from Ἀπὸ and Ἵημι, is beyond doubt. He explains that ν is often added to verbs having two adjacent vowels, for example: Τίω-Τίνω, Δύω-Δύνω. Probably our Ἀφίνω was found in some Greek dialect, instead of Ἀφίω. Korais then traces the development of Ἄφες, which appears in the Bible, to the Ἄφς of Byzantine times, and finally to the contemporary Ἄς.

ΑΓΑΠΩ. He cites the word's use with νὰ to mean "I am used to doing something" for example, Ἀγαπῶ νὰ λαλῶ. He says that the ancients used φιλῶ with the infinitive in the same way. Yet the contemporary usage was also influenced by the French: j'aime à me taire. Ἀγαπῶ is also used as an equivalent for ἐρῶ. This derives from hellenistic times. On analogy with Ἐραστής, Ἀγαπητικός should be

Ἀγαπητής. Finally, Korais speaks of correct love—i.e., love of one Greek for another, and love which surpasses bodily attraction. Such love will produce correct children and will sustain and save the political commonwealth.[30]

In all the arguments, schemes, and examples presented so far, we have seen Korais defending the contemporary language in a positive way (granted his superstitions and contradictions). He also defended it negatively, by attacking the extremist classicists and Atticizers. Here too, strangely, we find pronouncements that could easily be lifted from his writings and placed in the demoticist manifestoes of Kazantzakis' time. We have already encountered Korais' insistence that "we write not for the ancestors who have been dead for centuries." To those who held that it was the duty of modern Greeks to resurrect the ancestral language, Korais answered: "It would be a fine thing, naturally, if we lived in those times when the dead were raised up, and the gift of tongues effortlessly disseminated, but miracles do not happen every day."[31] As for the education then being imposed upon Greek youth, Korais compared it to the impossible labors of Sisyphus, and reminded the archaizers that even after all the Sisyphean sweat, the resulting idiom that their students wrote was not that of Plato or Xenophon, nor even that of Polybius or Diodorus, nor even yet that of Plutarch or Julian, but instead a hodgepodge with elements from everyone and everywhere.[32] And as if that were not bad enough, this education kept the modern Greeks nearly illiterate in their own tongue: "The pedagogues have undertaken to teach their pupils Plato and Xenophon, and have left them

30. Sources of the five entries, respectively, are: Korais, *Atakta*, I, p. 65; *Syllogi*, p. 440; *Syllogi*, pp. 424–25; *Syllogi*, p. 446; *Syllogi*, p. 413.
31. Korais, *Epistoli*, p. 42.   32. *Ibid.*, p. 45.

writing the common language worse than water-carriers and haulers of wood."[33]

KORAIS' HELLENISM

After all this eloquence on behalf of the common language, after all these appeals to democracy, contemporaneousness, pedagogical liberalism, and mother's milk, Korais in his other guise—his hellenism—may seem perverse or hypocritical. Yet I hope that my earlier discussion of the humanistic background may help us to appreciate how the contradictory elements in Korais could derive from the single, basic assumption that language and nationality are the same.[34] We have seen that, according to this assumption, the character of modern Greeks can be expressed and known only through the language suckled with their mother's milk; by the same token, however, the character of ancient Greeks can be known only through the ancient idiom in which they expressed themselves. It was precisely this frightening consistency that forced Korais (and others) into a paradoxical inconsistency. All his progressivism arose from an allegiance to the past; his hopes for a new Greece were at the same time hopes for a resurrected old Greece.

I have already spoken about the hellenic allegiance implicit in Korais' humanism. We must remember as well that professionally, although he was trained as a physician, he considered himself a classical philologist and was honored as such throughout Europe.[35] His ideological allegiance to Western liberalism/

33. Korais, *Syllogi*, p. 142.
34. This assumption is considered by some to be the prime source of Greece's future woes. On this see Sherrard, p. 182, who cites Arnold Toynbee, *A Study of History* (Oxford, 1954), Vol. VIII, p. 191, and N. Kaltchas, *Introduction to the Constitutional History of Modern Greece* (N.Y., 1940), p. 4.
35. Clogg, *Burgess*, pp. 44, 46, 52.

humanism was thus reinforced in its hellenic element by the classicists and philhellenes with whom he came in contact professionally. Korais was caught, so to speak, between his progressivism and his professional milieu. We see his predicament all too blatantly in the following confession placed directly in the midst of a plea for the common language: "My notes, written in our common tongue, were ready for the printers when some friends of mine—philhellenes expert in our ancient but not our modern language—eventually persuaded me to hellenize [my notes] so that they might be understood . . . by the scholars of Europe, who are ignorant of Modern Greek."[36] Despite all of Korais' protestations about the dignity of the spoken tongue, the fact remains that he did write for European philhellenes as well as for Greeks and—more importantly—shared with these philhellenes a romantic (and sometimes preposterous) vision of the hellenic past and of the moral, cultural, and intellectual effect that a revival of that past would have upon the Ottomanized modern Greeks.

This brings us back to Korais' ideological assumptions, which expressed themselves in turn in a philosophy of history. "A devoted reader of Gibbon, Korais saw civilization in terms of a 'classicism' which had been born in the Greece of Pericles, preserved through the Hellenistic and Roman period, was submerged in the 'dark' Christian Middle Ages, whether Latin or Byzantine, had been reborn in Italy with the Renaissance, and whose present bearers were the enlightened and liberal spirits of the eighteenth century. Greece, the birthplace of this civilization itself, was cut off from the Western Eu-

---

36. Korais, *Epistoli*, p. 41. Ironically, some philhellenes were soon to become fascinated with Modern Greek in its own right, stimulated by Fauriel's collection of the demotic ballads (1824–1825).

rope where it was now flourishing by the abominable and barbaric Turk, and, worse still, the inhabitants of Greece, successors of the ancient Greeks, had fallen, in their captivity, into a state of ignorance and depression that sadly compared with their past glory. What, therefore, was demanded was the reeducation of Greeks through the study of the classics, which, just as they had brought enlightenment to Western Europe at the time of the Renaissance, would revive in Greece itself a consciousness of its ancient heritage and provide the incentive to throw off the 'barbarian yoke,' restore to Greece her cultural eminence, and allow her to assume her rightful place among the nations of the civilized world. In short, what Korais envisaged was the 'emancipation' of Greece in terms of the secular liberalism and humanist enlightenment of the contemporary West." (Sherrard, p. 180.)

When we add to this the humanistic axiom identifying national character with language, we see that the enlightenment of modern Greece, for Korais, would be procured not simply by the sentiments preserved in the ancient classics but by the language itself. The classics had to be read, therefore, in the original, and if this was too much to expect, then at least in a *koine* that had been corrected and purified in such a way that it reminded one of the ancient as much as possible. Just how preposterous Korais' adoration of the Hellenic language could become is indicated by his conviction that its very subtlety and elegance would ennoble those who spoke it, making them peaceful, freedom-loving, and virtuous.[37] "Along with other points of excellence," he claimed, "Greek has another exceptional charm: it refines the habits of the young, making them more elegant and wise. It is a rare thing (this has been proved to me by the experience of the youth in other nations) for one to submit to physical slavery [despotism] if one has

37. Chaconas, pp. 63–64, 71. Also cited by Sherrard, p. 183.

once managed to drink to the full the charm of the Hellenic
language."

The result of this ideological position, reinforced by the romantic philhellenism of the West, was that Korais' major energies went not so much into the translation of ancient texts as
into the meticulous editing and publishing of the ancients in
the original. The many volumes he produced formed his famous Hellenic Library which, with the financial help of the
merchant Michael Zosimas, he distributed far and wide for
the edification of his compatriots. The texts themselves were
prefaced by long essays in the *koine* setting forth Korais' political and linguistic objectives and exhorting the Greeks to
awaken. As he indicated in his autobiography, having observed
that the spread of education in France was what gave birth
there to the love of liberty, and having resolved to work toward
a repetition of this situation in Greece, he conceived the means
of "publishing the Hellenic writers with lengthy prefaces in
the common tongue so that they might be read not only by
scholars of ancient Greek, but by laymen as well."[38]

PURIFIED "KOINE"

In sum, we see a contradictory man devoted at one and the
same time to the new and the old Greece and attempting to
honor the language of each. Since he knew that the Greeks
could never be made to write like Plato, and had convinced
himself that their contemporary tongue was still essentially
Greek, he endeavored to enable the old to shine through the
new to the greatest degree possible, while still preserving the
modern idiom that he also professed to honor. As partners in
this wedding of old and new he chose classical and hellenistic
Greek on the one hand (his anti-clerical prejudices helped him

38. Korais, *Syllogi*, pp. κδ′–κε′. Also cited by Chaconas, pp. 30–
31.

minimize the ecclesiastical idiom of Byzantium and the *tour-kokratia*),[39] and the written language of contemporary educated Greeks on the other. In this way he hoped to steer a course between extreme Atticism and extreme vulgarism. As might be expected, he justified this by invoking the ancients: "What other road is open to the nation's literary men but the middle one, leading away from vulgarity, for it is probable that neither the Platos nor Isocrates wrote like the galley-slaves of Athens; far also from hellenism or hellenic macaronism, for it is likewise probable that the Platos and Isocrates wrote in such a way that the galley-slaves could understand them."[40]

But he also justified his anti-vulgarism in terms drawn from his own narrow (and yet noble) conception of himself as enlightened and thus the enlightener for others: "If, on the one hand, it is tyrannical for a person to depart from common spoken usage to such a degree that he becomes unclear to the intellect and entirely strange to the ear, it is demagogic, I feel, for him to display a vulgarity so great that it becomes disgusting to those who have been well brought up. When I say that the entire nation partakes of its language with democratic equality, I do not mean that we must entrust the cultivation and creation of that language to the ochlocratic imagination of the vulgar. The mob is everywhere a mob."[41]

Implied in these statements are precisely those elements in Korais' program which were to be attacked so fervently by the demoticists ninety years later. In squirming to avoid the charge of undemocratic linguistic legislating, Korais arrived at the view that "correcting" the language was in no way depriving the people of their democratically shared "property."

39. This is the Greek term for the period under Turkish rule.
40. Cited in article on Korais in the Eleftheroudakis *Encyclopedia.*
41. Korais, *Epistoli*, p. 50.

We remember his defense of demotic as neither barbarous nor hellenic, but a new language of a new people, daughter and heir of ancient Greek. But he adds immediately afterward: "He who speaks or writes will be excused if he makes accustomed words regular and stylistically pleasing so that they become as seemly as possible, but not if he inserts other, ancient words in their place simply because these words are older."[42] Again, what seems like a defense of the common language against incursions by Hellenic turns out to be a defense of Korais' right to correct this language at will, and yet to be considered at the same time a defender of the people's common, democratic property. Though Korais acted in good faith, he naturally left himself open to easy attack by future populists.

Another element implicit in Korais' scheme, and open to subsequent attack, was his conviction that the written word, not the spoken, must be the basis of correctness. As though invoking some universal law, he declared that the legislators of the language spoken by a nation are "naturally the educated men" of that nation.[43] The whole medium of linguistic improvement had to be literacy, the written word. The class to whom Korais directed his efforts was the literate class, those who "at least know how to read, and have a definite desire to be enlightened."[44] From here the path was simple. If such people pored over books written in a "beautified" language, they would gradually learn to improve not only their writing but their speech, and would then transmit this improvement to the writers of succeeding generations. In any case, grammatical rules were to be based wherever possible on written, not spoken, usage.

Korais lacked any appreciation for the fact that the great vitality of Modern Greek (and surely, originally, of ancient

42. Korais, *Atakta*, IV, p. η′.
43. Korais, *Epistoli*, p. 52.   44. *Ibid.*, p. 51.

Greek as well) came from its oral tradition, that its true culti-
vators and creators were the illiterate "mob." The best he could
do was admit that a perfectly correct grammar could never be
constructed because of the "irregular elements" that must be
termed "exceptions to the natural laws."[45] It behooved the
grammarian to know the grammar of the spoken word, and
yet how much more "enlightened" everything would be if language could be molded systematically and logically in the
educated man's study.

   Full of contradictions, attempting to reconcile irreconcilables,
Korais wisely chose to make a virtue of his defects. By both
admonition and example, he presented patience, moderation,
and tact as guidelines for the linguistic reformation: "Write
with care and study. Uproot from the language the weeds of
vulgarity, not however all at once with the pitchfork, but rather
a few at a time, by hand, one after the other. Sow the language
with Hellenic seeds, but also by hand, not by the sackful."[46]
His object, we will remember, was to rid the language of Turkish, Italian, and other borrowings, replacing them wherever
possible with Hellenic items already preserved somehow or
somewhere in demotic. These, in turn, were discoverable (a)
through etymological commentary showing the genuineness of
contemporary forms which might otherwise be purged, and
(b) through the cherished pan-hellenic dictionary. If no *koine*
word could be found, then it was legitimate to borrow from
ancient or hellenistic Greek. But here, too, Korais elaborated
cautions. Since the ancient language was so rich, the contemporary writer should amass all the various synonyms for the
word he needed, and then "choose from among these the one
most easily comprehensible to those uninstructed in ancient
Greek."[47] If this was impossible, then the ancient word must

45. Korais, *Syllogi*, p. 117.   46. Korais, *Epistoli*, p. 51.
47. Korais, *Atakta*, iv, p. θ'. In a footnote on the same page he

be employed in such a way that it became immediately intelligible to the uninstructed because of its context.[48]

Theoretically, this was fine, but in practice it became all too easy for learned men to misjudge just what the uninstructed could or could not comprehend. In any case, despite Korais' cautions and despite what he felt was an allegiance to the living language of the people, he robbed that language of some of its most basic expressions because they were foreign in origin. We shall see this when we come to the impassioned campaign by the leading demoticists and by Kazantzakis for the restoration of these expressions.

Korais attempted a similar moderation in his efforts to correct existing words in order to make their Hellenic origins more apparent. But here, too, he failed to appreciate that although the change from τυρί to τυρός or from παιδί to παιδίον seems slight on paper, on the lips it robs the language of familiar, cherished forms, replacing them with others felt to be foreign and artificial. Yet, in comparison with the extremists, Korais was admirable in his restraint. Changes should be made, he argued, only when there is an "imperceptible alteration" involving just one or two letters.[49] For example, many verbs with "barbaric endings" can have their genuinely ancient forms easily restored, so that we may write συνάγω for συνάζω, φράσσω for φράζω, φυλάσσω for φυλάζω, etc.

Korais' etymological excursions, used both to convince himself and others of a word's Hellenic parentage, and hopefully to unearth a "more genuine" form that could imperceptively replace the barbarized one, we have already seen in the examples from his dictionary. The corrected language would employ

---

gives examples. Why should we write *proparaskevázo* instead of *proetoimázo?*

48. Korais, *Epistoli*, fn., pp. 51–52.

49. Korais, *Atakta*, iv, p. θ´.

(to cite an example already familiar to us) Ἀλωπὼ or at the worst Ἀλωποῦ, rather than the barbaric Ἀλεποῦ, because this imperceptible change would enable the ancient form Ἀλώπηξ to shine through. Another example is the substitution of ὀψά-ριον for ψάρι. In the notes on Ptohoprodromos, Korais traced the word back to ὄψον, which originally meant "that which is used for food aside from bread."[50] As far back as Menander's time, the term was used specifically for fish. Ψάρι is obviously the barbarized remains of ὀψάριον, the diminutive of ὄψον. Thus, if it is too much to expect the contemporary Greek to write ἰχθύς, he at least can modify ψάρι "imperceptibly" so that its ancient heritage shines through. An analogous case is the correction of μάτι to ὀμμάτιον.[51]

Korais also formulated rules for pleasing style.[52] Good writers, for example, should avoid unnecessary words. Instead of Ἦλθα διὰ νὰ σ᾽ ἐπάρω, they should write Ἦλθα νὰ σ᾽ ἐπάρω. I call attention to this because Psiharis was later to question the right of a non-literary man such as Korais to legislate on stylistic matters. As the demoticist consciousness developed, it came to be felt more and more that the only legitimate stylistic legislators were the poets, in addition to the people themselves. Kazantzakis, among others, reflected this changed attitude.

Korais' own writing was meant to be a stylistic embodiment of the new *koine*, not just a list of rules or series of admonitions. In actuality, it displayed the balanced periods, the sophistication, the love of subordination, the dignity and elegance, of the European Enlightenment, and thus was perhaps more foreign than Greek in character. (Psiharis was to say later that most of *katharevousa*'s locutions were literal translations from the French!) Though his theoretical aim was to steer a safe course between comprehensibility and crudity, in practice his

50. *Ibid.*, v, part i, p. 271, and i, pp. 96, 198.
51. Article on Korais in the Eleftheroudakis *Encyclopedia.*
52. Korais, *Atakta*, iv, p. ια᾽.

style sacrificed too much comprehensibility in order to please the educated Greek and foreign philhellene.

This is where Korais' system broke down. For, despite all his moderation and tact, his language could not be understood by the populace, and was therefore no longer Modern Greek. The trouble, of course, was what I have already indicated: Korais' emphasis upon the written language of educated writers as opposed to the vulgarisms of the illiterate mob. Only because of this narrow conception of his readership was he able to say with confidence when he prepared a sample translation of the New Testament, for example: "Regarding the style, I need not give answer to anyone, for the reader will readily be able to judge if I speak his usual language or some other that is strange."

Korais printed his own rendering together with the original and also a previous translation.[53] If we compare his version with the earlier (from 1638), we see that Korais tended to return to words found in the original. The text is Paul's Epistle to Titus 1:11:

Original text
Οὓς δεῖ ἐπιστομίζειν· οἵτινες ὅλους οἴκους ἀνατρέπουσιν διδάσκοντες ἃ μὴ δεῖ, αἰσχροῦ κέρδους χάριν.

Old translation
Τοὺς ὁποίους πρέπει νὰ τοὺς ἀποστομώνωμεν· οἱ ὁποῖοι ὁλάκαιρα ὀσπήτια γυρίζουσιν ἄνω κάτω, ἔστωντας νὰ διδάσκουσιν ἐκεῖνα ὁποῦ δὲν πρέπει, διὰ ἄσχημον κέρδος.

---

53. That of Maximus of Gallipoli, 1638. See Bibliography. Vlastos, *Greek Bilingualism*, pp. 48–53, explains the reasons for this translation and the involvement of the Patriarch, Cyril Loukaris, whose prologue to the volume is a significant demoticist manifesto. See also Kordatos, *Istoria*, pp. 34–36. Both Loukaris and Maximus were made to suffer excessively on account of their progressivism. As for the translation itself, after first being sanctioned, it was condemned and officially burned in 1704.

New translation

Τοὺς ὁποίους χρεωστοῦμεν νὰ ἐπιστομίζωμεν. Αὐτοὶ ἀνα-
ποδογυρίζουν ὁλοκλήρους οἰκίας, διδάσκοντες, διὰ κέρδος
αἰσχρὸν, ὅσα δὲν πρέπει [νὰ διδάσκωνται].⁵⁴

It should be remembered that according to Korais' own principles, a version of the Bible ought to have made comprehensibility its primary objective. He set up distinctions whereby
books dealing with mathematics, metaphysics, physics, medi-
cine, etc., should be written in an appropriately scholarly
language, but books on ethics and religion, "since they are intended for use by all members of the nation without exception,"⁵⁵ must never employ "either words or syntactical patterns which are unintelligible to the reader." The New Testament, of all books, obviously ought to have been the first to
conform to this prescription; if Korais was confident that it
did, it was only because by "reader" he did not mean the
average man. How far his version departed from the true
vernacular can perhaps be appreciated by comparing it with
the racy translation of Genesis 1:1 and 3 found in the Soncino
polyglot edition of the Pentateuch published in Constantinople in 1547:

Εἰς ἀρχὴ ἔπλασεν ὁ Θεὸς τὸν οὐρανὸ καὶ τὴν
ἤγῆ, . . . καὶ εἶπεν ὁ Θεός· ἂς εἶνε φῶς
καὶ ἦτον φῶς.⁵⁶

Further evidence of the gulf between Korais' language and
the demotic of his time comes, strangely, from the archives of
the British and Foreign Bible Society. In 1808, long before

54. Korais, *Atakta*, iii, pp. 284–85.
55. *Ibid.*, iv, p. ί. But Korais allows that technical terms may be
used in such works.
56. Cited in Clogg, *Bible Society*, pp. 77–78. Meant for the Jewish community of Constantinople, this volume offered the Hebrew
text along with translations into Spanish and Greek printed in
Hebrew characters.

Korais published his own sample of the New Testament, the Society consulted him regarding its projected Modern Greek Bible.[57] Korais' advice, which was followed, was that the existing 1638 version should be used, though in a revised form. When the results were published in 1810, however, certain Greeks complained to the Society that the translation was unacceptable to them because it contained "many foreign words, particularly Turkish." They asked the Society to consult Korais once more, with the hope of commissioning a new translation "into the pure language [which] would be generally acceptable and intelligible to readers in all the provinces, although the colloquial dialects vary." The Society then put the matter to its chief informant on the Greek situation, the Rev. John F. Usko, a Prussian who had lived many years in Smyrna (Korais' birthplace), had married a Greek native of that city, and who spoke the language fluently. Usko's memorandum dated November 6, 1811, was unequivocal:

". . . Mr. Corai's language is, in my opinion, so exalted, so much approaching to the hellenistical idiom, at least in words, if not in phrases, and so difficult to readers who have not learned the Ancient Greek, that it cannot be supposed to be generally understood by all the Greeks. . . . I do not mean to detract anything from Mr. Corai's great and eminent knowledge of the Ancient and Modern Greek, and I must declare his noble efforts very praiseworthy, to bring the modern dialect (his native tongue) as near the ancient language as it is practicable by its idiom and phraseology. However, I must confess that his modern language is fit for learned treatises and investigations rather than for the common understanding of the Greek Nation in general, and better adapted for men

57. The remainder of this section is drawn from Clogg, *Bible Society*, pp. 71, 80, 81, passim. Clogg, in turn, draws from "An Account of all the translations circulated by the Society" (in manuscript) by T. P. Platt, the Society's honorary librarian.

versed in the ancient Greek, than for those who have no idea of it, as is the case of the greatest number of the Greeks who live in the Ottoman empire."

The sad truth about Korais, as Petros Vlastos says, is that "although he accepted the Romaic as the lawful language of the nation, he had not the courage to do it openly and whole-heartedly. . . . Instead of the great reformer that he might have been, he remains a mere erudite, babbling of liberal in-stitutions."[58]

SUPPORTERS OF KORAIS' REFORMS

Korais' linguistic program obviously elicited a great deal of controversy. It was first attacked as insufficiently pure by the Atticizers; then, with the conscious and systematic growth of the demoticist movement from about 1890 onward, it was at-tacked with equal venom by the opposite camp as fabricated, foreign, and (here we come full circle) un-Greek.

But Korais also had (and has) his supporters. In his own day, given the philological assumptions and superstitions of that time, his program seemed to make linguistic sense. In ad-dition, there were political factors; Korais, after all, spoke for a particular ethos and—if one judges at all from the Marxist interpretation of the Greek struggle for independence—for a particular class. Various factions took sides on the language question, with Korais' supporters, so it is claimed, belonging chiefly to the rising merchant-bourgeoisie class that, "conscious of its growing importance and glaring lack of political author-ity, envisaged a cultured Greek state, independent and republi-can, with themselves as prominent members of the national government."[59]

58. Vlastos, *Greek Bilingualism*, pp. 60–61.
59. Chaconas, p. 82. For this interpretation, Chaconas is indebted to Kordatos.

Korais found additional support from the intelligentsia, which as a class had been nurtured like himself on the ideals of the French Enlightenment and had been infected by the romantic philhellenism of the West. Finally, he won adherents as a result of his educational endeavors, for the schools founded at least in part because of his inspiration, supplied with the volumes of his Hellenic Library and naturally using his *katharevousa* in the classroom, produced a new generation anxious to support his views.[60] These three groups—bourgeoisie, intelligentsia, and educated youth—were strong enough during and after the revolutionary period to have Korais' *koine* recognized in King Otho's educational laws of 1834 and 1836 as in effect the official language of the Greek state, a sanctioning that it still enjoys today.[61]

OPPOSITION TO KORAIS

The opposition, if we are to continue with the same interpretation, was centered in the ruling class of semi-autonomous Greece, i.e., the archons and other civil administrators who had prospered under the Sultan's rule.[62] In addition there were certain of the ecclesiastical authorities and the Phanariots, both groups identifying themselves with Byzantine culture and favoring an archaic style. Korais became a common target for all these elements. He was accused of being illiterate, of having learned his Greek in Paris from merchants, of using dialect, coining words, wishing to overturn religious and political tradition, of being unpatriotic, an atheist, etc.[63] It is instructive that many of these same accusations were subsequently hurled at his opponents, the demoticists.

60. *Ibid.*, pp. 82–83. 61. Hourmouzios, p. 1,442.
62. Chaconas, pp. 68, 77, 78. 63. *Apology*, p. 55.

The Atticizers and Psiharis

The Atticizers

Opposition continued after the Greek state was established, with the period 1830–1890 seeing constant pressure for further purification. The result was an increased distance between demotic and *katharevousa*; an equal consequence was the growth of linguistic anarchy. The more people learned to write "correctly," the greater the possibility of variations, mistakes, and solecisms. As Kazantzakis was to argue at the beginning of the twentieth century, Greece by that time had acquired not one but hundreds of *katharevousas*. This growth of linguistic anarchy stimulated increasingly strident exhortations about correctness, and a tendency to offer Attic Greek as the only clear standard. People like Alexandros Rankavis (Rangabé) found Korais' language barbarous; others like Panayotis Soutsos and Konstantinos Kontos joined in this appraisal, catalogued specific deficiencies, and offered their own prescriptions. In the period from approximately 1830 to the outbreak of the demotic revolution in 1888, the purifiers' originally reasonable, humanistic attitude toward the past all too often degenerated into what Λ. Hourmouzios has described as "shallow patriotism, hollow rhetoric, and romantic bombast which was manifested, quite consistently, in a *katharevousa* 'worthy of the ancients.' "[1]

SOUTSOS

Panayotis Soutsos is a good example. In 1853 he published a book entitled Νέα Σχολὴ τοῦ γραφομένου λόγου ἢ ἀνάστασις τῆς ἀρχαίας ἑλληνικῆς γλώσσης ἐννοουμένης ὑπὸ πάντων (New school of the written word, or resurrection of the ancient Hellenic language comprehensible to all). The opening chapter of this astonishing document accuses Korais of basing his language on the speech of the mob. The resulting idiom, says Soutsos, is not only meager in its vocabulary but lacks the various cases, tenses, moods; the majority of prepositions, adverbs, and conjunctions; and most participles and pronouns. In addition, "since this sagacious man [ὁ σοφὸς αὐτὸς ἀνὴρ] brought about the transference into Greece of the philosophical and political beliefs of France, he introduced an infinite number of French phrases into this meager language."[2]

1. Hourmouzios, p. 1,447.
2. Soutsos, p. 4.

Soutsos himself will of course have none of this. He is scandalized that Korais' barbaric tongue, adulterated still further with French and German locutions, is the language written by "university professors . . . , the journalists of Athens, Hermopolis, Smyrna, and Constantinople, all authors, and all the translators of European writings."[3] He reminds his readers that Attic showed its superiority in the past when it became the common language, and he makes the extraordinary assertion that this same Attic was then spread to the Indies by Alexander and used for both the Septuagint and New Testament, with degeneration beginning only after the rise of Byzantium. Thus he will take upon himself the audacious task of throwing down Korais' "poor, Frenchified edifice and raising from the tomb the Hellenic language of our forefathers, that called of yore the common tongue, making it easy and comprehensible to all."

Toward this noble end, Soutsos provides both general rules and specific examples.[4] Here are the rules:

(1) The language of the ancients and of us modern Greeks shall be one and the same; their grammar and ours shall be one and the same.

(2) The only acceptable words and phrases shall be theirs; every foreign word or foreign phrase in Greek words shall be rejected.

(3) Our syntax shall be . . . easily apprehended, regular and simple, as in the ancient poets Homer and Hesiod, and the historians Herodotus and Xenophon.

(4) . . . Every word, phrase, and idiom of the ancient Greeks can be employed if it is easily comprehensible to the select elements of Greeks and does not offend the ear.

Here are some of the examples:

3. *Ibid.*, p. 5.
4. *Ibid.*, pp. 5–6, 6–16, 20–21.

FORM TO BE ABANDONED	RECOMMENDED REPLACEMENT

Gallicisms, etc.

ἀπὸ καιρὸν εἰς καιρὸν
   (de temps en temps)
τόσον περισσότερον ὅσον   τοσούτῳ μᾶλλον ὅσῳ
   (d'autant plus que)
ὡς τόσον   ἐν τοσούτῳ
   (Italian: in tanto)

Verb forms

γράφουν   γράφουσι
ἔγραφα   ἔγραφον
θὰ γράψω   γράψω
ἔχω γράψει   γράψας ἔχω
   (modeled on French:
      j'ai écrit)
εἶμαι, εἶσαι, εἶναι   εἰμὶ, εἶ, ἐστί
ἂς ἔλθῃ   ἐλθέτω

Locutions

ἐστάλην διὰ νὰ ἀναγνώσω   ἐστάλην πρὸς ἀνάγνωσιν
μ' ἕνα λόγον   ἐν ἑνὶ λόγῳ
καθὼς ἦλθε τὸ ἔαρ   ἐλθόντος τοῦ ἔαρος
μὲ τὰ σωστά του   ἀληθῶς

Pronouns

μου, μας   ἐμοῦ, ἐμοί, ἡμῶν, ἡμῖν
σας   ὑμῶν
τὸ βιβλίο τους   τὸ βιβλίον αὐτῶν
δικός μου . . .   ἐμὸς, σὸς, ἡμέτερος
ὁ ὁποῖος . . .   ὅστις, ἥτις, ὅ, τι
κάποιος   τις
καθένας   καθεὶς

We should remember that throughout his book Soutsos attacked Korais repeatedly, and that most of the linguistic elements he sought to purge were from the *"koraistika."*[6] We should also remember that Soutsos was legislating not only for scholars, professors, and journalists, but also for writers of fiction, drama, and even poetry. Nor was he an isolated crusader; others shared his archaizing zeal. This can be seen in the language of P. Kalligas' *Thanos Vlekas*, a well-known Greek novel published in 1855, just two years after Soutsos' *New School*. Kalligas' work is an early example of naturalism (though not in language); yet in this supposedly realistic portrait of Greek agrarian life, a jug of cool water becomes an ἀγγεῖον ψυχροῦ ὕδατος, and even the sighs have been hellenized, the Attic Αἴ! replacing the demotic Ἄχ![7] But Alexander Rankavis in his history of Greek literature published in 1877 cited Kalligas' style as exemplary.[8]

KONTOS

To return completely to the ancients, as Panayotis Soutsos wished, was easier in theory than in practice. Although officially his Atticism dominated throughout a good part of the nineteenth century, in actuality the language of science, literature, and journalism remained Korais' *katharevousa*.[9] The one place where extreme Atticism did make more headway in

6. This term of derision is a pun on *korakistika* (or *korakistiká*), which means "tramps' jargon, gibberish," and which was used by the Phanariot Rizos Neroulos as the title for an anti-Korais satirical play (1813) showing a scholar trying vainly to teach peasants *katharevousa*.

7. Kalligas, pp. 33, 34.

8. Rangabé, vol. II, p. 271. The novel, says Rangabé, is "écrit dans un style qui peut servir de modèle." On Kalligas and Rangabé, see Hourmouzios, p. 1,445.

9. Glinos, *I Krisi*, p. 8.

practice as well as in theory was education, which fell prey to "Kontismos," the program of linguistic reform laid out in Konstantinos Kontos' Γλωσσικαὶ Παρατηρήσεις (Linguistic Observations) of 1882.

Kontos—like his intellectual ancestor Phrynichus—was a serious and learned classicist. If he seems pompously foolish to us, it is because we have outgrown presuppositions that were perfectly normal for men of his time. Taking the language's fallen state for granted, he saw Korais as the culprit.[10] He conceded that Korais was the first to cleanse demotic, and confessed his appreciation of this, but he then accused him of introducing barbarisms and of leaving the door open for his followers to introduce many more. The result, he claimed, was a linguistic anarchy characterized by ignorance of Attic grammar and manifesting itself in horrible solecisms such as: incorrect doubling of consonants, omission of the iota subscript where it belonged and insertion where it did not, faulty declensions, and hesitation regarding augment so that such multiple forms as ἀμφέβαλλον, ἀμφίβαλλον, ἠμφίβαλλον could be found.[11]

Thus Kontos took upon himself the much-needed task of correction, proscription, purgation—for a cleansed language, he said, is the one sure sign that a nation is progressing toward wisdom. Regarding the method, how else could this be accomplished but by "the study and exact teaching of our ancestral tongue"?[12]

The bulk of his book consists of two hundred "observations." I shall give just four or five examples (in paraphrase). From these it will be seen that Korais' effort to replace foreign words with Greek opened a Pandora's box of difficulties. Which Greek words or forms were "correct"? Since no one actually

10. Kontos, p. α'.
11. Ibid., pp. η', θ', ι'.
12. Ibid., p. α'.

spoke any of them, the decision rested solely on the etymological ingenuity (or imagination) of the philological expert. The arbitrariness and pettiness of the attempted purification of Korais' reformed language is nowhere more evident than in Kontos' strictures:

Observations 123–124. The form βιβλιόφιλος is not Greek. The Greek form is φιλόβιβλος on analogy with φιλότιμος, φιλάργυρος, φιλόλογος. Βιβλιόφιλος is unacceptable. Similarly, Ἑλληνόφιλος must be rejected in favor of φιλέλλην.

Observation 46. The nouns δημοκράτης and ἀριστοκράτης must be rejected in favor of δημοκρατικός and ἀριστοκρατικός, which the ancients applied to those embracing the democratic or aristocratic cause. Δημοκράτης and ἀριστοκράτης are non-hellenic; in addition, they can only mean τὸν κρατοῦντα τοῦ δήμου, τὸν κρατοῦντα τῶν ἀρίστων.

Observation 188. In his *Atakta*, Korais uses the word σιδερόκολλα for solder. From this he derives the verb σιδεροκολλῶ and the compounded verbal noun σιδεροκόλλησιν, which Herodotus expressed analytically: σιδήρου κόλλησιν. "By no means," says Kontos, "do we sanction the noun σιδηροκόλλησις." (I should add that Kontos has a general aversion to compounds, and gives long lists of those which are to be proscribed. Ease of compounding is of course one of the loveliest features of demotic, much exploited by Kazantzakis in all his writings and especially in his translation of the *Iliad*, where he strove to find a demotic equivalent for each of Homer's compound epithets.)[13]

Observation 150. Ὑπερηφανία must not be spelled ὑπερηφάνεια, because it derives from ὑπερήφανος. Do not be misled by the ει in a word like ἐπιφάνεια, which derives from ἐπιφανής.

13. See Kontos, section 102, pp. 279–81 where he gives long lists of compounds that bother him; also p. 504.

Observation 151. Περιέργεια is wrong and must be rejected in favor of περιεργία, deriving from περίεργος.

Observation 1. Καθομιλουμένη should be καθωμιληένη.

Observation 2. Καταχωρίζω must give καταχώρισις, not καταχώρησις. But in any case the correct form is καταχωρισμός.

The Turning Point

Kontos and Kontismos marked a turning point. The very extremity of Kontos' archaism and his tone of assured self-importance had the fortunate result of eliciting resistance. The problem had been a lingering one; all through this period there were those who understood that Korais, being fallible, would inevitably drive other purists to an unquestionable authority: Attic. As long as the basic assumption remained that modern Greeks were meant to be ancient Greeks resurrected, the original compromise had to move in this logical way toward Atticization. Yet no one could write Attic Greek. In short, the whole ideal was bankrupt.

Kontos became a turning point because he helped to make this realization unavoidable. In more specific terms, he provoked a direct rebuttal two years later from Dimitrios Vernardakis, a professor of history at the university and himself a purist. Four years after that, in 1888, came a more generalized and comprehensive rebuttal from the father of the demotic movement, Yannis Psiharis, in his crucial book Τὸ Ταξίδι μου (*My Journey*). Here, with tongue in cheek, Psiharis has his fictional grandmother give him the following prudent advice before he begins his journey:[14]

> Μ' ὅλους ὄμορφα, παιδί μου,
> Νὰ φερθῆς μὴ λησμονήσῃς

14. Psiharis, p. 50.

—Καὶ στὸν Κόντο νὰ μὴν κάμῃς
Γλωσσικὰς Παρατηρήσεις.

(Behave yourself, my boy,
Heed my stipulations,
—And to Kontos do not make
Linguistic Observations.)

Vernardakis, as we shall see, simply exposed the particular arguments Kontos used. Psiharis did much more: he exposed and fought the entire ideology. These sparks quickly lighted others, and the demotic movement exploded. A brief example of the chain of transmission can be seen in the statement in 1903 by the great demoticist Alexander Pallis: "My eyes were first opened theoretically by Vernardakis, practically by Psiharis. The internal need which required me to change was common sense."[15]

REBUTTAL BY VERNARDAKIS

Let us first dwell on Vernardakis very briefly, then discuss Psiharis at greater length. After that we shall review the nineteenth-century situation to see what elements were lying in wait, ready to lend strength to Psiharis' cause.

Vernardakis called his book Ψευδαττικισμοῦ Ἔλεγχος ἤτοι Κ. Σ. Κόντου Γλωσσικῶν Παρατηρήσεων Ἀναφερομένων εἰς τὴν Νέαν Ἑλληνικὴν Γλῶσσαν ἀνασκευή (The Inspection of False-Atticism, Namely the Refutation of K. S. Kontos' Linguistic Observations Regarding the Modern Greek Language).[16] We should note at once that although Vernardakis stated flatly that the only possible basis for Modern Greek must be the living language and not the dead ancient Greek, much less Attic, a dialect thereof, he himself still wrote in *kathare-*

15. *Apology*, p. 123.
16. See Triantafyllidis, *Apo ti glossiki*; also Mihailidis.

vousa.[17] (Looking forward to Psiharis for a moment, we must realize how much of his influence came from the simple fact that his book extolling the living language was also written in that language.) After accusing Kontos in a general way of arrogance, slander, and faulty scholarship, Vernardakis responded to the "linguistic observations" one by one.[18] He went out of his way to defend Korais from Kontos' insults and misrepresentations. For example, Kontos, as we have seen, accused Korais of coining the word σιδηροκόλλησις and then pompously refused to sanction this word. Vernardakis replied: "I merely serve notice upon the Linguistic Observer that the Greek people, without his sanctioning and in ignorance of Korais, have been calling soldering σιδηροκόλλησις from time immemorial, so let him do what he likes!"[19]

Not content with exposing Kontos' faulty knowledge of Modern Greek, Vernardakis examined the Observer's knowledge of ancient Greek as well. Kontos had insisted that ὑπερή-φανος must yield ὑπερηφανία not ὑπερηφάνεια. But in ancient Greek itself, claimed Vernardakis, there are many exceptions to this rule. Βοηθός, for example, yields βοήθεια, ἐνεργός yields ἐνέργεια. The moral is that the ancients were not slaves to grammatical laws. In addition, what makes Kontos so sure that ὑπερήφανος is the parent, when ὑπερφανής is found in Xenophon? This would then yield ὑπερηφάνεια, according to Kontos' own rule.

Kontos was just as limited in his remarks on βιβλιόφιλος, δημοκράτης, and ἀριστοκράτης. The real problem here, wrote Vernardakis, and the one that Kontos should have exposed, was gallicism.[20] These words were obviously blind mimicry of the French *bibliophile, démocrate, aristocrate*. The bankruptcy

17. Vernardakis, p. 3.   18. *Ibid.*, p. 42.
19. *Ibid.*, p. 354.
20. *Ibid.*, pp. 251, 345, 247–48; pp. 5–6.

of purism was evident in the fact that what purported to be the language of Plato was really French thought and locution dished up in Attic syntax. "Le pavillon couvre la marchandise." (Gallicism masquerading as genuine Hellenic also aided Psiharis in his attacks upon the official language.)

Perhaps the most significant parts of Vernardakis' book were those where he refused to argue on Kontos' own terms. It is one thing to point out the grammatical flexibility of the ancients or to challenge etymologies, and quite another to throw up one's hands, so to speak, and exclaim: "I will not contend with you because I simply do not share your premise that we must rule ourselves by ancient precedent." Thus in reference to Kontos' exclusion of both καταχώρισις and καταχώρησις in favor of καταχωρισμός, which occurs in St. Basil, Vernardakis replied curtly: "What Basil the Great said in the 4th century A.D. is one thing, and what we say and ought to say today is quite another."[21] Elsewhere he was even more tersely sardonic.[22] Kontos wanted such-and-such, his reason being that it was used by the ancients; this, said Vernardakis, was no reason.

The refusal to argue is significant because it reduces the whole matter to the crucial, primary question of differing intellectual orientations. In trying to define our being, are we to look backward, forward, or all around us? Are we ancient Greeks, Ottomanized Byzantines, Europeans, or something unique and different from any of these? Vernardakis, like so many of his contemporaries (he lived from 1834 to 1907) was caught in the middle. Thus we find in his book both a continuation of the old philological orientation initiated by Korais and reminiscent of foreign humanists, the orientation in which one invoked the ancients even when arguing against their

21. *Ibid.*, p. 142.   22. *Ibid.*, p. 150.

domination, and also a recognition of how petty and hopeless all such controversies had become.

Psiharis

Vernardakis was obviously not alone—a fact that we shall see when we consider the groups lying in wait, ready to take up Psiharis' cause. But to throw up one's hands and refuse to argue, though a perfectly honest and apposite response, was not the kind of response that could convince borderline cases or move to practical action those who had already been convinced in theory. It is not surprising that Dimaras has characterized Vernardakis' book as a "marvelous personal libel"[23] against Kontos, rather than a truly effective apology for demotic. Even those who were disillusioned with the archaism we have seen in Soutsos and Kontos were so accustomed to philological argumentation, having been subjected to it throughout their schooling, that they could not respond to bare assertions of common sense; they needed something more intellectually intricate and at the same time intellectually familiar. This need, it seems to me, explains Psiharis' astonishing success.[24]

Psiharis appeared on the scene at precisely the right moment and in precisely the right way, for in him the potential demoticist crusaders found a man who not only threw up his hands regarding the old ideology and the old philology, a man who not only made bare assertions of common sense, but a scholar who substantiated this with an immense erudition which was still philological in character.

23. Dimaras, p. 357.
24. A special issue of *Nea Estia* (Vol. vi, 1929, pp. 931 ff.) is dedicated to Psiharis and contains an appreciation by Triantafyllidis (reprinted in his *Apanta*, v, 366–80). See also *Nea Estia*, xxvi (1939), pp. 1,433ff. and lv (1954), pp. 561ff.; E. Kriaras' *Psiharis* (Thessaloniki, 1959); and Mirambel.

Psiharis' philology was entirely different from that flourishing in the University of Athens. It was contemporary, comparative in its orientation, and concerned not with correctness but with the rules that govern the permutations of all languages in time. Its aim was to record and systematize, not to dictate; it was descriptive, not prescriptive or proscriptive.[25] As Psiharis himself wrote, he wished "neither to manufacture languages nor to lay down rules for them." The purpose of linguistic research was rather "to discover their hidden rules, their natural laws, to listen to how the people speak them, and to understand how they were made." Despite these essential departures from the older approach, however, the fact remained that Psiharis seemed intellectually respectable and also intellectually familiar because his approach was philological. Nor should we underestimate the model he set for others by actually writing in demotic; we remember Pallis' remark that Vernardakis opened his eyes theoretically, Psiharis practically. Psiharis' epochal book not only preached—but demonstrated— the path that others had to take.

My Journey took upon itself the double task of demolishing the old and constructing the new. Furthermore, it did both in an entertaining, imaginative fashion, for Psiharis was interested in style as well as content. In a prologue added to the second edition, he took pride in the fact that people had called him a poet. This being the first "serious" book composed in demotic by a learned scholar, Psiharis was continually aware of his responsibility to write in an aesthetically pleasing way, and the extent of his success is the claim, by some at least, that *My Journey* has remained the model for Modern Greek prose style.[26] In any case, Psiharis asserted categorically that he who pretends to solve the language question, a question largely literary, must himself have the attributes of the literary man:

25. Psiharis, p. 154.   26. Asteriotis, p. 723.

skill, poetry, imagination, a lively style.[27] If he had known that he was a linguist and nothing more, he would never have dared to involve himself. But what about Korais and Kontos? Why has no one in Greece thus far wondered if such men have the right to teach the nation philology, for the true philologist— the "lover of words"—is the literary man. Those in whom we must place our hopes are the poets; here Psiharis invokes Malherbe and Dante, poets-turned-linguists in time of need.

DEMOLISHING THE OLD

Despite his grandmother's stipulations, Psiharis now proceeds to demolish Kontos by the "literary" means of jest, anecdote, exaggeration, and irony, as well as by philological argumentation. When his journey brings him to Athens he discovers that a Kontosian disciple has written an entire book on the Master, attempting to discover whether the name Kóntos existed in ancient Athens, and whether the correct pronunciation ought not to be Kontós.[28] Psiharis is glad to see that Kontismos is prospering among the fashionable ladies of this great city. Yes, ancient glory will be restored even to the most intimate domestic relations, as women will now call to their infants: Τὼ μαστὼ ἐπέχω σοι, βρέφος· σὺ δὲ ἔλξον κατασιωπῆσαν;

Korais receives kinder treatment as a person but not as a thinker; Psiharis minces no words when he comes to Korais' ideal of linguistic compromise or to the actual results that ideal produced. The only certainty we can predict for *katharevousa*, he says, is that it will destroy both modern and ancient Greek.[29] As an ideal, it is founded on a distinction between "noble" and "vulgar" which offends common sense. Vernardakis spoke of the pavilion covering the merchandise, referring specifically to the Attic "packaging" of gallicisms. Psiharis

27. Psiharis, pp. 26–27.   28. *Ibid.*, pp. 217–19.
29. *Ibid.*, p. 241.

carries this much further, making unmistakable the connection between the language question and what he feels is a huge and debilitating self-deception in modern Greek culture. Nobility cannot be conferred by outward forms; it is a thing of the soul. Indeed the continuous attention to outward forms characteristic of Greece, and seen most blatantly in the official attitude toward language, is precisely what has been blinding the Greeks to their considerable lack of inner nobility. The groundwork for true nobility, according to Psiharis, is to accept yourself for what you truly are, and to stop pretending you are something else.

Psiharis illustrates this by means of anecdote and hyperbole. On the ship from Constantinople to Chios he converses with a schoolteacher and happens to say νόμισα.[30] The teacher corrects him: ἐνόμισα. When Psiharis asks why this is preferable, the teacher replies: "Ancient Greek is nobler; the form becomes more noble by means of the epsilon." This of course invites the full blast of Psiharian sarcasm: "Pay attention to the form. All the nobility of the soul resides in the form. With this system you can utter abominations; you can insult people and they won't become angry, nor will you appear vulgar. The teacher will take it amiss if you call him γαϊδούρι, and with just cause. But if you call him ὄνος you are flattering him." Similarly, if you change κουρέλλι to κουρέλλιον the rag will become fragrant, if you write μέσπιλον instead of μούσμουλο, the putrid medlar will be transformed into a rose. It is a grand thing to be instructed in nobility by this teacher, Psiharis concludes. Now I can be noble; I can even steal without fear of the police, because if I speak ancient Greek to them they will become immediately aware of my innocence. If a policeman calls me a thief, I'll reply: "Κύριε ἀστυνόμε, οὐκ ἐνομίζω. Ἄπιθι εοῦν· κλὼψ γὰρ εἰμί, οὐχὶ δὲ κλέφτης."

30. *Ibid.*, pp. 129–38.

Though Psiharis does not invoke Korais here, his (very serious) fun is all at Korais' expense. It is the ultimate reply to all the romantic philhellenism that could believe, in the embarrassing words of Korais that we have already seen, that the Hellenic language "refines the habits of the young, making them more elegant and wise." Eloquence and wisdom, for Psiharis, are incompatible with linguistic faking.

Psiharis continues his demolition of *katharevousa* by pointing out its many and often ludicrous inconsistencies. He does to some degree attack the old-style philologists on their own ground. For example, his anecdote about ἐνόμισα leads him to the subject of over-correction. The craving for nobility has been so strong that the purists add epsilon even where it does not belong, writing ἐμέ and ἐσύ for example although the ancients said μέ and σύ.[31] Next, *katharevousa* produces hopeless mélanges.[32] Psiharis once heard a boy say to his mother: Μάννα, θὰ πάω καβάλλα, whereupon the mother angrily corrected him: Θὰ ὑπάγω νὰ ἱππεύσω. Which of the two sentences is barbarous? The mother's, answers Psiharis, for it yokes the modern θά with the ancient ἱππεύσω and the medieval ὑπάγω. Yet this mélange is supposed to be Hellenic. "I understood then," Psiharis comments, "that the only foreign language in Greece is *katharevousa*."

Arguing further, Psiharis reminds the purists that even after they have changed Μάρτης to Μάρτιον or Κωσταντίνο to Κωνσταντῖνος, these words are still Latin.[33] Conversely, when they wish to eliminate πόρτα as a supposed barbarism taken from Italian, they forget that it has been in the Greek language since the reign of Justinian. Worst of all, purification becomes nonsense unless the modern pronunciation is also abandoned in favor of the ancient, since in the speech even of the purists

31. *Ibid.*, pp. 131, 137.   32. *Ibid.*, p. 241.
33. *Ibid.*, pp. 238–39.

themselves it is impossible to distinguish ὑμῖν from ἡμῖν, ἐδήχθη from ἐδείχθη, λέξις from λέξεις, τοῖς from τῆς, omega from omicron, and so forth.[34]

Psiharis is particularly expansive on the subject of gallicisms. At the start of his journey, when he has first arrived in Constantinople, he picks up some Greek newspapers with great expectation, sighing that now, at last, he will be able to read his beloved Greek instead of the French he has been forced to read in Paris. And he will read the Greek of Pericles and Socrates! But as he peruses the papers he has a strange sensation: he is really reading a series of French phrases in literal translation:[35]

> ἀναλόγως τῶν περιστάσεων
> *selon les circonstances*
>
> Θίγει χορδὴν εὐαίσθητον.
> *Il touche à une corde sensible.*
>
> ἐν δεδομένῃ τινί στιγμῇ
> *dans un moment donné*
>
> Εἶδεν ἑαυτὸν ἠναγκασμένον.
> *Il s'est vu forcé.*
>
> Τὰ μέτρα ταῦτα ἔδει νὰ ληφθῶσι.
> *Ces mesures devaient être prises.*
>
> Ἡ λύσις ἐγγίζει.
> *La solution approche.*
>
> Δὲν ἠδύνατο νὰ ἀρθρώσῃ λέξιν.
> *Il ne pouvait articuler une parole.*

34. *Ibid.*, p. 244.
35. *Ibid.*, pp. 80–91. On p. 269 Psiharis affirms that all these phrases were indeed found in newspapers, and that he did not invent any of them.

This, then, is the language of Pericles. In a dream, Psiharis sees all of Europe laughing at the Greeks, saying: "Is this your Greek, you descendants of Pericles? . . . With the pseudo-purist you speak you have made a fine hash of the language of Pericles. Now you have really become barbarians. . . . Do you think you speak Greek? No indeed! You have been gallicized. Speak your own language so that the world may listen to you."

In Psiharis' view, at least, those European philhellenes who are true lovers of Hellas must now come full circle. Instead of applying pressure for an archaic idiom they themselves can understand, they must ask the Greeks to be genuinely themselves. And this, precisely, is Psiharis' plea: "We have made a new language, have altered the pronunciation, from somewhere have taken other blood into our veins. Our first duty is to recognize this and admit it. A nation exalts itself when it shows that it does not fear the truth. When it does fear the truth, this means that its people fail to honor and revere themselves; they adorn themselves with foreign clothes. . . . Let us not be ashamed to reveal what we are. In this way we shall appear more dignified."[36]

BUILDING THE NEW

Psiharis did much more than merely exhort his fellow Greeks to give up old paths and enter a new one. He took the first steps along this new path himself by laying down linguistic axioms and, most importantly, by giving an extended example of demotic Greek in the actual text of his book. On the constructive side, therefore, *My Journey* offers both a method and a demonstration.

Psiharis' axioms, the fruit of his scholarly researches in com-

36. *Ibid.*, p. 49.

parative linguistics, were systematically presented in his *Essais de grammaire historique néo-grecque* (2 vols., 1886–1889) and in the many articles and monographs he produced subsequently during his illustrious career in Paris as director of studies at the Ecole des Hautes Etudes.[37] *My Journey*, which Psiharis would like us to believe was intended primarily "to entertain people with a little imagination and poetry,"[38] does not present the axioms or methodology in any complete or organized way, but it nevertheless gives enough here and there for Psiharis' readers to realize that philology had suddenly become something very different indeed.

I have already spoken of the basic axiom: the aim of linguistics is to describe, record and systematize, to discover laws rather than make them. The first and most important law that Psiharis discovered was that languages change, and furthermore that they change not in an arbitrary or random way, but according to patterns that can be discovered.[39] This view throws an entirely new light on the so-called "mistakes" or barbarisms of Modern Greek. To the old philology, these were naughty departures from some supposed logicality seen in Attic; to the new philology, the altered forms were just the re-

37. See G. Rouillard, *Notice biographique et bibliographique de Jean Psichari* (Melun, 1930). Selections of Psiharis' articles: *Etudes de philologie néo-grecque*: recherches sur le développement historique du grec (Paris, 1892); *Quelques travaux de linguistique, de philologie et de littérature héllenique* 1884–1928 (Paris, 1930). It is important to realize that the authority of Psiharis' studies is now questioned. Because he assumed (wrongly) that vernacular texts exactly mirrored the spoken language of their time he "succeeded in dating most developments much too late, and in postulating their occurrence in an order which makes no sense. . . . Hatzidakis . . . pointed out that the proportion of old to new forms depends largely on the degree of education of the writer." (Browning, p. 18; see also Mirambel and Bachtin.)

38. Psiharis, p. 269.   39. *Ibid.*, p. 223.

verse: they offered confirmation of the logicality, regularity, and predictability with which all languages change.

By way of illustration, Psiharis claims that there were definite reasons causing πατήρ to become πατέρας and not πατῆρος; ἄνθρωπος to become ἄθρωπος and neither ἄνρωπος, ἄρωπος, nor ἄνθωπος; ἡμέρα to become μέρα and not ἡμέρ.[40] Once the fact of linguistic change is accepted and the initial rules discovered in the only possible way—by observing, recording, systematizing—then the methodology for the future becomes clear. "You must seek out the true and only laws in the language of the people; the grammar of the people must be followed faithfully."[41] In short, like Korais before him, Psiharis advocated expeditions to the villages to record peasant speech. But the reasons were very different. Korais, we remember, wished to discover and preserve all the "genuinely Hellenic" elements still surviving in the villages; Psiharis wished simply to discover the various forms used, in order to extract from them their inherent natural grammatical canons.

There is another crucial element in Psiharis' program, and another crucial axiom. Here we are led back to the language question as formulated in its most elemental way: What shall be the language of the Greek nation? In other words, what common language, what *koine*, can all the Greeks write? How can they solve the problem of regional differences? Psiharis' axiom is that this problem solves itself—or, to put it more accurately, is solved by the people themselves and perhaps by the poets, but certainly not by the grammarians. He thinks back to Homer in this regard, and formulates his view of the Homeric question.[42] We are dealing here, he insists, with oral traditions; the bard was illiterate. Furthermore, there was not just one Homer but many. Homer's poem displays a hodge-

40. *Ibid.*   41. *Ibid.*, p. 228.
42. *Ibid.*, pp. 143–46.

podge of forms, and this leads us to conclude that it originated in various regions, each speaking a localized variety of Greek. Yet somehow in the course of time the separate proto-epics and linguistic variations were able to coalesce and then to be promulgated and understood throughout the land. Each of the four ancient dialects developed naturally, in the same way, from the diverse village-languages of the region. Even the revered Attic of the purists, Psiharis reminds us, "was nothing else in the beginning but a peasant language, sluttish, vulgar, and spoken in the villages."[43]

From all this he concludes that the problem of modern Greek regionalism will be solved in the same way: by time and by the poets. He thinks of the demotic ballads that originate from the various regions and display a hodgepodge of forms.[44] Out of these, some day, unexpected by anyone, may come a new *Iliad*. (I should add here, in anticipation, that Kazantzakis' *Odyssey* was among other things a conscious— and probably unsuccessful—attempt to force various linguistic elements to coalesce into a unity and thereby help create a pan-hellenic demotic.)

If we take the second crucial axiom—that a *koine* develops naturally in time from village regionalism—and add to it the first axiom that linguistic change follows definite and discoverable rules, we arrive at Psiharis' methodology. This was simply: Go out to the villages and record peasant speech. This procedure is not in the interests of demotic alone. By studying village language, Psiharis argues, we can understand the workings of all languages, including ancient Greek. The teachers should sit at the feet of the peasant instead of reading Plato and Xenophon.[45] As for Psiharis himself:

43. *Ibid.*, p. 154. 44. *Ibid.*, p. 145.
45. *Ibid.*, pp. 154, 156.

"Ah, if only I could! . . . I would race all over Greece, would go to each village one by one with a pack on my back, a piece of paper in my hand, and collect, collect. Into my pack I would throw . . . every word, variant, pronunciation . . . in order to see how each region speaks, which idiom resembles which other, what distinguishes each from the other, how many linguistic centers exist in Greece, how a language forms itself little by little, how a peasant language devolves until it becomes a common tongue for all, how it spreads and is extended, how human speech changes little by little in the soul and on the lips. The village languages are disappearing before people realize their worth and how greatly the study of them will honor Greece."[46]

THE NEW "KOINE" EXEMPLIFIED

We have seen how Psiharis' book demolishes the opposition and how it lays down axioms and methodology for the demotic struggle. As I have already indicated, it goes one step further, for it provides an example of the new *koine*. Arguments against the purists and in defense of demotic were available elsewhere, both in Psiharis' own monographs and in the writings of others. But the text of *My Journey*—that is, an extended use of the vulgar language for serious (though entertaining) intellectual discussion—was unique.[47] Psiharis' aim was to demonstrate inflections, syntax, spelling, etc. As he said afterward in the prologue to the second edition, his Grammar was

46. *Ibid.*, pp. 152–53.
47. We should remember, however, that Solomos had used demotic prose in his *Dialogos* and also in the *Yinaika tou Zakynthos*, which was not published until the 20th century. Velaras also wrote demotic prose, including a translation of Plato's *Crito*, and Sophianos translated Plutarch's "On the Education of Children" into demotic in 1554.

written in effect with each word and form employed in *My Journey*.[48] Above and beyond this, his aim was to demonstrate demotic's ability to sustain the subtlety and breadth required for scholarly discourse, since, quite aside from its own riches, it could easily assimilate any terms that it lacked. Anticipating the inevitable accusation that the book must cheat, Psiharis declared in his famous preface to the first edition:

"I do not have a private language; I did not make up a language. . . . I write the common language of the people. When demotic lacks a needed word, I take the word from ancient Greek and try to fit it into the grammar of the people. This is what all the nations of the world have done, and what we shall do also. In this book of mine the language of the people has been written for the first time, I feel, with a certain order and unity. I have tried to write it correctly, preserving the laws . . . of demotic grammar."[49]

He added that each and every grammatical form in the book had been carefully considered.[50] Those lying in wait to pounce upon all the "mistakes" in his language should first read his theoretical monographs, which justified and explained everything.

Given his axioms and methodology, it is no surprise that the forms Psiharis uses in the book—quite aside from the spelling —are radically different from those imposed by *katharevousa*. Here are some examples: τὰ φώσια (= φῶτα), τὰ λάθια (= λάθη), συφωνῶ, ἄθρωπος, περσότερο, τὶς φημερίδες, πομονή, μὲ τὸν ἄμμο, τὸ ἄρφα (= ἄλφα), τὸ σκολειό, τὸ λοιπό,

48. Psiharis, p. 18.
49. *Ibid.*, p. 35. His claim to be the first writer of demotic prose is not justifiable, literally, if we consider the period before the 19th-century Atticism of Soutsos and Kontos. But he was the first scholar to offer demotic prose as a provocation in an effective way.
50. *Ibid.*, pp. 34–35.

τῶν παιδιῶ της, ἀφτά, ξεφέβγει, ὅτι κι ἄ σοῦ πούνε.[51] Most of
these represent rather an extreme divergence from puristic
forms, and some might be considered hopelessly illiterate. Actually, they do not characterize Psiharis' language fairly, for the
majority of his words (though not his inflections) remain
identical with their purist analogues.

The above examples, however, do point up very nicely Psiharis' insistence that the written language must be a phoneti-
cally accurate transcription of what people—the mass of people
—actually speak.[52] This is the full substance of his heresy. He
is ruled not by any standard of correctness imposed upon the
language from outside, but rather by what he would argue is
a standard imposed from inside. We have already seen his insistence that the modern divergences from ancient Greek are
predictable and regular, i.e., correct. But even beyond this, he
is ruled by the desire for comprehensibility. As he says at the
end of his prologue: "Πρῶτα πρῶτα καὶ πιὸ πολὶ ἀπ' ὅλα
θέλησα νὰ μπορέσῃ ὁ καθένας νὰ μὲ καταλάβῃ" (First of
all, and more than anything else, I wanted everyone to be
able to understand me).[53]

The particular forms offered by Psiharis in *My Journey*,
though responsibly presented as correct, do not matter nearly so
much as the axioms, methodology, and aims that I have been
discussing. Psiharis was not insisting that his words be reproduced letter by letter; he was calling upon others to continue
what he had begun. If Greece's language question is to be
solved, he argues, "Everyone must earnestly endeavor to learn

51. *Ibid.*, pp. 60, 269, 46, 10, 87, 91, 95, 150, 73, 65, 12, 50.
52. Many demoticists today would agree, however, that Psiharis'
language was in some ways just as "manufactured" and arbitrary as
katharevousa. He gave the imprimatur to what *some* people actually spoke.
53. Psiharis, p. 37.

the tongue he scorns out of ignorance, grammars must be made, our true language . . . must be taught in schools and at the university."[54] Psiharis was calling for allies in a crusade to overturn a century of deleterious theory and practice in official and educational circles. The call came at the right time; it was quickly answered.

ASSUMPTIONS SHARED WITH KORAIS

Before considering those who responded, we must examine my earlier claim that Psiharis, for all his extremism, shared certain primary assumptions with the purists, and thus continued rather than negated the liberal humanism of men like Korais.

The first thing we must realize is that Psiharis did not wish to abolish ancient Greek. Our obvious reaction to forms such as ἄρφα, ἄθρωπος, etc., is that they weaken the chain connecting modern Greece with the hellenic past. This was the reaction of the purists and even of some of the less radical demoticists. It is true that Psiharis was always ruled by phonetic rather than etymological facts, and it is true that he despised the ancestor worship imposed on Greece by the Enlightenment.[55] But he honored ancient Greece and its language; furthermore, as a professional scholar of language, he honored Greece's linguistic continuity. His argument, as we have already seen, was that *katharevousa* would destroy ancient Greek as well as demotic. Instead of mixing the two in an impossible hodgepodge, teachers should speak demotic and truly study ancient.[56] Indeed, "in order to understand the historical worth of demotic, we must study ancient better."[57] In no way did Psiharis wish to dishonor the ancient tradition; he merely wanted that tradition to encourage rather than hinder

54. *Ibid.*, pp. 35–36. 55. *Ibid.*, p. 61.
56. *Ibid.*, p. 241. 57. *Ibid.*, p. 36.

modern Greek development, and in this he was not impossibly far from the thinking of Korais.

Psiharis also shared with Korais the assumption that a nation's glory is measured by its cultural achievement. Korais, being a man of letters, emphasized the ancient achievements in the medium of the written word: philosophy, history, drama. Psiharis, also a man of letters, did the same. For him, cultural achievement and the concomitant glory come when a nation produces a literature of its own. I have already dwelt on the way in which nationality came to be defined in the Enlightenment by language, and I have cited the dictum with which Psiharis opened and closed his book: "Γλώσσα καὶ πατρίδα εἶναι τὸ ἴδιο" (language and fatherland are the same).[58] He shared this assumption with Korais; the difference was that Psiharis wished that the modern Greeks might be allowed to become themselves, in order to develop their own culture. Psiharis insisted that his goal was precisely the goal of the purist educators: that the nation might make progress.[59] If you allow us to be ourselves, he told them, then one day we may achieve precisely what you wish—a culture that will make us worthy successors of the ancients. But, as things stand, "you are ruining a language that of and by itself can one day bring us a national literature, poetry, and renown."

Though we must not minimize the differences between Psiharis and the purists, we must be aware that in many ways he continued their nationalism and, more importantly, their belief in the continuity of Greek culture. Like Korais to some degree and like humanists of the past such as du Bellay, Psiharis combined a respect for the vernacular with a program for its enrichment through the assimilation of ancient terms. He had the same high standards, the same philological orien-

58. *Ibid.*, p. 34, p. 264.
59. *Ibid.*, p. 243.

tation, the same obsession with that elusive something called "Greekness." Thus he could appeal not only because of his thoroughgoing radicalism but also because he was at the same time familiarly within a tradition shared by all. This was the secret of his success, and perhaps of the success of others who have influenced history to a similar degree.

The Response

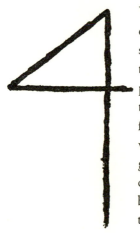We must now trace what must be called the "phenomenon" of the response, for it was truly phenomenal. In the half-century following Psiharis' appeal, Greece did indeed develop a literature, a poetry, a renown. This cultural florescence was so intimately connected with the linguistic and ideological program of the demotic movement that we can say—without risk of hyperbole, I believe—that it would have been unthinkable apart from that movement.

Demoticism sparked an extraordinary period of literary creativity.

ELEMENTS LYING IN WAIT

To understand the response, we must first look back on the nineteenth century to see what elements were lying in wait, ready to lend strength to Psiharis' cause. I spoke earlier of the Ionian islands: of how the demotic tradition that flowered in Crete in the seventeenth century was preserved in such places as Zante and Corfu throughout the eighteenth and taken up self-consciously by the poet Solomos in the nineteenth. In this way, an important precedent was set for the use of demotic at least in poetry.

We must next remember that these same islands remained outside the Greek kingdom until 1864.[1] Thus they were not affected by King Otho's laws requiring *katharevousa* in the schools and by the demands of Rankavis and Soutsos that the archaic language be employed for all modes of literary expression. Under these circumstances, Solomos' example was able to be invoked and imitated by succeeding generations of poets. Polylas, Solomos' pupil, translated Homer and Shakespeare, and defended demotic in the prologue to his 1859 edition of his teacher's works. Typaldos dedicated his poems (1856) to Solomos. Hiotis, the apologist for the Ionian poets, wrote a treatise on demotic, dedicating it to the purist Rankavis. Valaoritis continued Solomos' practice of looking to the demotic ballads for inspiration. In 1863, after the election de-

1. Venetian rule ended in 1797, when the islands were occupied by the French. In 1800 they were a federal republic under the protection of Russia and Turkey. In 1807 they were ceded to France. In 1809–1810 they were taken by the British. From 1815 to 1864 they were a protectorate under British control, and were then ceded by Great Britain to Greece.

termining *enosis* with Greece, he addressed the people of Levkas in demotic, reminding them that the language "of the
educated" was composed of the ashes and bones of the dead,
whereas demotic had been suckled by every Greek along with
his mother's milk. (How easily the trope passed from Korais
to his opponent!)[2]

These Ionian poets prepared the way, some living long
enough to respond personally to Psiharis' call. Polylas, for example, wrote a monograph entitled *Our Literary Language* in
1892. His student Mavilis, the last of the school of Solomos,
spoke for demotic in the National Assembly of 1911, and,
along with Kazantzakis, became one of the charter members
of the Educational Association, a demoticist lobby.

A second group that helped to prepare the way for Psiharis
was composed of certain literary and public figures in Athens.
These included (a) veterans of 1821 who remembered the
language of their illiterate leaders, (b) Ionians like Valaoritis
who had transported their demotic tradition to the capital, and
(c) purists who had become disillusioned because of the linguistic anarchy *katharevousa* had created. People spoke out
with increasing temerity. Tertsetis, who published the memoirs
of General Kolokotronis "from dictation," vaunted his pride
in speaking and writing the language of Kolokotronis, Miaou-
lis, and Botsaris in the capital of Greece. Justifying himself before Parliament, he declared: "How fortunate it would be,
gentlemen, if only we all spoke the language of 1821! Then
there was concord. . . . Now, if I am not mistaken, every Greek,
every citizen, has . . . his private grammar." Tertsetis' collaboration with Kolokotronis enriched the store of written demotic
prose with a text that would later be pillaged by Kazantzakis
for words. In addition, he must be credited with discovering

2. *Apology*, pp. 58–72.

Solomos' *Dialogue.* Another outspoken figure was Vernardakis, whose opposition to Kontos we have already seen.[3]

There was still a third group that helped to prepare the way,
composed of certain scholars who did not publicly join the
movement or cease to write in *katharevousa,* but whose studies
awakened people to the problem.[4] Most important were the
folklorists, and in particular N. G. Politis, who established
folklore studies in Greece in the 1870's with his *Neo-hellenic
Mythology* and the periodical *Laographia,* which became a
treasury of demotic words and forms. Systematic efforts to
discover and transcribe the country's folklore must have reflected a changed attitude toward Greek culture of the Byzantine period and the *tourkokratia.* Whereas the humanists had
intimated that "genuine" Greek civilization had died at the
beginning of the Christian era and had passed to Rome, Constantine Paparrhegopoulos, in his epochal *History of the Greek
Nation* (5 volumes, 1860–1872), attempted a synthetic view,
stressing the continuity from ancient times and the significance of Byzantium and the Turkish period for modern
Greece. This revised attitude helped to change the orientation of many intellectuals and to intensify the search for proof
that Greece's imaginative powers had not lain dormant. The
publication of the newly discovered medieval epic *Digenis
Akritas* in 1875 caused great excitement. As more and more
evidence of poetic creativity came to light, the Gibbonian view
of a dark age was necessarily qualified, and the purists' assumptions shaken. In addition, the folklorists made Greece
susceptible to the romantic German adulation of the *Volk,* and
thus to an ideology able to compete with the romantic French
adulation of the resurrected Hellenes. Once again, the purists'
assumptions were shaken. This Volk-cult was later to play a

3. *Ibid.,* pp. 73–78.   4. *Ibid.,* p. 93.

significant role in Kazantzakis' thought, and to become a banner under which demoticism and aggressive nationalism could march arm-in-arm.

As for Politis himself, although he continued to employ *katharevousa* and to espouse the ideals of ancient Greece, he could not help but recognize demotic's virtues. A man who enjoyed immense prestige, he aided the cause in his capacity as adjudicator in poetic contests. In 1889, just a few months after *My Journey* appeared, Politis awarded the prize to Kostis Palamas on the grounds that the poet's demotic was capable of evoking the "deep religious sense" of the ancients.[5] In short, barbaric demotic could serve the cause of Hellas. Eighteen years later, Politis was again one of the adjudicators when Kazantzakis' demotic play *Day Is Breaking* received praise and thus became the first theatrical work in demotic to achieve official recognition.

Folklore studies were not the only discipline to be imported from Western Europe into Greece in the late nineteenth century. The new philology, practiced by Psiharis abroad, was established in the University of Athens by George Hatzidakis.[6] A pupil of Kontos, Hatzidakis continued to employ the puristic language in his own writings, but since he was a student of comparative linguistics and thus able to view Greek bilingualism from a historical and objective standpoint, he campaigned for the simplification of *katharevousa*, recommending, for example, that it be relieved of the infinitive and optative. Most important, he enabled the systematic study of demotic to enter the sacred precincts of the purist university. (In the long run, however, Hatzidakis did not have the courage to apply his scholarly insights. He wavered between demotic and *katharevousa*, wrote a rebuttal to Vernardakis' *Inspection*

5. *Ibid.*, pp. 110–11.   6. *Ibid.*, p. 104.

of False-Atticism, eventually became one of the leading purists, and used his influence in the 1917–1920 Venizelist period to prevent a full turn to demoticism.)[7]

ROLE OF FRENCH NATURALISM

Each of these groups—the Ionian poets, certain men of letters in Athens, and the scholars of folklore and comparative linguistics—helped to produce conditions that by 1888 made Psiharis' seed fall on fertile and responsive ground. Each in its own way shared Psiharis' conviction that modern Greece had its own dignity and worth, quite apart from any reflected glory deriving from the ancient Hellenes. In effect, then, all these forces were seemingly moving Greek intellectual life away from the dominance exercised upon it by the liberal Enlightenment and the romantic philhellenism of eighteenth-century France—at the same time that they continued to share the Enlightenment's dictum that language and fatherland are one. That there was a shift in general attitude is undoubtedly true; that this shift tended to make Greeks more intellectually self-sufficient, less dependent on outside fashions, more interested in themselves, would seem to be equally true. But is it? We would be wrong, I believe, to think that receptivity to demoticism meant a move toward cultural isolation. It is true that modern Greece was looking inward and seeking its own identity, but part of what it had to discover was its cultural oneness with Europe. The challenge was not to escape Western influences, but to assimilate them in a fresh and creative way. The role played by outside fashion even in that most nationally self-centered of disciplines, folklore studies, has already been suggested. Nor should we forget, of course, that

7. Hadzidakis. The Vernardakis-Hadzidakis controversy is reviewed in Triantafyllidis, *Apo ti glossiki.*

philologists like Psiharis and Hatzidakis had been guided into their fields because of European influences.

What I would like to suggest now, in addition, is that the remarkable receptivity to the demotic crusade when it broke out in 1888 was conditioned—perhaps even made inevitable—by another European influence, namely the change in French literary fashion from romanticism to naturalism. Psiharis complained that a man like Korais had no right legislating for Greek writers because he himself was not a poet and had no concept of literature. I would qualify this by saying that Korais did indeed have a concept of literature, but that this concept was inevitably the aristocratic, courtly one of contemporary French romanticism. I would venture to assert, beyond this, that Korais' purified language was indeed a workable, fit vehicle for the Greek writers of his day.

Resident abroad, sharing the courtly view that saw literature as reflecting the "select" minority of society, these writers were chiefly occupied in editing the ancient classics, or translating and imitating French romantics such as Rousseau, Chateaubriand, Musset, Lamartine, and Hugo—in other words, engaged in projects that had no direct relation to the Greek people and culture, even though both the ancient and the romantic texts they produced were meant to be propaganda to teach the Greeks the value of liberty. As long as one's novel, poem, or play is a translation or imitation of a French original, most likely dealing in the old courtly manner with people and concerns very much above and apart from the vulgar herd, the artificiality of the language does not matter terribly, even in dialogue. Indeed, it may even be an asset. In any case, you can easily delude yourself into believing that your dialogue is an acceptable compromise.

A lovely example of this is found in E. A. Simos' translation of Mme de Staël's *Corinne* (1835).[8] Simos prefaces the book with a statement typical for that period: how beneficial the love and imitation of the ancients is for all peoples, and how indispensable for modern Greeks, whose new civilization will thereby be immeasurably strengthened. As far as the language of his translation is concerned, however, he claims that he sought a style that would be easily comprehensible and "removed as little as possible from common speech." A fine claim, but the result is dialogue that could never have been spoken by any modern Greek, even though a modern Greek might conceivably find it convincing for the speech of French ladies and gentlemen: Σήμερον, εἶπεν ἡ Κορίννα, θέλω σᾶς δείξει τὸ Πάνθεον. . . . εἶχα βέβαια ἐλπίδα τινά. Although Korais' language may have been appropriate for novels like *Corinne*, it was most inappropriate for novels like Zola's *L'Assommoir* or *Nana*. At least in part because of the change in fashion that brought letters steadily away from the courtly and toward the egalitarian, popular, and "vulgar," *katharevousa* became acutely impossible for literary men.

Even before naturalism reached its zenith in France with Zola, Greeks had begun turning to the "vulgar" life of shepherds and fishermen for their subject matter. At first—as might have been expected—they did this romantically, but as the European fashion changed they too felt an increasing need for the "scientific" accuracy that naturalism demanded. But how could a realistic picture of Greek life be conveyed in *katharevousa*? The attempts were bound to be grotesque, as we have already seen in the early naturalistic novel *Thanos Vlekas* with its ἀγγεῖον ψυχροῦ ὕδατος and its Atticized sighs. One of the "simple" characters in the novel complains when another character shows off his "Hellenic." Yet her own speech displays all of Korais' corrections: Σήμερον, δάσκαλε, θὰ εὕρῃς τὸν καφέ.

8. Hourmouzios, p. 1,442.

... Τί ἤκουσες διὰ τὸν Τάσον; And Thanos, the simple farmer, complains in unconvincing *katharevousa*: Εἶναι δέκα πέντε ἡμέραι ἀφοῦ ἐθέρισα, καὶ ἀκόμη δὲν ἐφάνησαν οἱ ἐνοικιασταί. . . .[9]

It is clear that once the dominant literary mode had ceased to be courtly—that is, deliberately removed from the people, deliberately imitative of romantic literature or the classics, deliberately artificial and elevated in tone—the use of *katharevousa* condemned imaginative writing either to superficiality (for how can a literary work capture the soul of the people it treats when it refuses to use the language they speak?) or to a grotesqueness accentuated, if anything, by halfway compromises. Thus I would add this change in literary fashion to the other factors making Psiharis' proclamation of the demotic revolution inevitable, and preparing the ground for the strong response by literary men. The various compromises attempted by puristic artists in their effort to approximate naturalistic speech had convinced ever-increasing numbers that the language question now had to be seen in terms of either/or. This is what helped determine the demoticists to insist upon uncompromising fidelity to the vulgar spoken tongue.

IMMEDIATE RESPONSE TO PSIHARIS' CALL

Almost immediately after *My Journey* appeared, δημοτικισμός established itself as a conscious movement, intent upon battling Ἀττικισμός and καθαρευουσιανισμός, the parties of Kontos and Korais respectively. It would be an oversimplification in the long run to call *dhimotikismós* the party of Psiharis, for the radicalism of Psiharis' language eventually repelled certain adherents, and various factions developed within the movement; but, at the start at least, Psiharis was the propelling force. As I have tried to show in the preceding sections, his

9. Kalligas, pp. 35, 34, 33.

well-timed message fell on fertile ground, and the result was an astonishing amount of activity over the next twenty years. I should like now to give some indication of this activity and the people involved, for we shall see that almost all the figures mentioned will have some connection with the career of Kazantzakis. Also, the specific details of their involvement—the type of literary work they did, the societies they formed, the newspapers and periodicals for which they wrote—add up to a literary culture that a young man born in 1883 and maturing in this intellectually exciting period would inevitably enter if he had literary aspirations.

My Journey was hailed and embraced at the start by men already influential or soon destined to become leading figures in Greek intellectual life. The novelist Roidis supported Psiharis in 1888 and five years later in his widely read *Eidola* he suggested that the written language be gradually simplified.[10] Eftaliotis, one of the most radical of the demoticists, praised the book and communicated his enthusiasm to Psiharis, saying that the only language was the national language and that the struggle was a great and holy one.[11] We will gain some sense of his own contributions when we consider demotic translations and scholarly treatises. A third figure who must be mentioned is the journalist Ghavriilidis, who wrote for the liberal paper *Akropolis*, as did Kazantzakis later. In 1907, Ghavriilidis was responsible for one of the few objective, non-partisan reviews of Kazantzakis' first play, even though at that time Kazantzakis was not yet a "pure" demoticist.[12] In 1888, he had this to say: "The people speak Romaiika [demotic], the educated speak or write Chinese. . . . What's the result? Graduating

10. *Apology*, p. 87. Vlastos in *Greek Bilingualism* (pp. 69–70) testifies to the effect of this book on the younger generation. It was *The Idols*, he says, that cured him of ancestor-worship.

11. Psiharis, p. 24.   12. Ghavriilidis, *Lakonika*.

from the high schools we have non-spellers, from the university non-scholars."[13] Lastly, there was Grigorios Xenopoulos, who contributed so much to the demoticization of the theatre circa 1900–1910, when Kazantzakis was also doing his share. (Xenopoulos eventually fell out of sympathy with the movement.)[14]

PROMULGATING THE GOSPEL

These were only some of the men who came in at the start, but they are perhaps sufficient to illustrate the variety of talents that offered themselves to the "great and holy struggle." The first task was to make the demoticist rationale and program known to the entire intellectual community. This promulgation of the gospel was done in various ways, through periodicals, newly formed societies, and the continued examination of the language question in scholarly treatises. Let us give a few examples of each.

Periodicals have always played a central role in Greek literary life as the organs for specific groups or cliques and very often as crusaders for particular literary styles. We shall see later, for example, how Kazantzakis, as he veered from a compromising language toward extreme demoticism in the first two or three years of his career, necessarily veered away as well from a compromising periodical to the radically and crusadingly demoticist *Noumas*.

The complete radicalism of this organ was possible because the way had already been prepared. *Estia* opened its columns to Psiharis, Pallis, Eftaliotis, Palamas, and Polylas as early as 1891–1894. *Techni*, published by Kostas Hatzopoulos in 1898–1899, used systematically written demotic as its "house style" and thus became the first demotic periodical. *Noumas*, which

---

13. *Apology*, p. 120. On Ghavriilidis, see also Kordatos, *Istoria*, pp. 121–22.

14. *Apology*, p. 138.

began publication in 1903 with Dimitrios Tankopoulos as its energetic director, did not therefore have to fight this battle from the beginning, and was able to extend its demotic crusading beyond the question of language itself to broader social and educational problems. It need hardly be added that demoticist periodicals proliferated in the succeeding years. Even *Nea Zoi*, published in 1906 by a professor of mathematics at the university, saw fit to write its literary section, at least, in the "language of peasants."[15]

Societies played an equally important role, though their effect was sometimes restricted to a given locality unless, like the Educational Association, they published a journal. In Athens in 1904, Markos Tsirimokos, Ion Dragoumis, and Manolis Triantafyllidis—crucial figures whom we shall encounter elsewhere as well—were among the founders of the Society for the National Language (Ἑταιρεία ἡ Ἐθνικὴ Γλῶσσα), whose purpose was "to aid the study, extension and use of the living Greek language in all sectors of social life and in all types of writing."[16] A linguistic Brotherhood was established in Constantinople in 1908, the first such center outside of Greece.[17] In 1909 the Solomos Society for the National Language sprang up in Hanya (Crete), its sixty-six members taking upon themselves the broad task of "striking down superstition."[18] A few months later, in response to opposition encountered by the Hanya group, another chapter was formed in Irakleion, with

15. *Ibid.*, pp. 114, 122, 141. *Noumas* lasted until 1922. Other early demoticist periodicals were Vokos' *Periodikon mas* (1900–1902), K. Hatzopoulos' *Dionysos*, Axiotis' *Kritiki* (1903 ff.), and Vlachoyannis' *Propylaia* (1901 ff.). *Panathinaia* (1901–1912) favored "simplified *katharevousa*" but welcomed articles in support of demotic. See Kordatos, *Istoria*, pp. 132–33.

16. *Apology*, p. 133. Dimaras, p. 399, gives the date of founding as 1905, not 1904.

17. *Ibid.*, p. 147.   18. *Ibid.*, p. 148.

Kazantzakis as president and spokesman. We shall see the manifesto he wrote in this capacity when we begin to follow his early career. We shall also at that time learn about the activities of what was undoubtedly the most important group of all, the Educational Association, founded in 1910 with Kazantzakis as one of the charter members.

Finally, the gospel preached by Psiharis was promulgated by means of treatises that continued to examine the linguistic problem and to explore its wider ramifications. We have already seen that Polylas, friend and pupil of Solomos, defender of demotic as early as 1859, produced his little monograph on *Our Literary Language* in 1892.[19] Fotis Fotiadis, a Constantinopolitan physician, brought out in 1902 a collection of essays on the demoticists' responsibility to reform the curriculum in the schools.[20] In the same year, the famous German philologist Krumbacher, founder of Byzantine studies in the West, published *Das Problem der neugriechischen Schriftsprache*, which circulated afterwards (1905) in translation, together with an "answer" by George Hatzidakis. The effect of this book on twenty-three-year-old Dimitrios Glinos, then studying at the university and destined to become one of demoticism's most persistent and radical proponents, has been recorded by a fellow student: "Glinos did not conceal his enthusiasm . . . for the wise defense of demotic by the Bavarian byzantinist and for the sophistic and clearly contentious answer by our reactionary professor of linguistics."[21] Krumbacher was important to the movement because in his studies of Byzantine civilization he tried to show how the demotic tradition, hidden be-

19. *Ibid.*, p. 65.
20. *Ibid.*, p. 129. The title of Fotiadis' book was "The Language Question and our Educational Rebirth." For comment on Fotiadis, see Triantafyllidis, *Apanta*, Vol. v, pp. 440–52.
21. K. Varnalis, "O Glinos daskalos," in *Sti mnimi*, p. 57. For data, see under Sotiriou.

hind the official Atticism of the state, had continued to nourish the nation.[22]

PHILOLOGICAL APPLICATION

The demoticists were not content with simply spreading their ideas to others. They themselves had to get on with the job, for as Psiharis himself had emphasized, *My Journey* was only a beginning. There was a dictionary to be compiled, a definitive grammar to be produced; and—of utmost importance— there was the challenge of applying demotic to all forms of written expression so that it could prove its worth as a literary and scholarly medium. (There were also pedagogical reforms that began to occupy the demoticists in the second decade of the century and that I shall treat when we come to the movement's broader implications and to Kazantzakis' personal involvement in the effort to produce demotic primers.)

A great dictionary along the lines of the *New English Dictionary on Historical Principles*, one not only recording all the known words in the language but using demotic itself for the definitions, has yet to be produced. (Even in desk dictionaries, the use of demotic for the actual text is only just beginning.)[23] Later, we shall encounter Kazantzakis' abortive attempt to bring this goal a bit nearer. In this context, however, I might mention the name of Petros Vlastos in order to give some idea of the spadework that eventually was done, although in this case not until somewhat later.

Vlastos has an added relevance for us because he was so admired by Kazantzakis, and because his family illustrates the continuity of Greek culture. A descendant of one of the nobles

22. Palamas, L. pp. 106–07. A Greek translation of Krumbacher's study appeared in 1901. See *Bibliography*.

23. A good example is the *Epitomo lexiko dimotikis glossas*, published by Haris Patsis.

dispatched by the Byzantine emperor Alexios II Komnenos in 1183 to rule Crete, Vlastos had behind him a family tradition of service to state, church, and letters. One of his ancestors, for example, was instrumental in the establishment of the first Greek publishing house in Venice in the sixteenth century.[24] Petros continued this family tradition of serving Greek letters from abroad. Like Pallis, whom we shall encounter in a moment, he worked for the Rally Company, residing in Liverpool as director of the branch there. His contributions include his own poetry; his work for spelling reform; a demotic grammar (1914); two racy lectures on "Greek bilingualism and some parallel cases," delivered at King's College, London;[25] and a pioneering lexicon called Συνώνυμα καὶ Συγγενικά, Τέχνες καὶ Σύνεργα (1931) in which he compiled terms for the operations and implements used in the various trades—thousands of words that had never found their way into any dictionary before. Kazantzakis eulogized Vlastos as a "fearless Akritas of our language," used his books as source materials for his own lexical projects, and maintained a friendship with the author, enjoying his hospitality in Liverpool in 1939.[26] Indeed, Vlastos seems to be one of the few people for whom the hypercritical Kazantzakis had nothing but kind words.[27]

Regarding grammars, Menos Filintas as early as 1907 produced, in his *Grammar of the Romaic Language*, a demotic grammar actually written in demotic.[28] This pioneering at-

24. See Geanakoplos; also the article by Layton.

25. Published in Athens in 1933. See *Bibliography* under Vlastos.

26. Kazantzakis, *Japan-China*, p. 223. Prevelakis, p. 490.

27. Kazantzakis, *England*, pp. 107–08. Here, Kazantzakis says: "Ion Dragoumis and Peter Vlastos are, I believe, the two people I have most respected and loved in my life."

28. *Apology*, p. 144. Vol. I, 1907; Vol. II, 1910. Filintas did have some predecessors. Vilaras' *Romeiki Glossa* (1814) was written in

tempt helped to lay the groundwork for the more systematic and definitive grammatical studies published by Triantafyllidis in the 1930's and culminating in his *Neohellenic Grammar* of 1941.

APPLICATION IN JOURNALISM AND SCHOLARSHIP

It is in the applications of demotic to many (alas not all) forms of written expression that we see most clearly the extraordinary amount of creative energy the movement released, not only in its first two decades, which we are considering now, but also in the following three decades. I can give only the barest sketch here of the works produced and the people involved circa 1890–1910, confining myself for the most part to figures who had some connection with Kazantzakis' career. The important thing to remember is that the question was not simply one of vocabulary, grammar, and syntax. Those who applied demotic were doing so in an effort to develop a true culture for modern Greece; they were trying to discover, project, and honor what they felt was the real Greece, which had so long been obscured by a romanticized conception of resurrected Hellas.

Among the areas where demotic was applied were journalism, scholarship, translations, and all genres of imaginative literature: poetry, prose-fiction, drama. The movement was far from successful in some of these areas while completely successful in others.

Among the journalists, Ghavriilidis was the first to attempt

---

demotic and was extremely radical, especially in its call for spelling reform. The earliest grammar was produced in the mid-sixteenth century by Nikolaos Sophianos, but remained unpublished except for the section on parsing, until Legrand's edition in 1870, 2nd ed., 1874. A grammar by Girolamo Germano (1622) was published by Pernot in 1907. There is also Christopoulos' grammar of 1805.

a simplified idiom.[29] In general, the newspapers resisted a demotic as radical as Psiharis', preferring some degree of mixed
language. We shall have occasion later to see Kazantzakis'
continued clash with editors in this regard.

In the realm of scholarship, an early application of demotic
was made by Eftaliotis in his *Istoria tis Romiosinis*, 1901.[30]
Dedicated to Psiharis, and written shortly after Greece's hu-
miliating defeat by the Turks in 1897, this book took the inevitable step of extending demoticism beyond pure linguistics
to questions of national identity and destiny. Both because it
spoke about the breadth of demoticism's revolutionary concern
and because the language in which it was written constituted an
incursion into the purism of scholarship, it was resented and
fought by the opposition. Though various books of a scholarly
nature have subsequently appeared in demotic, the purist tradition in this realm has remained strong.

TRANSLATIONS: PALLIS

Eftaliotis, one of Psiharis' earliest and most energetic supporters, leads us into the crucial realm of translation, for he
attempted a rendering of Homer's *Odyssey*, his version being
one of those Kazantzakis kept open before him as he composed his own translation of the *Iliad*.

The extraordinary energy the demoticists devoted to translation might best be illustrated by Alexander Pallis, another
immediate adherent to the cause. In Pallis we encounter a perfect example of the chains of transmission so important in
Greek literary life. We have already seen Pallis' indebtedness
to Vernardakis and Psiharis; soon we shall see Kazantzakis'
indebtedness to Pallis. Secondly, in Pallis we have a better
representative than Eftaliotis of demoticism's initial stage, since

29. *Apology*, p. 120.   30. *Ibid.*, p. 124.

his energies were focused chiefly upon linguistic problems rather than the social, political, or educational implications of the movement.[31] Third, Pallis was a rigorous, uncompromising disciple of Psiharis, believing that the written language must conform in all respects to the spoken. He therefore illustrates a radicalism that we often do not find in later demoticists or in those like Ghavriilidis whose incomes were at stake. Fourth, though Pallis did not devote himself to the wider implications of demoticism, his translations made those implications all too clear, as we shall see in a moment.

A director of the Rally Company and serving in their offices in Bombay, Manchester, and Liverpool, Pallis continued the tradition of businessmen contributing to Greek cultural life. In his spare time he translated Thucydides; plays by Shakespeare, Euripides, and Sophocles; the *Iliad* (1892, 1904); and the Gospels (1901).[32]

Psiharis, we remember, had declared provocatively in *My Journey* that Homer did not exist, that the great epics were coalescences of various oral ballads originating in different regions of Hellas, and that modern Greece had analogous proto-epics in its demotic songs, from which someday a new *Iliad* might emerge. Influenced by these theories of Psiharis (and others) on the Homeric Question, Pallis omitted Homer's name entirely from the title-page of his translation, treated the poem as a collection of ballads, and thus attempted to duplicate the language and atmosphere of these ballads, now available to all, thanks to the folklorist publications of N. Politis.[33] So relentless was he in his allegiance to the spoken language that he even modernized the proper names—Ἑλένη for exam-

31. *Ibid.*, p. 116.
32. The 1892 edition of the *Iliad* was incomplete; the 1904 edition contained the entire epic. A revised edition came out in 1915.
33. Stavrou, pp. 121–22.

ple becoming Λενιώ—so relentless in his dream of making the classics familiar and contemporary that he dressed his ancient warriors in the τσαρούχια and τουζλούκια (moccasins with or without pompons; wrap-around leggings) of the heroes of 1821. The resulting verses have a klephtic ring.

Here is the opening:[34]

Τραγούδα, μούσα, τὸ θυμὸ τοῦ ξακουστοῦ Ἀχιλλέα,
τὸν ἔρμο, π᾿ ὅλους πότισε τοὺς Ἀχαιοὺς φαρμάκια
καὶ πλῆθος ἔστειλε ψυχὲς λεβέντικες στὸν Ἅδη.

And here is Hector in the famous scene in which he foresees his wife Andromache's enslavement and humiliation by the victorious Achaeans:

Καὶ σὰ σὲ βλέπουν ποὺ περνᾶς ἀχνὴ καὶ δακρυσμένη,
"νά το", θὰ λέν, "τοῦ Ἕχτορα τὸ ταίρι, ποὺ τῶν Τρώων
ἦταν τὸ πρῶτο αὐτὸς σπαθὶ στῆς Τροίας τοὺς πολέμους."
Ἔτσι ἴσως ποῦν κι᾿ ὁ πόνος σου θὰ ξανανοίγῃ πάντα
σὰ βλέπεις πῶς ἀπ᾿ τὴ σκλαβιὰ νὰ βγῆς δὲν ἔχει ἐλπίδα.
Μὰ θέλω νὰ μὲ φάῃ ἡ γῆς, ἡ μαύρη πλάκα θέλω,
πρὶν νὰ βογγᾶς, νὰ κλαῖς σὲ δῶ, πρὶν σκλάβα νὰ σὲ
σέρνουν!

It is perhaps hard for us to appreciate the remarkableness of such a major undertaking appearing only four years after Psiharis' book, or how truly revolutionary Pallis' undertaking was. We must be reminded again and again, as we are by the critic Siomopoulos, that the epics of Homer—indeed all the classics—were at that time just mummies existing in order to be scrutinized by experts.[35] The scattered translations that had already appeared were "scholastic and cold; they rendered the text's prose-sense but not its true spirit." Pallis changed all this,

34. The following passages are cited by Siomopoulos, p. 11. They are from Book I, 1–3 and Book VI, 459–65.

35. Siomopoulos, p. 10.

making the *Iliad* a living, comprehensible work for the ordinary reader. In addition, when the initial installment of Pallis' translation came out in 1892, it constituted for the opposition the first major demonstration of demotic's great poetic potentiality. (Solomos' poems were not then generally known to Athenian intellectuals, and Palamas' significant works had not yet appeared.) In his *Iliad*, Pallis destroyed the myth that demotic was incapable of expressing the entire range of human emotions.[36] On the other hand, he unwittingly helped to initiate new myths about the demoticists' desecration of ancient treasures, about coining of words, and so forth. The real storm, however, was yet to come.

In Greece, no new translation of the Scripture is allowed without prior authorization by the Holy Synod of Athens.[37] In 1901, when Pallis published his translation of the Gospels into pan-hellenic demotic, the reaction was so great that rioting occurred in the streets. Added to the hue and cry about demoticism's coining of new words, its advocacy of everything vulgar and barbarous, its desecration of the ancient classics, was the charge that the demoticists sought to undermine religion. To us, who remember Korais' anti-clericalism, this charge seems strange, coming from Korais' supposed disciples; it seems even stranger when directed against Pallis, a religious man who read the Gospel to his children each Sunday and drew his justification from Saint Paul's admonition to the Corinthians: Οὕτως καὶ ὑμεῖς διὰ τῆς γλώσσης ἐὰν μὴ εὔσημον λόγον δῶτε, πῶς γνωσθήσεται τὸ λαλούμενον; (So also ye, unless ye utter by the tongue speech easy to be understood, how shall it be known what is spoken?").[38] Yet there is no

36. *Ibid.*, p. 11. 37. Campbell and Sherrard, p. 198.
38. I Cor. 14:9. Pallis used this as his epigraph. Note that Pallis published various Biblical commentaries, in English: *A few notes*

doubt that Pallis unwittingly helped to initiate an increasing suspicion and hostility toward the radical demoticists—already known as *malliarí*,[39] "the hairy ones"—a hostility now exhibited not only by the educated class, which felt constrained to protect its nineteenth-century inheritance of romanticized hellenism, but also by the peasants, who were led to believe that their religion had come under attack. Their religion did come under attack by certain demoticists later on, but not by Pallis in 1901.

Here is a sample of his translation. It is unpretentious, clear, and unadorned, in keeping with Paul's admonitions:[40]

Στην αρχη ειταν ο λογος κι'ο λογος ειτανε με το Θεὺ και Θεος ειταν ὁ λογος. Ειταν εκεινος στην αρχη με το Θεο. Ολα τα παντα μεσο του εγιναν, και χωρις του τιποτα δεν εγινε που γινηκε. Μεσα του ειτανε ζωη κι'η ζωη ειτανε το φως των ανθρωπων, και το φως μεσα στο σκοταδι φεγγει και το σκοταδι δεν το κυριεψε.

2. Βγηκε ενας ανθρωπος σταλμενος απο το Θεο· τ'ονομα του Ιωαννης. Αφτος ηρθε προς κηρυγμα, για να κηρυξει το φως, που να κανει κι'ολοι να πιστεψουν. Δεν ειταν εκεινος το φως, παρα για να κηρυξει το φως. Το φως τ'αληθινο που φωτιζει καθε ανθρωπο

on the Gospels according to St. Mark and St. Matthew, based chiefly on modern Greek (Liverpool, 1903; London, 1932). *Notes on St. John and Apocalypse* (London, n.d.). *Notes on St. Luke and the Acts* (Edinburgh, 1928). *To the Romans; a commentary* (Liverpool, 1920). Also see Duckworth, who compares Pallis' translation with that published by the British and Foreign Bible Society, and comments philologically on Pallis' inflections.

39. The term was first used in 1898 and is attributed to the journalist Kondylakis, who made fun of the long-haired poets in a certain café. Since poets were demoticists, the term was then applied to all the Psiharists. See Kordatos, *Istoria*, p. 133.

40. Pallis. The selection is the opening of the Gospel According to St. John.

ερχοτανε cton κοcmo· cton κοcmo ειταν κι᾽ο κοcmoc
mεco toy εγινε, κι᾽ο κοcmoc δεν τον αναγνωριce. Στα
δικα toy ηρθε, κι᾽οι δικοι toy δεν τον παραδεχτηκαν·
ομωc οcοι tone δεχτηκαν, toyc εδωκε εξουcια να γινουν
toy Θεου παιδια, c᾽αφτουc πoy πιcτεψαν τ᾽ονομα toy,
πoy οχι απο αιματα μητε απο θελημα cαρκαc μητε απο
θελημα αντροc, παρα απο το Θεο γεννηθηκαν.

I spoke earlier of Pallis as a link in a chain of transmission. He carried forth the work not only of Vernardakis and Psiharis, but also of Korais, who wanted the Bible to be understood by all. Then, his own work became an inspiration and challenge to future translators, including Kazantzakis. In 1933, when Kazantzakis was revising his translation of the entire *Divine Comedy* into relentless pan-hellenic demotic, he held Pallis out as his model, stating to Eleni Samiou that he wished his rendering "to be on the same level as Pallis' *Iliad*."[41] A decade later, when he undertook his own *Iliad*, he dedicated his work to Pallis' memory, even though he now viewed the older translation more as a challenge for him to surpass than as a model. He felt that Pallis had bypassed some of the extraordinarily difficult problems presented to a translator determined to find a living equivalent for every Homeric word.[42] For example, Pallis had omitted Apollo's epithet ἑκηβόλος and had weakly transformed the mouse-god Σμινθεὺς into Σμινθέας. Kazantzakis aspired to do better. But this does not mean that he had lost his appreciation of Pallis' pioneering achievement or his sense of discipleship; indeed, true discipleship for Kazantzakis always meant the effort to pass beyond one's master.

41. *Biography*, p. 281. It is interesting that when Kazantzakis was soliciting subscriptions to enable him to print his translation of Dante, Pallis was one of the few who responded. See Prevelakis, pp. 397, 401.

42. Prevelakis, p. 508.

Those who know Kazantzakis' career will marvel at the energy he devoted to translations over the full fifty-year period of his creative life. He aspired in each case to put his beloved language to the proof, and to leave a legacy of the world's classics demoticized. We cannot understand this zeal unless we remember his vivid sense of following in the tradition of fearless demotic translations, a tradition initiated in large part by Pallis.

POETRY : PALAMAS

As important as the translations were, the demoticists obviously could not be happy simply with clothing the classics of Hellas and Europe in demotic robes. The great hope of both Korais and Psiharis had been that modern Greece might create a literature of its own. Indeed, Psiharis' decision to abandon every iota of purism was prompted to a degree by his feeling that Greece had not yet fulfilled Korais' hopes, and could never do so while *katharevousa* remained the literary medium. Thus, while a great amount of energy went into putting demotic to the proof by means of translation, even more went into original, creative production in all the genres of imaginative literature.

To trace the applications of demotic in poetry, prose-fiction, and drama, even if one were to speak only of the period 1890–1910, would require an entire book. I obviously cannot even make an attempt at anything comprehensive, yet I do wish to skim the subject, once more with the purpose of introducing the necessary background to Kazantzakis' career.

Everyone would agree, I think, that poetry was the most important and impressive genre in this period; it was also the first in which demotic achieved an unquestioned sovereignty. Poetry possessed a demotic tradition in the nineteenth century because of the Ionian school. But this in itself was not sufficient, and indeed the Ionians had been eclipsed in general sophisticated consciousness by the purist poets of the so-called Old School of Athens. The situation called for a great figure who by means of his energy and unquestioned talent could focus in himself the scattered impulses toward change and thus effect the total demoticization of his craft. Such a figure appeared in the person of Kostis Palamas.

Palamas had begun using demotic for his own poetry as early as 1880.[43] By 1900 he was convinced that demotic should enjoy universal use, not only in poetry but everywhere. By 1910 he was a "national poet," the symbol of the demotic idea in its widest possible implications. By 1922 he could be characterized in all sincerity, even by a demoticist who had grown hostile to him, as "the supreme hierophant of Greek letters, the scimitar of demoticism, the literary conscience of the era of renaissance."[44] Palamas revived interest in Solomos and Valaoritis, supported the movement to translate the Bible, forged the links between demotic and nationalism, evoked the unity and continuity of the Greek spirit throughout the ages, campaigned for the awakening of neo-hellenic consciousness, proved that demotic could answer to the most sophisticated and cultivated artistic needs. A follower of Psiharis, he made no secret of his allegiances:

". . . My joy above all things, and my glory, is the language which I write and knead and extol: the language of our heroic ballads . . . and of Solomos. . . ."

"The modern language must be made official, must become the language of the State . . . , the universal instrument of national life. . . ."

43. *Apology,* pp. 125–26. For a fine appreciation of Palamas, see Seferis, pp. 41–52.

44. Glinos, *I Krisi,* p. 16. Though published in 1924, this article was written in 1922, as Glinos tells us on p. 3.

"I know that I am . . . absolutely *malliaros*, and . . . I consider it to my credit . . . to be called *malliaros*, seeing who else is marked with this label. I've said it and I say it again: *Malliarismos* is my virtue."[45]

These statements should make it clear that Palamas was a polemicist as well as a poet. From the late nineties onward he became the real leader of the entire demotic movement, propagandizing for it in countless articles and book reviews, the extent of which can be appreciated by anyone who peruses his *Collected Works*.[46] Perhaps Palamas' real virtue, seen more comprehensively, was his bridging of factional divisions. The myth had it that the *malliari* sought to desecrate the ancient culture, yet we have already seen that Palamas could be cited by Politis, in the poetic contest of 1889, for evoking the ancients' deep religious sense.[47] His nationalism appealed to a certain segment who did not necessarily share his *malliarismos*, and his emphasis on the continuity of culture, with language as base, carried forward the original assumption of Korais and the other humanists.

Thus it is not surprising that Palamas, radical though he was in certain respects, eventually found himself part of the literary establishment. In the late 1880's he was being officially recognized by university professors; in 1897 he became Secretary of the university. It would be entirely misleading to imply by this recognition that Palamas' demoticism was generally accepted at this time, or that his position within the establishment was comfortably secure. In 1903, for example, a production of the *Oresteia* in demotic translation caused commotions similar to those provoked by Pallis' Gospels two years earlier. Because a

45. *Apology*, pp. 125, 128. The date of the first utterance is 1903.
46. Palamas, K. See in particular, "Yia tin idhea ti glossiki," in *Apanta*, vi, 156–87.
47. Dimaras, p. 392.

poem by Palamas had been declaimed before the opening, students marched through the streets shouting, "Down with Palamas," and his Secretaryship was endangered.[48] The fact remains, however, that he did not lose his position; indeed, he retained it for thirty years and respect for him grew continually.

All this bears on Kazantzakis' career. In the period 1906–1910, when the young and unknown Cretan was establishing himself in Athenian circles, Palamas stood at the height of his power and prestige (his most significant works appeared in this period: *Immovable Life* in 1904, *The Twelve Lays of the Gypsy* in 1907, and *The King's Flute* in 1910). Owing in large part to him, the battle for demotic had been won for poetry, and this victory gave impetus to the remaining battles for demotic in prose, on the stage, and in the schools, precisely the areas to which Kazantzakis soon turned his energies.

Nor was Palamas' influence felt only in this question of language. A group of satellite poets known as the New School of Athens had come to revolve about him, sharing his intellectual orientation as well as his demoticism. It was only natural that a young writer like Kazantzakis should be influenced by this dominant force in the literary scene; in particular, it was partly through Palamas' example that Kazantzakis veered at first toward the modes of the Parnassians, D'Annunzio, Hauptmann. It was just as natural that such a strong-willed person as Kazantzakis should revolt eventually against Palamas' domination. When Kazantzakis began to form a new intellectual orientation in the 1920's, rejecting Greek nationalism along with the modes of D'Annunzio and the French (which he had rejected much earlier), it is not surprising that

48. *Ibid.*, p. 399. Palamas was again threatened in 1911 when he affirmed himself a *malliaros* in the midst of the linguistic controversy in the assembly. Kordatos, *Istoria*, pp. 162–64.

he also began consciously to think of Palamas as an influence that had to be surpassed.[49] In 1929 he complained in print of Palamas' "violent conservatism," though admitting and honoring his continued allegiance to demotic.[50] His final verdict is to be found in the letter he wrote to Sikelianos just after Palamas' funeral in 1943: "You know how foreign this poet is to me, except for a few of his lyrical things. A small poeta major. . . ."[51]

We are interested in the first decade of the century, when Kazantzakis was happy to acknowledge the master and receive his help. As Secretary of the university, Palamas had signed Kazantzakis' diploma;[52] as leader of the intellectual community, Palamas had helped to establish the young author's name when he praised Kazantzakis' first published work, the novella *Snake and Lily*, even though the language employed in this work was far from "irreproachable" demotic. In the years that followed, Palamas' patronage became the single most important factor in opening all doors to the ambitious Cretan.[53] In return, Kazantzakis apostrophized the purists in one of his newspaper articles dispatched from Paris in 1909. In Greece, he wrote, we have better poets than Rostand but we scorn them. "How many today recognize Palamas, a great—the greatest—glory of our land?"[54]

PROSE-FICTION

If Kazantzakis had chosen to inaugurate his career with a work in verse, he clearly would have written in uncompromis-

49. See Kazantzakis, *Epistoles*, pp. 144, 159.
50. Kazantzakis, *La littérature grecque contemporaine.*
51. *Biography*, pp. 417–18.
52. *Ibid.*, p. 40.
53. Tea Anemoyanni, interviewed by the author, April 22, 1967.
54. Kazantzakis, "Ellinika poiimata," *Nea Estia*, Sept. 1, 1958, p. 1,288.

ing demotic. But he began with a novel, employing a less pugnacious demotic indicative of that genre's transitional state around 1905–1906. I should add that his second novel, done in pure demotic and published in 1909, shows how rapidly things were changing.

There are various reasons why prose-fiction did not become fully demoticized as quickly as poetry. Chief of these is probably the meagerness of any previous tradition capable of augmenting the *élan* provided by Psiharis. On the contrary, by the time of Kazantzakis' student days, fiction in *katharevousa* was represented by authors of high quality such as Papadiamantis and Roidis, so that a respected puristic tradition had established itself. Papadiamantis was a particularly important factor in this because of his great popularity, his stories being serialized in the newspapers and read aloud in village cafés. That prose-fiction should eventually become demoticized, however, was inevitable given the example set by poetry and the internal needs of the novels themselves. All in all, the time-lag was at most one or two decades.

I have already touched upon some of the factors contributing both to the lag and to the change. Here I should like simply to gather these together and fill in several gaps, following in general the account given by Campbell and Sherrard.[55] The first demoticists, as we have seen, had behind them a wealth of demotic poetry in the folk ballads, in Solomos and Valaoritis. Demotic prose, by contrast, offered them little to begin with and still less that was both "alive" and available. The memoirs of Makriyannis were then unknown; the fairy tales were not collected as early or with as much zeal as the ballads, and in any case had never found their Solomos or Valaoritis.

Even if we look for prose not in demotic there is very little

55. Campbell and Sherrard, pp. 237–44.

before the nineteenth century. The hellenistic novels were too
remote, and were eclipsed by ancient poetry. Strangely, one
area in which we find demotic prose to some degree is the
ecclesiastical. Though in general the Church has been puristic
since early Byzantine times, its need to combat the proselytiz-
ing propaganda of other faiths led it occasionally to encourage
the "simplification" of religious texts. The Bible was translated more than once, as we have seen; monks busied themselves with paraphrases of patristic writings and hagiography.[56]
Indeed, the saint's life in demotic prose (συναξάρι) has remained a living form for the Greek people and was to become
a very conscious influence upon Kazantzakis, who originally
called his most famous novel *The Saint's-Life of Zorba*.[57] But
these religious texts, circumscribed as they were in style and
content, were hardly enough to stimulate modern literature
in demotic prose. In sum, before Korais' time, written prose-
fiction did not exist as a living genre in contemporary Greek
culture, and before Psiharis' it did not exist as a genre in
demotic.

When the novel entered Greek cultural life at the time of
the Enlightenment it did not emerge from anything indigenous. The first novelists were educated Greeks who lived
abroad and were largely ignorant of Greek ways. Translations
and imitations of romantic or courtly prototypes were the rule,
with Mme de Staël, Dumas père, Sir Walter Scott, and Rousseau among the favorites. As for the language, we have already
seen a sample in Simos' rendering of Mme de Staël's *Corinne*.
As I said earlier, a remote, elevated, and artificial *katharevousa*
was quite appropriate for this alien and derivative material.

56. Dimaras, p. 49.
57. Prevelakis, p. 387; *Biography*, p. 401. For the absorption
with which the young Kazantzakis read the *synaxaria*, see *Report
to Greco*, ch. 8, pp. 71–74.

This type of writing continued for a century, though the romantic obsessions of the Parnassians were grafted to the gothic melancholy of Scott or the neo-paganism of Rousseau. Kazantzakis' *Snake and Lily* was one of this plant's last and weirdest blossoms, being a mélange of defiant paganism and sickly weariness, tinted with the Parnassian formulas of Leconte de Lisle and the lushness of D'Annunzio. Its language is appropriately mannered. Needless to say, the work has nothing whatsoever to do with contemporary Greece.

Change, as we have seen, came with the advent of naturalism. Zola was translated in the 1880's, inspiring in Greek writers the desire to treat a different kind of subject matter in a different kind of way and with a new freedom of language.[58] Translations of Dostoevsky reinforced this movement, as did the folklore studies that were then flourishing. Novelists now aspired to treat Greek life—which perforce meant village life— in a realistic way. The problem was, however, how could this be done in *katharevousa*, since it was unthinkable in those pre-Psiharian times to employ the vulgar tongue? We have already encountered Kalligas' *Thanos Vlekas*, where strict *katharevousa* is employed for narration and an often painful attempt is made to approximate demotic in the dialogue. True, Kalligas was a precursor; but those who came later and developed the "ethographic school" did not at first alter his basic approach. The situation is perfectly exemplified in Dimitrios Vikelas, who in his poetry switched from *katharevousa* to demotic after reading Valaoritis, who wrote epigrams against the purists as early as 1859 but who retained *katharevousa* for his novel *Loukis Laras* (1879), which is an early example of the ethographic genre.[59] Papadiamantis, the most

58. The appearance of *Nana* in 1880, translated by I. Kambouroglou, had a great effect. See Dimaras, p. 372.

59. *Apology*, pp. 79–80.

widely read of the naturalistic novelists who flourished circa 1880–1910, employed demotic for dialogue and puristic for narration.

This was the situation when Psiharis published *My Journey*. There was no Solomos, no Palamas who had already turned to demotic. Thus it is understandable that the full demoticization of prose should have lagged behind that of poetry. As we have seen, however, support for Psiharis in some quarters was both strong and rapid. Among those who responded were prose writers a decade or so younger than Papadiamantis (b. 1851). Karkavitsas (b. 1865), for example, though beginning with the *katharevousa* of his fellow ethographic writers, embraced the linguistic revolution to such a degree that he even went back and translated some of his early stories into demotic.[60] In general, the merger of demotic and the ethographic tradition benefited both the novels involved and the language. For demotic, with so little written tradition behind it, "had need of being enriched by the unadulterated vocabulary and the plain manner of expression which survived far from the unformed miscegenation of Athens. All these writers, who came from the Greek provinces, brought the popular language with them as a living contribution."[61]

One way that Psiharis helped to accelerate the transition was by stimulating a sub-genre: the naturalistic novel of urban rather than rural life. His own productions in this sub-genre deal with the only cities he had experienced, those outside Greece.[62] But soon a new generation of novelists who knew

60. Dimaras, p. 426.   61. *Ibid.*, p. 424.
62. Psiharis' literary (as distinguished from philological) works: in Greek—*T'oneiro tou Yanniri*, 1897; *Zoi ki agapi sti monaxia*, 1904; *Ta dio aderfia*, 1911; *Agni*, 1913. In French—*Jalousie*, 1892; *Cadeau de Noces*, 1893; *Autour de la Grèce*, 1895; *Le Rêve de Yanniri*, 1897; *La Croyante*, 1898; *L'Epreuve*, 1899; *Soeur Anselmine*, 1918; *Le Solitaire du Pacifique*, 1922, etc.

Athens and whose style had not already been formed in the puristic mold were writing about urban life in Greece. Grigorios Xenopoulos is an example. It is interesting that Kazantzakis' second novel, *Broken Souls*, published in 1909 and composed in demotic, has an urban setting, Paris; that its concerns, despite the foreign locale, are obsessively Greek. In the novels of his final period, beginning with *Zorba* (written 1941–1943), Kazantzakis fused his crusading demoticism with (a) the ethographic tradition of the naturalists, and (b) the artificiality, sublimity, neo-paganism, and gothic melancholy of the romantics. His background, one might almost say, was his being.

DRAMA

Although known now almost exclusively for his novels and the epic *Odyssey*, Kazantzakis for a great part of his career considered himself primarily a playwright. Because of this, and because his activities as playwright produced his most significant contributions to the demotic movement in the crucial first decade of the century, we should glance at the situation in the theatre in the years before he arrived in Athens. Demoticization in this area kept pace with that of prose-fiction. Until nearly 1900 *katharevousa* and French farces were the rule, even though the great shadow of Ibsen was already looming. If a character wished to don his gloves he was forced to declaim: Ἂς θέσω τὰς χειρίδας μου, and if he was fed up with his wife he accused her of being a γυνὴ ἄνευ καρδίας.[63]

After the publication of *My Journey*, various actors and directors who sympathized with Psiharis began to make his influence felt, the change gathering momentum in this last decade of the century and leading to the remarkable theatrical

63. Rodas, p. 1,453.

rebirth circa 1900–1910. By the end of this decade, eventual victory for demotic was assured, although the common language was by no means yet taken for granted in the theatre. It is perhaps difficult for us to imagine the tenacity of the Kontosian penchant for "linguistic observations," or the degree to which audiences could be scandalized when, for example, the playwright Spyros Melas made a character say τοῦ κυμάτου instead of τοῦ κύματος, or when words like τσιτσίδι or κλοτσοσκούφι appeared in a translation of *Antigone*.[64]

Two important new troupes, the Nea Skini and the Vasiliko Theatro, appeared in 1901. (We should remember that Kazantzakis spent the years 1902–1906 in Athens as a law student at the university, and was thus directly exposed to all these developments.) The Nea Skini, as one historian has put it, was founded in a spirit of holy dedication.[65] The Vasiliko, though directed at first by a purist, eventually came under the influence of the demoticist Thomas Oikonomou, whom we shall meet later as the director of Kazantzakis' first play, *Day Is Breaking*. The new troupes naturally needed scripts in demotic. Thus a significant amount of the activity in this decade was prompted by direct commissions that involved many of the outstanding literary figures of the time, including Palamas himself.

It is of interest, however, that much of the creative energy went, not into original plays, but into translations of works that would presumably stand greater chance of box-office success. Classic authors such as Shakespeare, Goethe, Molière, and the ancient Greek tragedians were performed, but so were contemporary dramatists then in vogue. Palamas translated

64. *Ibid.*, p. 1,456. *Apology*, p. 131. The translator in question was Konstantinos Christomanos.
65. Rodas, p. 1,455.

D'Annunzio, for example;[66] the much-admired Ibsen was given demotic dress;[67] Kostas Hatzopoulos translated Hofmannsthal and helped to impress upon Greeks the importance of Maeterlinck.[68] It was Hatzopoulos who translated Goethe's *Faust* for Oikonomou, who in turn produced the play with Marika Kotopouli in the role of Margarita.[69] I cite this in particular because here, once again, we see various linkages. Hatzopoulos, one of Psiharis' earliest adherents, was the publisher of *Techni*, the first demotic periodical, as we have already noted. A pioneering demoticist translator like Pallis, he helped to create a tradition that was inevitably in the minds of future translators like Kazantzakis, if only as a level of achievement calling out to be surpassed. When Kazantzakis undertook his own translation of *Faust*, he declared his aim to improve upon the Hatzopoulos version by employing "a language that is richer and more universally Greek"—in other words, a pan-hellenic demotic reaching into the remotest villages for its vocabulary.[70] As for the demoticist actress Marika Kotopouli, probably the most admired star Greece produced in this period, we shall meet her again in connection with both of Kazantzakis' early plays, and even as the subject of a theatrical anecdote told by Alexis Zorba![71]

The theatrical renaissance of 1900–1910 elicited original plays and produced playwrights of note, such as Spyros Melas, already mentioned, and Grigorios Xenopoulos, whom we met as a novelist of urban life and as one of the first to answer

66. *Ibid.*, p. 1,456.
67. See Dreux; also Karandonis, p. 134 passim.
68. Karandonis, pp. 134–36.
69. Rodas, p. 1,456.
70. *Biography*, pp. 336–37. The Hatzopoulos version still holds its own, however, and is preferred by many.
71. Kazantzakis, *Zorba*, pp. 95–96. On Kotopouli, see *Nea Estia*, Oct. 1, 1954, pp. 1,397–1,427.

Psiharis' call. Nor did Palamas eschew this challenge.[72] The problem was to create a truly neo-hellenic style almost out of a vacuum, since no prototypes for a demotic theatre existed at all, except the few works that survived from the Venetian period in Crete and the Ionian flowering of the nineteenth century.[73] In addition, the playwrights had hanging over them as a kind of curse the glorious classicism of the ancients and the seductive modernity of the fashionable Europeans. They had to take elements from these sources, yet avoid servile imitation, and all the ingredients somehow had to be made relevant both to contemporary Greece and to "eternal" Hellas. This was the challenge facing dramatists when Kazantzakis came upon the scene.

72. See Kostes Palamas, *Royal Blossom* or *Trisevyene*, tr. A. E. Phoutrides (New Haven, 1923). The play dates from 1902. An excellent summary of its political and cultural background is in Laourdas, *Trisevyene*. Among other plays written in answer to this challenge were: *O yios tou iskiou*, by Spyros Melas; *Maria i pentayiotissa*, by Pavlos Nirvanas; and *I Rodopi*, by Nikos Poriotis.

73. Besides the well-known dramas from the Cretan revival there is *Vasilikos*, written by Antonis Matesis (1794–1874), who lived on Zakynthos. This play was discussed by Angelos Terzakis in his paper, "The First Drama of Ideas in the Modern Greek Theatre," read at the 1969 symposium of the Modern Greek Studies Association. (*Modern Greek Writers.*) The 19th century also saw drama in *katharevousa*. Particular mention should be made of the plays of Dimitrios Vernardakis, whom we have already met as an opponent of Kontismos. See Dimaras, p. 345.

Later Developments

SIMPLICITY OF THE INITIAL RESPONSE Though the foregoing account of the spread and application of demotic circa 1890–1910 is filled with names, dates, and titles, I have tried to keep it simple and to limit myself to demoticism in its original, philological guise, though brief references to the movement's wider implications in the political and educational realms have been unavoidable.

These wider implications began to be consciously discerned before 1910, but I have delayed considering them, first because they become truly pronounced chiefly after this date, and, second, because I wished to give a sense of demoticism as a relatively uncomplicated phenomenon, drawing to its service men who could give themselves to it wholly and without second thoughts. These pioneers gained a kind of legendary stature among demoticists in later, sadder, and more intricate years. We see this in the terzina that Kazantzakis dedicated to Psiharis in 1933. These terzinas were devoted to people he considered the "bodyguards of his spirit"—to his masters, gurus, or hero-saints. In this case, he conveys Psiharis' heroism by paraphrasing the opening lines of a famous ballad[1] about the warrior Kolokotronis and fusing this with the legend of Saint George the dragon-killer:[2]

> Astride he writes, astride eats bread,
> Astride makes war . . .[3]

Following the majestic leader come the original stalwarts (πρωτοπαλίκαρα), Pallis, Eftaliotis, Palamas, Filintas; they encounter screeching Hatzidakis; Psiharis becomes a legend, and a thousand years later a grandmother recites his story to her grandchildren, equating it with the tale of Saint George, who rescued the princess from the monster that had poisoned the drinking fountain. The key to this allegory should be all too clear![4]

COMPLEXITY OF THE SUBSEQUENT RESPONSE:
POLITICIZATION

Matters did not remain so uncomplicated for long (if indeed the saints had even been either so pure or so unified, and the

1. Politis, p. 71.   2. Prevelakis, pp. 402–03.
3. Kazantzakis, *Tertzines*, p. 155.
4. Prevelakis, p. 403. All the foregoing is Kazantzakis' own summary of the poem.

dragon so unquestionably monstrous). Factionalism developed within the crusaders' ranks, with one group fighting for pan-hellenic demotic, another for the speech of Athenians, while still another favored a compromised demotic assimilating to itself certain elements from *katharevousa*. Politics and demoticism became uneasy and sometimes disparate bedfellows. The result was a tangle that makes any generalization such as "Demotic was espoused by the left and fought by the right" a very risky one indeed.

To untangle this skein of allegiances (if it ever could be done at all) most certainly lies outside the limits of the present essay. I simply wish to indicate that the politicization of the language question was predictable and indeed inevitable. The very passion brought to the supposedly philological aspect of the problem in the early stage is a hint that much more than philology was involved. The added implications, deemphasized and perhaps only subconscious at first, very soon became all too conscious, so that what initially seemed a movement to cultivate the genuine neo-hellenic language became a movement to cultivate a "genuine neo-hellenic civilization." Greek intellectuals looked back on the preceding century, remembered the hope that the new state would enable Greeks finally to achieve cultural self-identity, élan, confidence, yet concluded that this had not yet happened. Especially after the defeat of 1897, which left Greece despondent and directionless, they reacted against the foreign impositions that—like the puristic gallicisms of the nineteenth-century archaizers—had masqueraded as forms appropriate to Greece. They began to ask comprehensive questions such as: What was Greece? What is it? What can it become?[5]

5. *Apology,* p. 124.

DRAGOUMIS

One of the first figures to link his demoticism in this way with the broadest possible social and political problems was Eftaliotis, whose *Istoria tis Romiosinis* (1901) we have already encountered. But the person who best represents this politicization, and who has the added importance (for us) of being undoubtedly a crucial influence upon Kazantzakis during this period, is Ion Dragoumis, in whom the demotic struggle and a specific kind of nationalistic politics or "mystique" became synonymous.

Dragoumis developed his position in the course of an active political life, beginning in 1897, when as a youth of nineteen he served in the disastrous war against the Turks, and ending with his tragic assassination in 1920.[6] After the defeat of 1897 Dragoumis helped to organize the Macedonian Greeks in their resistance against the Bulgarian *comitadjis*; here he worked with Pavlos Melas, whose death in 1904 he exploited in his effort to waken public opinion in Greece and abroad about the Macedonian question. Later he campaigned to arouse nationalistic consciousness among the Greeks of Constantinople and the Dodecanese; took part in the Goudi rising of 1909, which led to Venizelos' first premiership; was a founding member of the Educational Association; personally negotiated the surrender of Salonika to Greece in 1912; served as Venizelos' minister in Petrograd, Vienna, and Berlin; advised King Constantine to side with the Entente so that Greece might win back Constantinople; became a Member of Parliament in 1915; began publishing the periodical *Political Revue* in 1916; split with Venizelos in 1917, when the Allies forced King Constantine into exile, and was himself exiled to Corsica; re-

6. Palamas, L., p. 99.

turned two years later to Greece, where on August 13, 1920 (new style), the day that the news of the attempt on Venizelos' life in Paris' Gare de Lyon reached Athens, he was shot in retaliation by Venizelist security-police.

A prolific writer from 1907 onward, Dragoumis promulgated his nationalistic gospel in the manner that Psiharis had advised—entertainingly, vividly, by means of anecdote, irony, eloquence, and imagination. Of his major political books the most systematic was the last, *Greek Civilization*, published in 1913. Here, Dragoumis took the demoticists' admiration for the spoken language and widened it until he made the demotic tradition the source of Greece's creative life from the first centuries A.D. to the present, and thus the one and only basis for the craved neo-hellenic culture that still had not appeared. "The demotic tradition," he wrote, "is inside us, like the footprints of our soul; following and ascending it we discover our soul, the true well-spring of neo-hellenic life. The demotic tradition will guide us so that we may draw near to this well-spring and drink."[7]

What we must realize is that by the demotic tradition Dragoumis meant here not only a certain language but an entire way of life with specific political and social as well as linguistic manifestations. Elsewhere he emphasized the local autonomy of each community, and the generally Eastern customs, such as: "women confined to the home, the separation of men and women, no walks, much church-going, much worship of ikons, much crossing and repenting, much fasting"—in short, everything "in its place, Byzantine survivals, a distilled life, the outcome of old civilization and ages."

This way of life was most seriously compromised, ironically, precisely when the Greeks finally won their freedom in the early nineteenth century, for what they "won," claimed Dra-

7. Cited by Palamas, L., p. 106; also by Sherrard, p. 190.

goumis, was a foreign way of life imposed upon them by "enlightened" Western philhellenes and such Westernized Greeks as Korais. After 1821, Greece in effect replaced the local village community with the national government, the bishop and patriarch with the nomarch and king. "And thus a greater revolution took place than had taken place against the Sultan. And since everything was slowly turned upside down, nothing remained in its place, and that is our situation now. . . ." "What conspires against us are Western ideas, contemporary civilization with its masonry, its philanthropy, its 'altruism,' its constitutionalism, its levelling that makes all men equal with the most base—all that contemporary civilization . . . which eliminates distinctions. . . . It is the influence of that civilization which we must fight if we wish to live."[8]

So Dragoumis preached, and by active example helped create, a nationalism meant to liberate the "genuine" demotic tradition from its foreign enslavement. What he suppressed was the fact that his own assumptions were themselves borrowed from the West. Nationalism itself—especially a nationalism based as was his on the identification between fatherland and language and thus striving to "liberate" all Greek-speaking peoples from foreign rule—was a Western concept reaching its most articulate expression in the German thinkers Johann Gottfried von Herder and Friedrich von Schlegel and shared by Korais, as we have seen. Furthermore, certain of the qualities and attitudes that Dragoumis cited as "genuinely" Greek were those which Nietzsche in particular had embraced in his effort to save "genuine" German Kultur from French egalitarian Civilization, which was based in turn on a romantic, liberal, rationalistic misrepresentation of ancient Greece.

8. The quotations in this paragraph are cited by Sherrard, pp. 188, 189, from *O Ellinismos mou kai oi Ellines* (Athens, 1927), pp. 23, 72.

Dragoumis' indebtedness to Nietzsche and also to the militant French nationalist Maurice Barrès is undeniable.[9] Instead of separating out truly Greek characteristics from a Western adulteration, he was in effect condemning one Western mode only to replace it with another, insisting just as Korais had a century earlier that this would magically awaken the dormant soul of modern Greece—or, to return to Kazantzakis' figure, that it would rescue the princess from the foreign monster that had poisoned Greece's well-springs.

Though Dragoumis presented his position most systematically in *Greek Civilization*, the basic ideas were all developed earlier, and can be seen in the books he published between 1907 and 1911, precisely when Kazantzakis was most susceptible to his influence. In Ὅσοι Ζωντανοί, published in 1911, Dragoumis placed his hero in Constantinople and made him dream of a reestablished Byzantine Empire with Greeks once more at the helm. This was the Μεγάλη Ἰδέα, the Great Idea, which Dragoumis (and others) invoked as a crucial part of the demotic tradition. "The Great Idea," he wrote earlier in *Noumas*, "is a memory which has remained, thrusting itself deep into the soul of the Greeks and nestling there since 1453, when the Turks took Constantinople. It is the memory that the Greeks, with Constantinople as their capital, ruled the East in former times."[10]

In Ὅσοι Ζωντανοί this nestling memory was presented as much more than a simple nostalgia; rather, it was a spur to Greek regeneration in the future. If it seemed too ambitious or unrealistic, Dragoumis replied that great dreams help to nourish the masses.[11] What he meant was that infinite dreams produce finite gains: out of the myth of a restored empire

9. See Theotokas, *Dragoumis kai Barrès*.
10. Dragoumis, *Megali Idea*.
11. Palamas, L., p. 106.

might come at least the capture of Salonika. Was it accidental that in France the Nietzschean thinker Georges Sorel was at precisely the same time stressing the need of sublimity, myth, and the infinite (in the form of a general strike) if his syndicalist movement was to win finite victories?[12] At the heart of both men's philosophy was the dictum: behave *as if* the impossible were obtainable—a dictum Kazantzakis never ceased to honor. Once more we see that what both Dragoumis and Kazantzakis preached in order to stimulate the Greeks to rediscover their Greekness was simply a current fashion of extremist thought in Western Europe. *Plus ça change, plus c'est la même chose.*

This is evident as well in *Samothraki* (1909) in which Dragoumis, like Psiharis before him, employed a journey as pretext for polemic and exhortation. In this book he presented a catalogue of Nietzschean doctrine: heroic pessimism, the strong have a particular right to live, liberal ideals of equality and compassion are symptoms of weakness, voluntarism is superior to rationalism, truth is made rather than discovered, egoism is superior to altruism, egoism is in the best interests of the state, nationalism is an irrational, mystical bond to folk and land. All this was then applied as an exhortation to the Samothrakians, who seemed content to languish under Turkish rule instead of fulfilling their duty to themselves and their nation. When we come to the details of Kazantzakis' crusading demoticism in the year this book was published, we shall see how he consciously viewed his anti-purism as a nationalistic duty, and how he used Dragoumis' book as a pretext for his own exhortations. We cannot understand Kazantzakis' early demoticism apart from its role within a nationalistic mystique to which Dragoumis was the key.

Nor, without a sense of this nationalism, can we truly un-

12. See *Réflexions sur la violence*, first published 1908.

derstand Kazantzakis' continuing demoticism after the mystique was destroyed. The whole problem with Kazantzakis' demoticism circa 1920-1940 was its autonomy, its lack of context. The improvement in his final period, circa 1940-1957 (if my hypothesis is correct) was possible because his demoticism found a new context in a new and mellowed nationalism, wedded itself to a renewed love of Greece, and produced the final novels.

Dragoumis was relevant not only to the early period of the Great Idea but to all the later stages as well, though in lesser degree. Dragoumis' assassination in 1920 symbolized for Kazantzakis the bankruptcy of Greek political life, which meant by extension the bankruptcy of the Great Idea—a situation confirmed overwhelmingly by the disaster of 1922.[13] Seeing his countrymen deal in this way with the very person who had fought hardest to resurrect them, and seeing them reject Venizelos himself several months later, Kazantzakis developed a scorn for Greeks—at least for "official" Greeks—and a determination to make his career elsewhere. Politically, he replaced Dragoumian nationalism with communistic internationalism. But he did not forget Dragoumis, especially after his communism had waned and, disoriented, he began groping for a new allegiance.[14] In the later 1930's Dragoumis seemed to be continually in Kazantzakis' mind. Thus we find him remembered in 1935 as "a brilliant man full of contradictory forces and lofty anxieties";[15] in 1937 as the man whom Greeks should admire if they were to create a truly neo-hellenic civili-

13. See Alexiou, E., p. 119; also Vrettakos, pp. 63, 748.
14. But he also remembered Dragoumis before this, in 1926, when he wrote a tribute on the occasion of the sixth anniversary of his friend's death. See Vrettakos, p. 748. The piece was called "I ekti epeteios."
15. Kazantzakis, *Japan-China*, p. 166.

zation (Kazantzakis enjoyed repeating Dragoumis' words: "I too like to feel that I am one of the many and fleeting archons of Hellenism, that it must pass through me in order to advance");[16] in early 1940, along with Petros Vlastos, as one of "the two people I have most respected and loved in my life. Companions in the great Hellenic solitude, champions in a struggle which transcends fatherland and language and mutely travels beyond their frontiers. Would that it might be the fate written for me that I should travel with them after my death!"[17] Finally, in October 1940, just a few weeks before the Italian invasion, Kazantzakis dedicated a poem to Dragoumis in which he invoked him as an Akritas guarding the Greek race in its present danger.[18]

Although Kazantzakis never returned to the Great Idea or to the old Dragoumian mystique, he did return in 1940 to a concern for his country, and his memories of Dragoumis during the five-year period of political disorientation preceding the Italian invasion help to indicate to us his growing need to anchor himself once again in his homeland. This, as I hope to show later, had a decisive and salutary effect on his demoticism, wedding it at last to subject matter and concerns that were truly Greek—indeed much more Greek, I would venture, than Dragoumis' amalgam of Nietzsche, Sorel and Barrès.

I spoke earlier of how politics and demoticism sometimes became disparate bedfellows, resulting in a tangle of allegiances that should make us wary of generalizations. Dragoumis is an example of a demoticist most basically at home—intellectually at least—with the radical right; others such as Dimitrios Gli-

16. Kazantzakis, *Journey to the Morea*, pp. 9, 172; Alexiou, E., p. 119.

17. Kazantzakis, *England*, pp. 107–08.

18. Kazantzakis, "Hairetismos ston Iona Dragoumi."

nos, who was also associated with Kazantzakis' career, could be adduced to show the links between demoticism and the left.[19]

Still others such as George Papandreou, who worked all his life for demotic in the schools, represented the political center. One might conclude that if demoticism was universally embraceable, it ought not to have been a political issue. Papandreou himself tried to argue this in 1914 in a quaint article, saying that demoticism should please everyone: it wishes to preserve the past and thus should appeal to the conservatives; it recognizes a people's freedom to choose its own language, and thus should appeal to freedom-loving liberals; it is the end-result of an evolutionary process and thus should please the progressives; it fights for the language of the proletariat, and thus should be attractive to socialists.[20] "The conclusion," Papandreou maintained, "is that demoticism is not a sociological system, nor does it belong exclusively to any such system; rather, it can be adapted to any."

But in actuality, demoticism did not achieve this universality, even though specific adherents belonged to disparate parties; nor did it leave the political arena. On the contrary, the spoken language's chief "pressure group," the Educational Association, eventually split in two because of political differences.[21] What we must realize, if we wish to understand the demoticists of Kazantzakis' generation, is that for every man, no matter what

19. Glinos' political radicalism developed gradually and rather late in his career. It wasn't until the founding of *Anayennisi* (1926) that he stood fully in the "radical progressive" camp. See Sotiriou, p. 49 passim.

20. Papandreou, "Ta oria . . ."

21. This happened in 1927. The conservative faction, under Delmouzos, wished to avoid identifying demoticism with any particular political party. The radicals, under Glinos, insisted that language reform must be linked to socialism. Glinos carried a majority of the members with him. The details are in Sotiriou, pp. 49–52.

his affiliation, the language question had become in large part a political question—which it still remains.

EDUCATIONAL DEMOTICISM

This politicization naturally helped to complicate things in the second broad area where the implications of demoticism were felt, namely, in education. By 1910 if not before, literature, politics, and education had become braided into a unity in which no one of these strands could any longer be perceived as independent. Thus even to treat pedagogical reform as a discrete aspect, a "second broad area," is to distort the subject in the interests of expository convenience. With demotic a plank in the platform of some political parties and not of others, with demotic hotly debated in the Assembly which was charged with revising the Constitution in 1911, any literary person or any teacher who took sides linguistically or pedagogically was also perforce taking sides politically. We should keep this always in mind as we examine the "separate" problem of the schools.

Educational demoticism began gathering momentum shortly after 1900 and by 1917 had won remarkable victories. The initial impetus came from Fotis Fotiadis' book *Our Language Problem and Our Educational Rebirth* (1902), to which I referred earlier when considering the initial promulgation of Psiharis' ideas. Using arguments that became staples of subsequent debates and can be seen, for example, in Kazantzakis' pronouncements at the end of the decade, Fotiadis awakened in demoticists a sense of responsibility to reform curricula and rewrite textbooks. "Even if children's minds can be educated with one or another foreign language," he wrote, "their hearts and souls cannot be educated in the interests of the nation except in one way: with the language, music, poetry and the other domestic and community customs which the people have preserved in a living form. . . . A national life and culture sprout from the dynamism of a single root, and the grub attacking this root is *katharevousa*, which explains why things that should be continually sprouting are dying."[22]

This pronouncement set the tone for the future. Note in particular how educational reformation, like the strictly literary reformation that had already partly occurred, was meant to foster "a national life and culture," namely, the establishment of a neo-hellenic identity. It should be stressed from the beginning, however, that although the educational demoticists naturally invoked the demotic tradition, as did Dragoumis, this did not mean that they were fiercely opposed to the ancients. Indeed, their complaint was that the ancients had been made inaccessible and hateful to Greek children (we shall see Kazantzakis arguing in this way), and much of their energy was devoted to remedying this inaccessibility by means of demotic translations of ancient authors. (Later, as an example, we shall see Kazantzakis' great desire to be commissioned to translate Plato for the schools.)

In all this, the educational demoticists were paradoxically continuing, not opposing, the humanism of their opponent Korais, and in particular Korais' dream of integrating the ancient and modern cultures. We should remember as well that Korais—liberal nationalist that he was, and believing in the Socratic dictum (so strongly attacked by Nietzsche) that knowledge is virtue—campaigned vigorously for universal education, and indeed education employing "the language of the people on which all of us have been nourished by our mutual mother, the homeland."[23] But Korais' conception of this *koine*, as we have seen, forced it to depart from demotic, and his conception of the actual methods of instruction in the classroom was

22. Cited in Triantafyllidis, *Quo-usque*, p. 134.
23. Chaconas, p. 64, citing Korais, *Syllogi*, pp. 42–44.

hardly likely either to bring the classics alive or to educate the child's heart and soul in the interests of the nation. An ideal classroom exercise, according to Korais, involved translating a passage from an ancient text into Modern Greek (i.e., *katharevousa*) and then back again into ancient, after which the pupils would be asked to comment on the linguistic problems involved and to find ways in which Greek words could be substituted for any foreign words in their modern renderings![24]

To appreciate what the demoticists were rebelling against, we should realize that this philological approach to literature (though not necessarily the exact exercise) had survived as a method of "literary" instruction in the Greek schools. Thus the living quality of the ancient texts was compromised, to say the least. The older students were made to wrestle with the classics in the original language, while those in the third grade were expected to whet their appetites on puristic versions such as the following (in use circa 1905):[25]

"Σοῦ ὅμως, ὦ ᾿Αχιλλεῦ, οὐδεὶς ὑπῆρξεν εὐτυχέστερος, διότι καὶ πρότερον ζῶντα σὲ ἐτιμῶμεν ὡς θεόν, καὶ τώρα πάλιν εἰς τὸν ῞Αδην εἶσαι βασιλεὺς τῶν νεκρῶν. Διὰ τοῦτο δὲν πρέπει νὰ λυπῆσαι διὰ τὸν θάνατόν σου".

Τότε ἐκεῖνος μοὶ ἀπεκρίθη: "Μὴ μὲ παρηγορῇς διὰ τὸν θάνατόν μου, ᾿Οδυσσεῦ. ᾿Επεθύμουν καλλίτερον νὰ εἶμαι δοῦλος πτωχοῦ ἀνδρὸς καὶ νὰ βλέπω τὸ φῶς τοῦ ἡλίου παρὰ νὰ εἶμαι εἰς τὸν ῞Αδην καὶ νὰ ἄρχω τῶν νεκρῶν. ᾿Αλλ᾿ ἔλα εἰπέ μοι, ᾿Οδυσσεῦ, τί γίνεται ὁ υἱός μου; ῏Ηλθεν εἰς τὸν πόλεμον ἢ ὄχι; Περὶ δὲ τοῦ γηραιοῦ πατρός μου τί γνωρίζεις;"

(Odysseus interviewing Achilles in Hades, Book xi)

24. Chaconas, p. 64.
25. Cited in Triantafyllidis, *Quo-usque*, p. 145. The passages are from Book xi, 482–93 and Book xvi, 25–26, 30–33.

" "Ελα, εἴσελθε, προσφιλὲς τέκνον, ἵνα χαρῶ ὁλοψύχως
βλέπων σε ἐλθόντα εἰς τὴν καλύβην μου ἀμέσως μετὰ τὴν
ἐπιστροφήν σου ἐκ τῆς ξένης χώρας. . . ."

Πρὸς αὐτὸν ἀπήντησε τότε ὁ Τηλέμαχος: "Πάτερ μου,
θὰ πράξω ὅ τι λέγεις, διότι ἐπίτηδες διὰ σὲ ἦλθον ἐνταῦθα,
καὶ διὰ νὰ σὲ ἴδω καὶ διὰ νὰ μάθω παρὰ σοῦ, ἐὰν ἡ μήτηρ
μου μένῃ ἀκόμη ἐν τῇ οἰκίᾳ μας ἢ ἐξέλεξεν ἄλλον σύζυγον".
(The swineherd Eumaios addressing Telemachus, Book XVI)

We should recall how the Greek novel, as far back as the
1850's, had begun to struggle with this problem of incongruity
between language and subject matter, and especially with the
incongruity arising in dialogue when swineherds are made to
speak "correctly." We have seen that the novel solved the
problem in two stages: (1) by using demotic dialogue while
retaining purist narration, (2) by using demotic narration as
well. The first of these stages had already been accepted by
1905; the second was to be accepted soon afterward.

But the schoolbooks reflected none of this. Instead, they
manifested the continued dominance of Soutsos-Kontos in all
realms outside the arts, even when the books were ostensibly
literary, as in the Homeric translations cited above. The uncompromising "correctness" of these texts, the thoroughness
with which *katharevousa* was made the medium of the child's
instruction and cultural development, can perhaps be illustrated by one further example, a simple tale, carrying with it
none of the sacrosanct aura which the humanists/philhellenes/
purists had given to the classics, yet offered to the pupils in
a language fully as "irreproachable" as that deemed necessary
for Homer:[26]

26. Cited in Triantafyllidis, *I glossa mas*, p. 51. For examples
from first-grade readers, 1908 ff., see Glinos, *Oi hoiroi*, pp. 38–43.

. . . κατὰ τὴν θαλασσοπορίαν ὁ πόντος ἐμελαίνετο, ἐκ δὲ
τοῦ ὕδατος ἀφρὸς ἐξήρχετο, πανταχοῦ τῆς θαλάσσης
ἠχούντων τῶν κυμάτων. Τεθορυβημένος καὶ περιδεής . . . .
βαθέος ὄρθρου εἰσπλεύσαντες ἐν τῷ λιμένι . . .

It was against all this that educational demoticism began to
rebel shortly after 1900. The tangible and immediate goals were
rewritten texts and modified curricula so that modern Greek
culture might be studied in its own right. Toward this end
the demoticists hoped to convince the Ministry of Education
to sanction their materials for actual use in schools; this in
turn required enabling legislation by Parliament, for we must
always remember that *katharevousa* was by law the official
language of the Greek Kingdom.

The more intangible goals were to foster a truly literary
sensibility in future generations and, especially, to promulgate
the demoticist ideology (including its political and cultural
implications) to the population as a whole.[27] This was a logical
sequel to the initial promulgation a decade earlier, when the
problem was to make Psiharis' ideas known to artists, scholars,
administrators, i.e., to a narrow circle of intellectuals. The demoticists were now assuming a much more difficult and extensive task, for a significant portion of the common people—
precisely those who might be expected to embrace demoticism
enthusiastically—had by this time been so indoctrinated that
they considered *katharevousa* identical with education and
thus saw it as the sine qua non of improved social status. Kazantzakis, at the height of his active campaign for demotic
in Irakleion, was hooted in the streets not by the professional
class, but by cobblers!

The most significant milestones along the route leading to

27. Glinos, *I krisi*, p. 9.

these tangible and intangible goals—milestones such as the founding of the Educational Association in 1910, the appointment of demoticists to the Ministry of Education, the enabling legislation by Parliament in 1917—are situated within the period of Kazantzakis' active interest in educational problems and need be only listed now, since they can best be considered in detail later, when we follow his career.

Here, I should like simply to provide additional background to that career by mentioning briefly the work of two men who, along with Fotiadis, formed a kind of triumvirate of leadership in the earliest years of educational demoticism. The first of these was Markos Tsirimokos, whom we have already encountered as one of the founders in 1904 of the Society for the National Language, along with Dragoumis and Triantafyllidis. Part of the Society's aim was to extend the living language to all sections of social life; Tsirimokos took the schools as his particular province, drawing his fellow demoticists' attention to the educational realm in his book *The Old and the New* (1905) and in subsequent writings. He was also one of the founders of the Educational Association.

The second figure who must be mentioned is Alexander Delmouzos, the first person actually to apply demoticism in a school.[28] The experiment was conducted in Volos, beginning in 1908 and ending in 1911 when public pressure, brought to a head by the controversy in the Revisionary Assembly regarding a linguistic clause for the new Constitution, forced Delmouzos' school to close. In devising his curriculum, he took as axiomatic that demotic and *katharevousa* were two entirely separate languages, thus rejecting any further experiments in compromise. We must not be misled, he wrote, by the small area in which the two tongues coincide. Nor must we be concerned only with glaring differences such as ἰχθύς-

28. *Apology*, pp. 159–60.

ψάρι, where the corresponding words have entirely different roots.[29] When *katharevousa* "corrects" demotic words retaining ancient roots, the result is just as bad. Changing δόντι to ὀδούς or πέφτω to πίπτω alters the "character, the soul" of the language. When we add to this the great differences between purist and demotic in syntax, declensions, etc., "only superstition and obstinacy are capable of denying that we have two different languages before us." Thus Delmouzos taught his girls (interestingly, the experiment was allowed only in a παρθεναγωγεῖον) to write νύχτα instead of νύξ, μέσα στὸ σπίτι instead of ἐν τῇ οἰκίᾳ, and so forth.

Here are some further examples which he himself has cited:

write	*instead of*
ζάχαρη, τῆς ζάχαρης	ζάκχαρις, τῆς ζακχάρεως
γείτονας	γείτων
γυναῖκα, τῆς γυναῖκας, οἱ γυναῖκες	γυνὴ, τῆς γυναικὸς, αἱ γυναῖκες
θάλασσα, τῆς θάλασσας	θάλασσα, τῆς θαλάσσης
τὸ μῆλο	τὸ μῆλον
ἄγριος-ἄγρια	ἄγριος-ἀγρία
ἔλεγα	ἔλεγον
γινόμουνα	ἐγενόμην
ἐπάνω στὸ τραπέζι	ἐπὶ τῆς τραπέζης
γιὰ τοὺς γάμους	ἐπὶ τοῖς γάμοις
βαρέθηκα περιμένοντας	ἐβαρύνθην ἀναμένων
ἕνα ζευγάρι κάλτσες	ἓν ζεῦγος ὑποποδίων

Delmouzos also taught his girls to use and appreciate demotic's wealth of synthetic forms such as κρυφομιλῶ (a resource that Kazantzakis always exploited to the full), and its expressive, varied diminutives and augmentatives—γιαγιάκα,

29. Delmouzos, *To protypon*, pp. 29–30. All the following material on his educational program is drawn from this source.

γεροντᾶκος, ἀγγελοῦδι, μανοῦλα, πατερούλης, μύταρος, πο-δάρα—forms whose nuances of feeling and meaning can never be reproduced in *katharevousa*.

Delmouzos' educational aims naturally encompassed much more than grammar and syntax. He wished to counteract the entire attitude that made the continued dominance of *katharevousa* possible. "The children I was given . . . by the official school," he proclaimed, were "sickly rayahs, drowning in fake romanticism." He therefore aimed to improve their bodies by means of games and excursions, their minds by teaching them subjects that would be of realistic use in later life. Unifying the entire program was a single craving: "to see the rise in our land of a real, national, neo-hellenic civilization."[30]

Such a curriculum aroused suspicion, since in many ways Delmouzos was attempting to undermine the "fake romanticism"—i.e., the imported philhellenism—which had masqueraded throughout the nineteenth century as truly appropriate to modern Greece. The result was that not only did public pressure close the school in 1911, as I have indicated, but that Delmouzos found himself brought to trial, accused of promulgating Darwinism, freemasonry, anarchism, and in sum of being "an enemy of religion, morality, and the fatherland."[31] The trial, which reminds us of the Scopes trial in the United States, took place in Nauplion in 1914. Despite the parade of witnesses against him, Delmouzos was acquitted. The whole affair became a *cause célèbre* in the demotic struggle, and through its sensational nature served to make Delmouzos' work more widely known than it could have been otherwise.[32]

Though the opposition continued, the fortunes of educa-

30. Papandreou, *I diki*, pp. 203, 204.
31. *Ibid.*, passim.
32. *Apology*, p. 160. In 1915 a complete transcript of the trial was published: *I Diki tou Nafpliou (16–28 Apriliou 1914), stenografimena praktika*.

tional demoticism prospered in these years. The preparation of new textbooks went on apace, with Kazantzakis one of the writers involved; in 1917 demotic was sanctioned as the exclusive language in the first four grades and as a partner with *katharevousa* in the fifth and sixth; Delmouzos and the demotic grammarian Triantafyllidis were appointed as overseers for the change.

All this leads us ahead of ourselves once more, but I wished at least to list certain events so that we might realize the decisive, though short-lived, victories achieved by educational demoticism during the period of Kazantzakis' involvement.

KAZANTZAKIS' CONTEXT

Much more important at this point, however, is a realization of all the interrelated endeavors that were already taking place at the time Kazantzakis began his career, and of the particular people involved. I have tried to sketch in the reasons why Greek bilingualism developed, the relation of the various factions to humanistic values, the pressures which made Psiharis inevitable. I have tried to convey the breadth and variety of the response to Psiharis' appeal—the "phenomenon" of the response—and how by 1906 its literary, political, and educational aspects had been twined together so closely that any one of them was now unthinkable without the others.

Above all, I have tried to convey the urgency with which so many people approached the language question, and the extraordinary amount of creative energy that the whole matter released—as seen in the remarkable advances in poetry, prose, drama; the treatises, societies, periodicals, dictionaries, grammars, translations, schoolbooks. In 1906, with the demotic movement gathering momentum, Greece was experiencing a general cultural awakening. Kazantzakis could not have chosen a better time to commence his literary career. Nor, once immersed in that career, could he have avoided committing himself one way or the other as far as the language question was concerned. He committed himself to demotic, indeed to the extreme pan-hellenic demotic advocated by Psiharis. This commitment deeply affected all of his subsequent writings, sometimes for ill sometimes for good, as I hope to show. It also brought him much pain. But once the commitment was made, Kazantzakis never swerved from it. For fifty years he remained a "fanatic" demoticist, a *malliaros* who without second thoughts could always say, echoing Palamas, "*malliarismos* is my virtue." Whether it was his virtue or not, and in what ways, we must now examine.

PART TWO

The Demoticism of Kazantzakis

Initial Development and Activism

INITIAL DEVELOPMENT, 1906–1909

Kazantzakis was not born with his extreme demoticism; he developed it during his first few years in Athens in response to the people and spirit he encountered there. He used demotic for his first published work, the romance *Ophis kai Krino* (*Snake and Lily*) but admitted puristic forms as well, as can be seen in the title. The distance of this book's language from the model set by Psiharis can be appreciated from phrases such as the following:

Κι ἀπὸ τὰ χείλη Σου στάσσει . . . ἵμερος
   τῶν Μαγνητῶν
Ἀπάνω στὰ χείλη τῶν ὡραίων γυναικῶν βλέπω τὰ
   φιλιὰ νὰ ἔρπουν
Ἔλα νὰ σπεύσομεν ἀφοῦ θὰ πεθάνομεν[1]

Because of this mixed language, the book was badly reviewed in *Noumas*, the crusading demoticist periodical whose
columnists were Psiharis himself, Palamas, Pallis, and Vlastos.
This periodical can be compared to *Scrutiny* in the effect it ex-
erted and also in its cantankerous narrowmindedness. Whereas Leavis disparaged authors who did not display moral seriousness, the reviewers in *Noumas* were notorious for dis-
paraging all authors who did not worship Psiharis and employ the *malliari* idiom.[2] The adverse review of *Snake and
Lily*, written, ironically, by Kazantzakis' subsequent friend
Petros Vlastos, objected to the intrusions of *katharevousa* but
conceded that the author could write well, which meant that
he could write in good radical demotic when he wished to.[3]

This novella, which I have already characterized as a mélange of defiant paganism and sickly weariness à la D'Annunzio and the Parnassians, has nothing to do with Greek
life as such, but is courtly and remote in character, very consciously arty in the *fin-de-siècle* mode; thus the dignified
mixed language rather suits it. But *Noumas* was crusading,
its aim was to impose upon literature an idiom identical with
the spoken language in every detail, and no questions of
aesthetic appropriateness could make it condone Kazantzakis'
"bilingualism."

   1. Kazantzakis, *Ophis kai Krino*, pp. 17, 69, 71. The form
"stassei" is apparently a Cretan variant. See Georgios E. Panka-
los, *Peri tou glossikou idiomatos tis Kritis*, Vol. III, p. 446.
   2. See Xenopoulos, *Skiamachia*.
   3. Vlastos, *Kritikes anapodies*.

But the book was praised by Palamas.[4] Writing in another periodical, he spoke of it as a "prose poem," hailed the talented author, and admonished him not to be so decadent in the future. As I remarked earlier, this was a vital aid for Kazantzakis, the start of a patronage that opened political, social, and literary doors.

During the next three or four years Kazantzakis moved slowly but steadily toward the *Noumas* camp as far as his language was concerned, and although he did not abandon his decadence, he transformed it from the "arty" type to a "healthy," vigorous Nietzscheanism more consistent with the *Noumas* mystique.

For the time being—that is, from his debut in 1906 until his return in 1909 from graduate study in Paris—Kazantzakis found his chief welcome in another periodical, *Pinakothiki*.[5] Dimitrios Kaloyeropoulos, its editor, was a moderate; though he personally preferred *katharevousa*, he opened his periodical to all who had talent. He had reviewed *Snake and Lily* favorably, characterizing its author as not a professional *malliaros*, but someone who seemed to use both demotic and *katharevousa* without any apparent system—in short, a bilingualist.[6] Kazantzakis wrote to Kaloyeropoulos thanking him, whereupon friendship and mutual admiration ensued.

This encouragement was sufficient to make Kazantzakis compose his next major work, the play Ξημερώνει (*Day Is Breaking*), in a modified demotic acceptable to Kaloyeropoulos but still—as we shall see—not sufficiently *malliari* for *Noumas*. Kazantzakis sent the work to his patron, accompanying it with a long explanatory letter dated August 22, 1906, a letter very important for our knowledge of his intentions in the play, but also significant because it shows that

4. Palamas, K., *Ophis*.   5. Markakis, p. 30.
6. Kaloyeropoulos.

even in his private correspondence he was not yet writing in demotic:[7]

    . . . Τὰς σκέψεις τοῦ γιατροῦ τὰς ἐπαναστατικὰς . . .
"Επρεπε . . . νὰ συντριφθῇ, διὰ νὰ γίνῃ . . . καὶ νὰ γίνει
ἀντιληπτὸ

(Note here, however, that a demotic spelling, γίνει, appears in the same sentence as the purist γίνῃ. It is also of interest that, as late as 1909, Kazantzakis sometimes wrote to his father in *katharevousa* while addressing familiar remarks to his mother and sisters in demotic on the back of the same sheet.[8] Some of the letters to his father were in full demotic by 1908, in contrast to the mixed language he employed in 1907 and the full *katharevousa* of 1902.)[9]

Nine months after his letter to Kaloyeropoulos, Kazantzakis had apparently begun to throw in his lot with the more radical of the demoticists. On the pretext of reviewing a new book by Triantafyllidis, whom we have encountered in connection with the Society for the National Language and who was to become the definitive grammarian of the spoken tongue, Kazantzakis wrote the first of his many demotic manifestoes.[10] Arguing the problem of whether so-called foreign words ought to be expelled from Greek, he asked quite sensibly: How can we know which words are "foreign" and which are not? Then he replied in what he called the only rational way: "Greek" words are those which live on the lips of the Greek people. By this definition, living words of foreign derivation are obviously Greek, while impeccably Greek words that have fallen out of use are foreign.

Kazantzakis went on to rebut the argument that the Ger-

7. Markakis, p. 32.   8. *Biography*, pp. 46, 48.
9. For samples, see *Nea Estia*, Christmas 1959, pp. 205–10.
10. Kazantzakis, *To glossiko mas zitima*.

mans were purifying their language of foreign words and that the Greeks ought therefore to do the same. The cases, he pointed out, were not at all analogous. The foreign words that the Germans wished to expel were incomprehensible to the people; the German purifiers wished to replace them with terms the people spoke. But the Greek purists were doing just the opposite: expelling terms the people spoke, and replacing them with others that were incomprehensible. Kazantzakis then exhorted the Greek people to break the chains of tradition, accept the contemporary spoken idiom, and stop being so chauvinistic as far as language was concerned. English, French, and Spanish were full of loan words. Why not Greek?

"DAY IS BREAKING"

Meanwhile, Kazantzakis had taken his play *Day Is Breaking*, written almost a year earlier in a language still not extreme, and had submitted it to the dramatic competition sponsored by the University of Athens. As a result it became the *cause célèbre* of the season.[11] True, the play's morality, not its language, was what chiefly inflamed the good bourgeoisie of Athens, for Kazantzakis in an Ibsenesque mood had proclaimed the right of his heroine to slam the door against a doting, responsible husband she does not love, in order to consummate an illicit affair with a romantic poet.

This play was so shocking, yet so good, that the judges were forced to compromise by praising it and it alone, but awarding no prize. Nevertheless, they had given it official recognition in a backhanded way, and indeed from the sacred precincts of the university, before an audience that included the Minister of Education and other dignitaries. The critical jury was the literary establishment itself: the folklorist Politis, at that time

11. Katsimbalis, *O agnostos Kazantzakis*, p. 745. Also *Biography*, p. 40.

chancellor of the university; Lambros, dean of the faculty of philosophy, eventually Prime Minister; and Sakellaropoulos, professor of Latin philology. The fact that such a jury had praised such a play was sensational, and not a small part of the sensation arose from the fact that this libel against Greek womanhood was written in demotic.

The importance of the language issue is seen in the adjudicators' official statement, where this is the first matter discussed. Lambros, the spokesman, observed interestingly that although some of the play's vocabulary stood above the social class of the characters, this was for the most part a demotic work. The controversy that followed in the newspapers involved extreme statements from the two linguistic blocs, with little or no attempt to judge the language from an artistic viewpoint—that is, to discuss its appropriateness to this particular play and these particular characters, as Lambros had so wisely done. One inflamed journalist asked indignantly what right the adjudicators had to praise such a play when many of the other entries were in *katharevousa*.[12] But *Noumas* found cause for jubilation even though the language was far from "irreproachable." The next issue bore a lead article by the director, Tankopoulos. Until now, he wrote, to win a dramatic prize you had to compose iambic twelve-syllable verse in *katharevousa*, and include a pseudo-Aristotelian catharsis.[13] At last a play with none of these qualifications had been praised, breaking the hold of the past on Greek letters and advancing the struggle for demotic.

It is true that at least one commentator—actually Ghavriilidis, whom we have met as the first journalist to embrace demoticism—escaped the partisan spirit and hailed Kazantzakis for attempting a new type of linguistic compromise, calling

12. See Tankopoulos, *Paragrafakia*, p. 5.
13. Tankopoulos, *O Pantelideios*, p. 755.

him neither a purist nor a Psiharist.[14] Tankopoulos, picking
this up, was forced to agree. In his remarks he gives us some
particular examples of the details the *malliari* were espousing.
If the author had been a Psiharist, commented Tankopoulos,
he would never have written ἐκτείνω τὰ χέρια μου or στὴ
πτῶσι and τὴ ψυχή, since no one ἐκτείνει his hands, or swal-
lows the ν when he chats about the πτώση or the ψυχή.[15]

Nevertheless, the way was now open for Kazantzakis to
enter into full association with the *Noumas* group, especially
since he had become a propagandist for demotic in the year
that intervened between his play's composition and its no-
toriety. In addition, his value as a worker in the demotic vine-
yard was confirmed when this same play was produced in
Athens two months after its official recognition.

The background to this production is interesting. Although
in his letters to Kaloyeropoulos about *Day Is Breaking* Kazantzakis confessed that he knew nothing about writing for
the stage, had no sense of entrances and exits, and was unable
to visualize his characters at all, he nevertheless dropped a
hint to his patron that Greece's most celebrated actress, Marika
Kotopouli, might perhaps be suitable for the lead![16] Never
lacking in self-confidence, Kazantzakis tended to aim directly for the top. In this case he failed to achieve Kotopouli,
but he did equally well. After withdrawing the manuscript
from a producer who wished to make changes, he submitted it
successfully to the distinguished director Thomas Oikonomou,
who played such an important part in the demoticization of
the theatre.[17] Oikonomou's particular mission was to restore

14. Ghavriilidis, *Lakonika*. See *Biography*, p. 41.
15. Tankopoulos, *O idios*, p. 8.
16. Markakis, p. 32.
17. Katsimbalis, O Agnostos Kazantzakis, *Nea Estia*, June 1,
1958, p. 848.

poetic drama to the stage, and this perhaps explains his attraction to Kazantzakis' play, for *Day Is Breaking* is lyrical in texture despite the Ibsenesque subject matter. With Evangelia Paraskevopoulou, a star of that day, in the leading role, the play achieved a glittering premiere before all the important literary and artistic figures of Athens—and prompted the expected controversy. The controversy centered mostly on its morals and defective dramatic technique, but language was still a sore point, one critic, for example, objecting to the word φοντάνα (fountain).[18]

These developments delighted the demoticists of *Noumas*, who had found in Kazantzakis the talented, articulate, and controversial figure they needed to place their claims before the widest possible public.

PARIS

The play *Day Is Breaking* was on the boards in the first part of July 1907. In September, the young dramatist, already famous or notorious in his own country, left for Paris to spend roughly two years doing graduate work. But though Kazantzakis was nominally studying political philosophy and preparing a dissertation to win himself a position in the Faculty of Law at Athens University, he was actually maturing as a writer.[19] With his usual industriousness, he completed in this period a major novel called *Broken Souls* and a major play, *The Masterbuilder*, as well as his dissertation on Nietzsche (written with admirable lucidity, one should note, in the obligatory *katharevousa*), another play or two, and journalistic dispatches sent to Athens.

18. See Rodas, p. 1,455; also Sideris, p. 1,030; Alexiou, E., p. 98; Theatis.

19. See the letters to his father, *Nea Estia*, Christmas 1959, pp. 208–09.

These works, and the newspaper articles in particular, show (1) a radicalism that took the form of increasing disgust with the bourgeois world of the respectable establishment, and (2) a nationalism consistent with Nietzsche's worship of strength and Bergson's belief in creative evolution.[20] Kazantzakis, fascinated with the radical right as manifested in those days in France, was preparing himself in effect to embrace the full nationalistic mystique we have mentioned in connection with Ion Dragoumis, a mystique that abhorred the bourgeoisie, humanism/liberalism and the romantic adoration of ancient Greece. Nor did he hesitate to smash humanistic idols. In one of his newspaper dispatches, for example, he told of the annual oration delivered at Korais' grave in Montparnasse on March 25, Greece's Independence Day. This year, said Kazantzakis, the speaker will omit the "threadbare and braggart ornaments of our rhetoricians, the triumphs of Marathon and Salamis; he will leave the past to lie rotted in the ground, will talk about the terrible crisis Hellenism is now enduring, and will suggest how each of us . . . can help the race."[21] In another article he characterized modern Greece as young and vigorous. If only the Greeks themselves would stop scorning modern civilization, they could command forces that would lead them to victory in the evolutionary struggle, enabling them to fulfill their manifest destiny. This is the article in which Kazantzakis admonished his countrymen to recognize such cultural glories as Palamas, and to stop worshipping the tired, decadent writers of France.[22]

This nationalism, swelling to an almost hysterical forte during the Paris years and immediately afterward, made it all

20. Katsimbalis, O Agnostos Kazantzakis, *Nea Estia*, Aug. 15, 1958, p. 1,208.

21. Kazantzakis, *Oi Ellines spoudastai*.

22. Kazantzakis, *Ellinika poiimata*.

the easier for Kazantzakis to enter the extremists' camp as far as language was concerned—for demotic, as we have seen, was a major component of the new nationalistic mystique.

He returned to Greece in April of 1909, bearing with him the manuscripts of his novel, play, and scholarly dissertation. All evidence shows him now a *malliaros* in matters linguistic. In October of the same year, for example, he wrote to his patron Kaloyeropoulos about new works he and his wife Galateia hoped to have published in *Pinakothiki*. But he obviously sensed that the old relationship would be difficult to maintain because of his linguistic radicalism: "You have always been gracious to us," he stated rather defensively. "However much you hate the *malliari* you have always managed . . . to put us in something of a special category." Then he added, more defiantly: "We are now working day and night on several novels, *malliara* unfortunately, because this is the only way we can express vibrantly what is circulating in our blood."[23]

As things turned out, he contributed nothing further of note to this moderate periodical. *Broken Souls*, the novel he had written in Paris, began to be serialized in *Noumas*, running from June 30, 1909 to February 7, 1910. Unlike Kazantzakis' earlier novel and despite the setting in Paris, this work offered subject matter that was Greek, and language that was pure vernacular in both narration and dialogue:[24]

ὀρθομένο . . . μπροστά του σὰν πελώριο ξεφουντωμένο κρίνο, . . . πότε πάλι . . . σὰν ἀγιόκλημα ὀλοάνθιστο ἢ σὰν φίδι

23. Markakis, p. 38.
24. Kazantzakis, *Spasmenes*. The citations are from Part I, ch. 11; Part II, ch. 2; Part II, ch. 4, which appeared in the *Noumas* issues of Oct. 4, 1909, p. 7, Oct. 18, 1909, p. 7, and Nov. 1, 1909, p. 2, respectively.

(Note that the ὄφις of Kazantzakis' first novel has been transformed now into a demotic φίδι.)

Ἐγὼ κάτι ἄλλο θέλω, ἐγὼ πνίγομαι στὴν ἀγκαλιά σου, ἐγὼ θέλω νὰ βγῶ ὄξω στὸ φῶς. . . — γιατὶ κάποιος ἄλλος εἶναι ὁ σκοπός μου ἐμένα.

μήπως δὲν ὑπάρχει Ἀλήθεια; Ἢ κι ἂν ὑπάρχει, μήπως εἶναι ἀδύνατο νὰ τήνε δοῦμε ἐμεῖς;

In the November 15th issue of *Noumas*—that is, before the serialization was completed—the novel was praised by Psiharis himself.[25] Thus it and its author received the ultimate imprimatur. Kazantzakis was now part of *Noumas*'s inner

25. This praise arose from circumstances that demand some explanation. Despite what I have said about Kazantzakis' new nationalistic fervor, this novel is not basically nationalistic in theme or content. True, it begins with the hero making a March 25th oration at Korais' grave, preaching an intellectual and moral revolution with Nietzsche and evolution as the rallying cries. But it then quickly becomes a study of the hero's inability to act at all, indeed of complete moral, physical, sexual, and intellectual frustration—thus the title, *Broken Souls*. Even before the serialization was well underway, Kazantzakis had received letters from friends asking why he had made his novel so pessimistic, sick, and negative. He felt obliged to defend himself, which he did in the *Noumas* of September 27, 1909 (reprinted in *Nea Estia*, Oct. 1, 1958, p. 1,498); hence we have the strange situation of a novelist publicly announcing his intentions before his readership has had an opportunity to complete the novel.

The question of language was no longer a factor here; thus this is not the place for further discussion of the novel's content or of Kazantzakis' self-defense. This is the background, however, to Psiharis' brief article (*Noumas*, Nov. 8, 1909), in which he agrees that Kazantzakis was premature in publishing an apology for his work, but then goes on to praise the young author's evocative and descriptive powers, and to claim that the characters are not broken souls at all: they are fresh, lively, deliciously young. One can only conclude that Psiharis had not read beyond the first four or five installments!

circle, or perhaps one should say "the joint chiefs of staff," for the demoticists were extremely militant. During the decade 1909–1919 he found himself at the center of the struggle, involved in all its facets: the political, religious, and educational, as well as the more strictly literary or philological. Indeed, his active and non-literary involvement was so great during these years that he produced very few major works of his own.

Activism, 1909–1919

I should like now to treat some examples of this active involvement, withholding discussion of *The Masterbuilder*, the ambitious play that Kazantzakis brought back with him from Paris, until we reach 1910, when this work became an actual factor, indeed a decisive *event*, in his career. In the meantime we shall learn more about the linguistic and nationalistic militancy that received pugnacious expression in that work.

In February 1909, shortly before Kazantzakis returned from Paris, the demoticists of Hanya, Crete (Venizelos' home town) formed a Solomos Society for the National Language. Since the founder, Christos Christoulakis, preached the collaborative effort of demoticism and politics against the forces of reaction, and since the Society's expressed aim was to "strike down superstition," it is no wonder that these demoticists met with opposition.[26] Things came to a head when they complained publicly about the headmaster of the local high school, whereupon the Metropolitan of the town denounced them as anti-religious.[27] The Society announced a lecture that would clarify its aims—for one of the oddest aspects of this situation was the reluctance of the Folk themselves to support the demoticists. As a result, the latter were constantly trying to explain their position to the people and correct any misconcep-

26. *Apology*, p. 147.
27. *Noumas,* May 31, 1909, p. 5.

tions. The lecture took place, but meanwhile the headmaster had ordered his students to gather outside the hall and hoot, shout, and whistle so that the speaker could not be heard. The following day, when it became known that Venizelos himself was involved in the Society, passions swelled even more, and the members, finding for a time that discretion is the better part of valor, did not venture out-of-doors.

This defeat roused the demoticists of Irakleion to support their brethren by forming another branch of the Solomos Society. Kazantzakis, newly returned from abroad, took the initiative and became president.[28] Thus, two months after he landed in Crete, he was leader of a holy crusade. Here, too, was his opportunity to suffer martyrdom bravely, to be consoled in adversity by the thought that he was witnessing for the truth just as had the early Christians or the Spanish demoticist de Leon. Kazantzakis apparently did suffer ridicule, if not actual physical abuse. One report states that the city's cobblers liked to toss their lasts at his head as he passed through their quarter; another, that they merely beat their hammers on their benches and hissed "zit-zit" whenever he came into sight;[29] another, that the only person willing to be seen with him in the streets was a Turkish boatman convinced that anyone who worked so clearly "against the national interest" must be a secret ally of the Sultan; still another, that he was imprisoned briefly for his campaign against the official legally sanctioned language and for desiring (as the opposition would put it) "to make us all speak and write like peasants."[30]

We are obliged to see all this in a double light. The first light is positive. How splendid, how genuinely heroic was his

28. *Apology*, p. 148.
29. Venezis, p. 5; Haris, M., p. 29.
30. *Apology*, p. 148; Nikos Saklambanis, Kazantzakis' nephew, in an interview with the author, April 1964.

involvement in this still very unpopular cause! How many youths—how many of us in our youth or at any time—have endangered reputation, career, and comfort for the truth? In this light, Kazantzakis was acting in the tradition of the great moral and religious leaders we universally admire; more relevant for our secular age, he was transmuting intellectuality into action and was thus consciously pushing human culture one tiny step forward.

But there is another light that is inescapable and in which we are forced to see Kazantzakis: newly returned from Paris with his Nietzschean belief in the superman plus his Bergsonian emphasis on the omnipotent will, acting with a somewhat Napoleonic bravura, reveling in opposition and difficulty for their own sake or rather as a test for his will, and perhaps really scorning the common people whose language was his joy. There is no doubt that he had a very low opinion of the provincials he was among; a year earlier he had written to Kaloyeropoulos: "I am ridiculed by twenty-five thousand—that is the population of Irakleion—and I ridicule twenty-five thousand back, so I get the best of them."[31] He liked the idea of being alone against the multitude, thus showing his strength.

MANIFESTO OF THE SOLOMOS SOCIETY

As president of the Solomos Society of Irakleion, Kazantzakis prepared a long manifesto stating the Society's program. This was published anonymously in *Noumas* on June 7, 1909. It shows Kazantzakis in both aspects I have described above. Positively, the manifesto displays the admirable mixture of passion and dispassionate logic that characterizes the best of his polemical writing; it is, moreover, indisputably sincere and well-informed. But negatively, especially toward the end,

31. Markakis, p. 37.

there is a certain cheap stridency in the tone, complacent superiority in the attitude toward the enemy, and a gloating
over martyrdom; in addition, there are some of the same
"threadbare and braggart ornaments" of patriotic rhetoric that
Kazantzakis liked to condemn—in others. The whole per-
formance is vituperative, very Miltonic, and, ironically, rather
in the style of the classical oration that Kazantzakis had studied to good advantage in the very school curriculum he was
now doing his best to abolish.

The manifesto begins by stating the purpose of the Solomos
Society: to convince Greeks that their written language should
be based on the language they speak. To this end, Kazantzakis says, he will (1) treat the history of the language question, (2) delineate the adverse effects of *katharevousa* on education, society, and the nation, (3) show why the written
language should be based on the spoken, proving that this is
(a) necessary because of national need, (b) possible, (c) imperative.[32] Lastly (4) he will indicate who must accomplish
this—not the teachers and literati, but the people themselves.
He adds at this point that the demoticists will speak out even
if they are hooted in the streets. Their opponents give them no
chance to explain their position; he and his colleagues bear
no grudge against the "teachers and demagogues" who treat
them so contemptuously, yet they will not remain silent.

Here, in paraphrase, are the chief points he makes:

(1) History of the language question. As soon as a child
enters school, he is taught to scorn the language he speaks. He
must never write ψωμί, νερό, κρασί, σπίτι, but rather ἄρτος,
ὕδωρ, οἶνος, οἰκία. The problem is that the teachers, blinded
by the splendor of the ancient tongue, have forgotten that languages develop. Though it did not take long to discover the
impossibility of returning to the idiom of Plato or even of

32. Kazantzakis, *Syllogos*; see also *Apology*, pp. 148–49.

Xenophon, the teachers failed to take the reasonable step of abandoning *katharevousa* altogether; instead, they began making compromises, mixing the old and the new, with the result that we now have thousands of different *katharevousas*.

The worst aspect of the problem is that the words we are told to suppress are the most living and common: terms for clothing (κᾳπέλλα, παντούφλες, γάντια, κάλτσες), for the tools of the various trades, for the most familiar things in ourselves and our environment: φωτιὰ (πῦρ), πόδι (πούς), χῶμα (χοῦς), χέρι (χείρ), αὐτὶ (οὖς).

(2) The consequences are catastrophic. In the educational realm, the child is made to feel confused, forced to learn words he will never hear. He ought to be instructed to love beauty, and, as in all teaching, this must be done through the medium of language. But can he be taught this with *katharevousa*? No!

Socially, the consequences are equally bad. Instead of learning something of practical value in school, we learn ancient Greek—that is, we learn to hate it, because Homer, Plato, and the rest are forever connected in our minds with the terrors of syntax, parsing, declensions. With this as a start, we come to hate all books, all learning, and develop a society that despises all books and learning, and is without idealism. If one in a thousand does emerge loving the ancient ideals "he is insulted and harassed until he is either assimilated to the rest, killed, or exiled."

As far as the nation is concerned, bilingualism creates a split between the learned and the people, because the books the professors write can never be read by the ordinary man. Bilingualism thus destroys the national unity and inhibits Greek progress.

In summary: "*Katharevousa* is unable to mold the child's spirit; it suffocates the mind and distorts the child's natural development. It makes us into superficial people full of hollow words and braggart phraseology; prevents us from loving books, study, everything serious and researched; breaks the nation's linguistic unity and little by little our very national integrity."

The remainder of the manifesto does not adhere very strictly to the outline announced at the start. It is more in the nature of an exhortation. Too many people, says Kazantzakis, cross their hands and say that the problem will solve itself. Why? Because they don't want to disturb their καφενειακὴ . . . μακαριότητα (café-bibbers' beatitude). What we need is workers: men who sense their great social and national destiny, women who will raise their children to love the Faith and Fatherland. (Kazantzakis makes this tactful concession to the Church, even though personally he had lost his faith while still a student in high school.)[33] It is a terrible thing, he continues, to see the teachers insulting the people by calling their language vulgar and barbaric, their ideals cheap, common. Yet when the demoticists proclaim that the ideals, joys, and pain of the people should be expressed in the spoken language, in the idiom of the demotic ballads—for poetry is always where a language is seen at its best—they are hooted and jeered, and by the people themselves.[34] This is all the result of a misunderstanding.

Demoticists do not want to touch religion or coin new words; they merely want demotic to be the common, accepted language throughout Greece. This is possible because the differences existing in the various regions are lexical, not syn-

33. Alexiou, E., p. 102.
34. Compare Vlastos, *Greek Bilingualism*, p. 81: "The masses of the people will be the last to be converted. They worship the *katharevousa* because it is something incomprehensible, ostentatious, and pseudogenteel."

tactical or grammatical. Demotic is a universal language for Greece, and it will triumph, just as a common idiom triumphed in Dante's Italy, Luther's Germany, and Lomonosov's Russia.

The Society's aim is to press the issue, making it a social and political one. Our opponents say: nothing is more perfect than the achievements of the ancient Greeks and therefore we must turn back and copy them. We reply: "Nothing is more beautiful than the works of our ancestors. Their language, literature, art—everything—is perfection. We have a great duty because we bear a great name; we must work along with other peoples to achieve something worthy of our ancestors, for life moves forward, it never turns back." Cretans pioneered in this; three hundred years ago Kornaros and Hortatsis were writing in demotic. "We have thrown off the Turkish yoke; now we Cretans shall be the ones to throw off the linguistic yoke that oppresses and enslaves our entire nation."

In the peroration, Kazantzakis offers his hand "fraternally to all, without any offense" (that is, to the opponents he had previously called sycophants, cowards, and demagogues!). He also includes the following strange confession of his yearning for martyrdom and his satisfied pride in doing his duty: "The man who leaves the great battle of Marathon . . . , who runs ahead of all others and proclaims the Victory (Νίκη) to the people of the city-state—he is the one who falls down dead, for he ran very much faster than the rest."

INFLUENCE OF DRAGOUMIS

Such was the manifesto Kazantzakis wrote for the Solomos Society in 1909. In connection with the final paragraph, it might be well to remember that as early as his university days Kazantzakis liked to sign his name using just the opening syllables Νι and Κα because they spell the imperative Νίκα—

conquer![35] Now, more than ever, Kazantzakis was a Marathon runner proclaiming Νίκη and willing to pay the consequences of being the first to do so. He was a Youth-Doing-His-Duty, calling upon other youths to do theirs. But he himself was responding to the call of another, thus forming the chain of discipleship that was so important to him throughout his life. The other in this case was Ion Dragoumis. All the motifs in the above manifesto—national unity; demotic ballads as respository for the soul of the nation; faith; fatherland; the folk infinite in its wisdom if only it will awaken—are the stock-in-trade of Dragoumis' mystical nationalism.

Precisely at the time Kazantzakis was spokesman for the Solomos Society of Irakleion, Dragoumis' book *Samothraki* was being serialized in *Noumas*. The contents of this exhortatory volume, and the way in which it presents a catalogue of Nietzschean doctrine, I have already attempted to indicate. We can suspect Kazantzakis' indebtedness simply from the arguments and attitudes in the Solomos Society manifesto, but we can be absolutely certain when we read the review he wrote of Dragoumis' book, which appeared in April 1910 in an Alexandrian periodical.[36] It is called "For Our Youth" and is principally a pretext for Kazantzakis' own Dragoumian comments on nationalism, in particular for his "proof" that nationalistic egotism is indeed altruism. He hails Dragoumis as a leader of youth, the prophet who will guide Greek manhood to the faith that is needed to return Greece to glory—"faith," because Dragoumis emphasized in his book that his nationalism was based, not on reason, but on a non-rational belief in the divine mission of Greece. Next, Kazantzakis stresses that for Dragoumis and himself the glory of Greece is a future glory, not a past one. On the contrary, the race is

35. Venezis. Cf. the "prosforon" in the liturgy.
36. Kazantzakis, *Kritika meletimata*.

in danger of drowning in an "ancestor-worshipping maras-mus"; if only we heed Dragoumis we shall learn to recognize this problem and solve it.

This utter disenchantment with the cultural dominance of the ancients, this evolutionary mentality pushing out the an-tiquarian, is the first way in which Dragoumis' program lends itself to demoticism. Another aspect dear to Kazantzakis was Dragoumis' voluntarism, very much in the Nietzschean-Berg-sonian pattern: the will is all-powerful, we can will ourselves to glory, to our manifest destiny, and also to demotic. Lastly, the Leader of Youth taught Kazantzakis that all this could be accomplished by means of a mystical faith in the people and the Greek land, the people and land of the present, not the past. Such are the Dragoumian ideas, or rather emotions, that lie in back of Kazantzakis' manifesto for demotic.

"THE MASTERBUILDER" AND THE EFFECT OF ITS FAILURE

The next event in Kazantzakis' career as a creative writer was his first and in many ways his last fully demoticist work—if by "fully demoticist" we mean the whole complex, the whole Dragoumian mystique of which the language question is only a part. I am referring to the major play written (at least in first draft) in 1908 while he was in Paris.[37] Encouraged by the success of *Day Is Breaking*, Kazantzakis submitted this new work to the dramatic contest of 1910, and it won first prize. The original title was Θυσία (*Sacrifice*), but this was changed afterward to the Ibsenesque Ὁ Πρωτομάστορας (*The Masterbuilder*).

The play is dedicated to Dragoumis, and no wonder, for it is Dragoumian through and through. Based on the folk ballad Τὸ Γεφύρι τῆς Ἄρτας and set in a village, it deals with peas-

37. Kazantzakis, *Masterbuilder*.

ants, i.e., the people, treats thematically the need to do one's duty, to reject happiness and all other forms of bourgeois lethargy, to assert one's egotism "altruistically," to follow faith rather than reason, to be constantly on the move toward future challenge and never satisfied with past achievement. The play is fiercely voluntaristic: the hero puts his will in the arena with fate itself and wins. It is also an interesting example of the efforts by many artists—Palamas first and foremost—to show Greece's cultural continuity; it does this by making an amalgam of modernism with ancient elements such as the chorus, all this in the service of modern Greek settings, characters, and obsessions. We should remember that Kazantzakis was among those striving to create a viable neo-hellenic theatrical form now that nationalism was dominant and demotic finding a more and more assured place in the theatre.[38] He was combatting not only the ubiquitous French farces that plague the Greek stage to this day, but a popular, patriotic-type play that apparently greatly attracted the man in the street, and that he characterized delightfully as "the yodeling of shepherds, mixed with religion, fatherland, and cheese."[39] To give artistic substance and depth to the new nationalistic movement, Kazantzakis tried to infuse his simple folktale with the religious urgency of the ancient drama, the shocking views promulgated by Dragoumis, and the intellectual excitement of the European theatre of ideas.

All this deserves elaboration elsewhere, for the play represents an important and fascinating stage in Kazantzakis' political, moral, philosophical and artistic development. I mention it here as much as I do simply to emphasize once again how wrong it is to discuss the language question in a vacuum. When we say that *The Masterbuilder* was Kazantzakis' most

38. Thrylos, p. 17.
39. Xenopoulos, *Skiamachia*, p. 1,564; Kazantzakis, *Ragiades*.

radically demotic work so far, we are speaking not simply of language but of the entire mystique that served him and certain others as a context for language. Indeed one of the great troubles with Kazantzakis as an artist in his middle period (I return to my hypothesis) was that he continued his radical demoticism but too often divorced it from a context that would make the purely linguistic elements artistically necessary and justified. It was only in the late novels and in the translation of the *Iliad* that this fault was overcome.

The fact remains that *The Masterbuilder* won Kazantzakis his first complete prize, since the adjudicators had merely praised *Day Is Breaking* but had denied it the laurel. In this case Kazantzakis, with his accustomed arrogance, his inner need to defy the establishment, refused to claim the laurel crown itself, though presumably he was happy to pocket the substantial award of 1,000 drachmas.[40] The adjudicators, who were the same as three years earlier, opened their statement as follows: "*Sacrifice*. Two-act drama, in prose, in pure demotic, with shades of Cretan dialect."[41] *Noumas* was again jubilant.[42] In the issue of May 23, 1910, it announced the decision and praised the adjudicators for choosing Kazantzakis' play "even though it was written in genuine demotic, even though it was made in a manner antithetical to the classical molds of the contest, even though blowing over and through it was an orgiastic breath that invariably frightens and enrages the shiny bald pates of critics." It noted finally that Marika Kotopouli was warmly in agreement with the adjudicators' choice, and suggested that they themselves should accept the laurel crown that the playwright had spurned.

But a strange thing happened after all this, considering

40. Katsimbalis, "O Agnostos Kazantzakis," *Nea Estia*, Oct. 15, 1958, p. 1,558.
41. Sakellaropoulos, p. 1,560.   42. Tankopoulos, *Oi Krites*.

Kazantzakis' reputation, the prize, and the general nationalistic climate: complete silence. The text was published, and a
newspaper announced in September that Kotopouli was about
to produce the drama; in the end, however, it failed not only
to reach the stage but to elicit any response whatsoever. No
reviews; no controversy. This was the first setback in a career
that had enjoyed rapid, flattering success until then. Kazantzakis, far from reacting graciously, published a vitriolic de-
nouncement of the theatrical scene in general and of the critics
in particular.[43] Anything, even abusive attack, is better than
silence, he cried. Abuse reveals lack of polish, but silence the
cowardice and lethargy of the rayah (the bondsman under the
Turks). Dragoumis in *Samothraki* had told the Greeks they
were still rayahs because of their indifference and inertia. Kazantzakis continued in this vein. "The true man" likes to
"throw stones into stagnant waters"; the rayah "crosses his
arms, compromises, is afraid of noise and light. . . . Where
among us are the youths who out of an overflowing of egotism always resist and deny. . . ?"[44]

Still, nothing happened. I have repeatedly termed this entire
episode an *event* in Kazantzakis' career, because the failure
of *The Masterbuilder* to be produced seems to have brought
the young author's theatrical ambitions to a sudden termina-
tion.[45] Since it is impossible to know the exact reasons for

43. Kazantzakis, *Ragiades*.

44. In all this can be seen the seeds of Kazantzakis' Odysseus,
and also of Odysseus' mellowed successor, Zorba, whose philosophy
is that the real man undoes his belt and looks for trouble. Kazantzakis' central ideas remain remarkably consistent throughout his
career; it is chiefly the contexts that change.

45. Ironically, the play, though never produced in its original
form, was staged successfully as a musical comedy six years later.
This version brought Kazantzakis a delayed bonanza of 180,000
(inflated) drachmas in 1943. (*Biography*, p. 411.)

Kazantzakis' abrupt disappearance from the theatrical scene, we can only speculate. Could money have been a factor? Kazantzakis was desperately poor at this time, as he was for most of his life. Although the theatre in those days was one of the best means for a Greek writer to make a living from his own creative work, obviously the returns were sporadic and unreliable, especially if a playwright chose to be as controversial and uncompromising as Kazantzakis. Immediate financial need may have been what turned Kazantzakis to other available means such as translating and textbooks (journalism, one additional source of reliable income, did not become an important factor in Kazantzakis' life until after his involvement with the Soviet Union in the 1920's). But Kazantzakis was notoriously indifferent to money, and struggled on principle not to allow financial considerations to influence him.

Thus we must continue our speculations. It would seem that his excessive fury against the critics was a kind of bombastic mask for his own inability to accept humiliation. Rather than expose himself in the future to the whims of public taste, or the organizational and financial difficulties of actually mounting a play, he would leave the theatre, abandon it to the rayahs. I probably exaggerate, but surely there is some small accuracy in what I say. As confirmation we have the fact that although the works that constitute Kazantzakis' astonishingly meagre production for the decade 1910–1920 are poetic dramas, they are consciously composed for the armchair rather than the stage, a way of avoiding the humiliation suffered when *The Masterbuilder* failed to be produced. The most theatrical of the group, *Nikiforos Fokas*, actually bears a headnote meant to allay any misapprehension: "This work was not written at all for the theatre."[46]

46. Mrs. Kazantzakis has informed me that between 1910 and 1920 Kazantzakis wrote many works that he later destroyed. The

The Masterbuilder's failure was followed by redirections much more comprehensive than the literary ones I have been describing. Or perhaps we should say that the nationalism, demoticism, and voluntarism that had found literary expres-

---

headnote appears in the original 1927 edition, but not in the collected edition of the plays. This play, together with *Christos*, is an exploration of the messianism that consumed Kazantzakis, particularly after the meeting with Sikelianos in 1914, and that slaked itself in admiration for Tolstoy, extended sojourns at Mount Athos, a pilgrimage to Nietzsche's birthplace, and dreams of founding a monastic community where Kazantzakis and presumably his disciples could turn their backs forever on the rayahs. The third play is *Odysseas*; the fourth—now lost—*Herakles*. All four works, with subjects drawn from the classic, Christian, and Byzantine eras, are attempts to exploit the Greek tradition and, taken together, to show the continuity of that tradition. In addition, most importantly, Kazantzakis was experimenting here with his new literary idiom, ultra-demotic, trying to make it bend to the pressures of eleven- and thirteen-syllable verse. Although he could not have known this at the time, he was limbering himself up for the verse-marathon that was to come: the *Odyssey*.

It is interesting that thirty years later, after the *Odyssey* had been published and Kazantzakis was resident again in Greece, he aspired once more to the stage, although he had scarcely better luck than before in having his plays produced. In 1938 he wrote to Eleni Samiou: "How I wish they'd accept *Melissa*. This will encourage me and I shall write other theatrical works. . . . A play is something utterly different from a poem. Poems I can write even if they are never published and even if no one ever reads them. But a dramatic work is . . . an autonomous organism that becomes detached from yourself and hankers to climb up on a stage. If it does not get there, your power to make another birth cracks." (*Biography*, p. 354.) This may throw further light on his original flight from the stage to the armchair dramas, i.e. pure poetry, of *Nikiforos Fokas, Christos,* and *Odysseas*. In any case, history repeated itself, for it was in part because of his second failure to have his plays produced in the theatre in the period following 1938 that Kazantzakis—still protesting "I'm a born playwright . . . . Novels demand a pulse-beat different from my own" (*Biography*, p. 395) —turned to his final genre and wrote *Zorba*.

sion in this play demanded more direct expression in terms of action. Whatever the reasons—whether financial, psychological, or ideological—the fact remains that the decade 1910–1920 was primarily a non-literary one for Kazantzakis. Though he turned his pen to translations and textbooks, and though he composed the closet dramas I referred to above, much of his energy went into politics, educational reform, government service (the mission to the Caucasus), and even business: an unrealized scheme to harvest timber from Mount Athos, an unremunerative mining venture with George Zorbas as foreman, a plan to export carob fruit to Switzerland.[47] It is interesting to speculate how much of this redirection would have taken place had Kazantzakis' play been a success.

ROLE OF VENIZELOS

Perhaps we should not be surprised at this shift in balance toward activism, for if ever there was a time in Greek history when enthusiasts of the demotic tradition and the Great Idea thought they saw a possibility of realizing their hopes, it was now. This optimism, in turn, was made possible by the political ascendancy of Eleftherios Venizelos during most of the decade; Venizelos was Prime Minister from 1910 to 1915, and again from 1917 to 1920. Kazantzakis' active involvements can be understood only if seen against the background of Venizelos' fluctuating fortunes and of the changes that the Venizelist regime brought about, especially in the field of education. The Prime Minister was a demoticist (Kazantzakis accused him afterward, however, of being so only out of expediency), an admirer of Palamas, an advocate of educational reform.[48] He was a Cretan, furthermore, and personally friendly with both Kazantzakis and his wife Galateia, though he later cooled

47. Prevelakis, p. 9; *Biography*, p. 71.
48. Kazantzakis, *La littérature grecque.*

to Kazantzakis as did Kazantzakis to him.[49] During the wars of 1912–1913 Kazantzakis served in the Prime Minister's private office; he was offered the post of sub-secretary in the Ministry of Education, but did not accept (his detractors say because such a low grade was beneath his dignity).[50] When the King forced Venizelos to resign in March 1915, Kazantzakis wrote to his sister: "Venizelos has fallen. You cannot imagine my sorrow. With him have fallen all the people who held power —and were my friends. Now everyone is unknown to me, and hostile." He continued by suggesting that he himself would like to stand for Parliament in the coming elections in order to have the opportunity of "fighting in Parliament, now that Venizelos has such need of friends."[51]

Kazantzakis did not stand for Parliament. What he did instead was to resume his writing; in other words, he returned to his old mode of life as soon as Venizelos was out of office. (The elections returned Venizelos to power, but only for a few months; he was forced to resign again in October.) It was most likely in this interim period that Kazantzakis, influenced by his new friend Sikelianos and consumed by a messianic zeal, composed the play *Nikiforos Fokas* and an early draft of *Christos*.[52] This interim period was also the time of his business ventures. After King Constantine relinquished the throne and Venizelos took up the reins again in Athens in 1917, ending the national schism, Kazantzakis did not at once resume his active life. But when Venizelos appointed him to the Ministry of Welfare in May 1919 he ac-

49. Alexiou, E., p. 88; *Epistoles*, p. 92; Prevelakis, pp. 11, 174; *Biography*, pp. 228, 279.

50. Neoellinas; Alexiou, E., p. 217.

51. Dimos Irakleiou, p. 32. The seat Kazantzakis desired was held by his brother-in-law, and Kazantzakis was suggesting that his sister convince her husband not to run for re-election.

52. See Prevelakis, pp. 8–9.

cepted, and in July set out on his mission to repatriate 150,000 Greeks from the Caucasus, acting now as a true servant of beleaguered Hellenism.[53] In August he was at Versailles to report the results to Venizelos. In the months following, he supervised the refugees' resettlement in Thrace and Macedonia. But in 1920 the wheel turned again. Venizelos suffered overwhelming defeat at the polls on November 14; Kazantzakis resigned from the Ministry, and on December 4 boarded the train for Paris and his first brief period of self-exile.

This summary should make clear the important parallelism between Venizelos' fortunes and Kazantzakis' activities during this decade and immediately afterward. His scorn toward Greece and his despair over his country's future, already awakened by the assassination of Dragoumis, were confirmed by Venizelos' fall and then of course doubly confirmed by the catastrophe in Asia Minor in 1922. It was only after the end of the Venizelist decade that Kazantzakis, along with many other Greek intellectuals, sought an outlet in communism.

ROLE OF OTHERS, ESPECIALLY IN EDUCATION

Important as Venizelos was, neither the directions taken by Greece in general nor by Kazantzakis in particular were of course determined by one man, however powerful. Both politically and linguistically Venizelos rested on a base of public support, though the opposition was still formidable in both domains. Thus, while recognizing the crucial role he played as leader and acknowledging the political and linguistic changes that occurred during his rule, we should not distort the situation by ignoring the part played by others or by minimizing the struggle that preceded every victory, a struggle that manifested itself later in the extreme reaction that deposed

53. Synadinou; also Fanourakis.

Venizelos in 1920 and then proceeded to nullify his decrees and to purge the people who had supported him. In examining these people and their struggles I shall focus on the question of demotic in the schools, for this is the area in which Kazantzakis was most involved.

The changes effected even in Venizelos' first period (1910–1915) are strikingly reflected in the ways Kazantzakis chose to make a living after his disappointment with *The Masterbuilder*. At the start of the decade he embarked on an ambitious series of translations, all in *katharevousa*, an enterprise that raised some eyebrows in *Noumas*.[54] By 1914, however, he was able to turn his energies to the composition of new primers for the schools, in demotic.

THE EDUCATIONAL ASSOCIATION

Let us now trace some of the factors and events that made this change possible. The first and doubtlessly the most important in the long run was the founding of the Educational Association ('Εκπαιδευτικὸς ῞Ομιλος) in 1910. Kazantzakis was one of the charter members; he served as secretary in 1910 and was still on the advisory committee in 1915.[55] We have already met some of the other founders: Dragoumis, Tsirimokos, Delmouzos, Ghavriilidis, Mavilis. The organization's stated purpose was "to aid the rebirth of education in Greece."[56] It was in effect a pedagogical lobby, a pressure group that argued for new laws permitting the use of demotic, and that in the meantime set about building up a collection of texts, primers, histories, and workbooks so that once the en-

54. For bibliographical data, see Katsimbalis' *Bibliography*, items 28–38. The authors involved were William James, Nietzsche, Eckermann, Laisant, Maeterlinck, Darwin, Büchner, Bergson, and Plato. See also Arharios.

55. Vrettakos, pp. 63, 748; *Deltio*, January 1911, p. 6; Arharios.

56. *Deltio tou Ekpaideftikou Omilou*, January 1911.

abling legislation had been passed, the teachers would have materials with which to work.[57] It also stimulated linguistic studies and attempts to arrive at an acceptable demotic grammar (favoring Athenian demotic over a pan-hellenic amalgam). The Association's headquarters became a meeting place, a center of discussion and intellectual life even in areas not strictly pedagogical or linguistic.[58] It was here, for example, that Kazantzakis first met Sikelianos (1914), and it was here too that he delivered his lecture on Bergson, which was then duly published in the Association's bulletin.[59]

Members of the Educational Association were naturally at the center of the controversy and ferment that filled the opening years of the decade. Delmouzos, as we have seen, had already opened his model school at Volos; Dragoumis had begun publishing his influential books. But successes did not come easily or at once. In the Revisionary Assembly called in January 1911 to update the Constitution of 1864, 300 of the 364 delegates were Venizelists, but only nineteen of these were committed to an enabling clause for the spoken tongue.[60] Language was one of the many issues heatedly debated by the assembly, with repercussions such as the closing of Delmouzos' school, as we have already noted. Members of the Educational Association such as Mavilis and A. Papanastasiou (who in his program of the Populist Party, 1910, had called for demotic in the schools) argued in the assembly against a linguistic clause extending *katharevousa*'s official sanction, but Venizelos was forced to bow to public opinion, and the clause was included:[61]

57. Arharios; also Delmouzos.
58. Theotokas, *Ta provlimata*.
59. Prevelakis, p. 7; Kazantzakis, "H. Bergson," *Deltio*, October 1912, pp. 310–334.
60. Campbell and Sherrard, p. 112; *Apology*, p. 114.
61. *Apology*, p. 72; 151–52. In his speech in Parliament, Mavilis

Ἐπίσημος γλῶσσα τοῦ Κράτους εἶναι ἐκείνη εἰς τὴν ὁποίαν
συντάσσεται τὸ πολίτευμα καὶ τῆς ἑλληνικῆς νομοθεσίας
τὰ κείμενα· πᾶσα πρὸς παραφθορὰν ταύτης ἐπέμβασις
ἀπαγορεύεται.

This did not stop Venizelos, however, from appointing the demoticist, I. Tsirimokos to the Ministry of Education. In addition, Dimitrios Glinos, who was intimately associated with Kazantzakis in the late 1920's, became Director of the Training College for secondary school teachers.[62] The tension between the government's demoticist ideology and the law was reflected in 1912 in the curious wording in a statement regulating an official competition for new textbooks: "Inasmuch as the requirements of linguistic form cannot now be made entirely compatible with the requirements of the students' linguistic apprehension, the former requirements will of necessity be taken into greater consideration."[63] In short, the status quo was to be preserved; yet the Ministry itself had proclaimed that *katharevousa* could be incompatible with the child's true linguistic apprehension.

The next logical step was to attempt to change the statutes. Tsirimokos accordingly introduced a bill into Parliament (1913). The preamble, written by Glinos, argued that the Greek elementary schools as presently constituted were obviously not successful in their linguistic instruction, and that

---

did not mince his words. "There is no such thing as a crude language," he declared; "there are crude people, and there are many crude people who speak *katharevousa*." Kordatos, *Istoria,* p. 225. See Kordatos, *Istoria,* pp. 156–57. The debate is printed in *Episima,* Session 37, Feb. 18, 1911, pp. 739–50. Kordatos, *Istoria,* p. 194, quotes Venizelos' speech in favor of demotic. The clause was removed from the Constitution in 1925, but reinstated in 1937.

62. *Apology,* p. 162; Sotiriou, p. 41. Glinos' appointment was made in September 1912.

63. Triantafyllidis, *I glossa mas,* p. 85, fn. 75.

this fact had to be admitted and confronted: "To turn our backs intentionally upon reality can have no other result but the enfeeblement of the nation through a pointless squandering of its energies. Our written language . . . presents pedagogical difficulties which the elementary schools of other civilized nations do not have to face." Added to this was a statement that children would learn their maternal tongue better, and would be able to use it with more ease, eloquence, and correctness, if they could seriously study "the creations of our national literature."[64]

The members of the parliamentary committee that reported on the proposed bill agreed enthusiastically: "They acknowledged that the elementary school graduate not only fails to learn his maternal tongue, but forgets . . . what he did know of it; they proclaimed that . . . elementary education has no influence whatsoever on the child's character, but instead destroys his intellectuality; and they therefore recommended above all that the State 'take intense and radical measures'" to have demotic become the medium of instruction in the first four grades.[65]

Despite all this effort, the bill was defeated. The debate itself constituted a gain, however, for it was the first official recognition, as far as education was concerned, of the independent existence of modern Greek culture. The broad and public discussion that the proposals elicited sowed a seed that was to germinate four years later.[66]

64. Triantafyllidis, *I glossa mas*, p. 59, fn. 50. Glinos also prepared the initial draft of the bill. See Sotiriou, p. 38. The preamble is published in Glinos, *Enas Ataphos*, pp. 1–157; also in Tsirimokos.

65. Triantafyllides, *I glossa mas*, p. 59.

66. Delmouzos, p. 1,466. Glinos' articles in response to critiques in the papers are reprinted in Glinos, *Enas Ataphos*, pp. 161–320.

The year 1914 reveals how the two sides in the debate continued their clash, yet how demoticism proceeded to make slow but decisive progress. This was the year, we should remember, of Delmouzos' trial at Nauplion. Demotic had now established itself unquestionably in prose and drama, as well as in poetry. The Balkan Wars of 1912–1913 had given Venizelos a new, practical argument for rapid demoticization, for Greece had acquired Macedonia with its many speakers of slavic. "If we wish the foreign-speaking populations of the new areas to master the Greek language quickly," he told Parliament, "they must be taught the spoken tongue."[67] (This argument was again a factor in 1917 when the Provisional Government set up by Venizelos in Thessaloniki actually established demotic in the first four grades.)[68] Even the official ministerial encyclicals had by now reflected the new climate to a small degree by permitting demotic poetry—though poetry alone—in certain readers.

Thus it was that when the Ministry of Education announced a competition for new textbooks in 1914, Kazantzakis and other demoticists felt that they could take part. They had to moderate their demoticist zeal in order to produce a language sufficiently "fitting"; nevertheless, they felt that they could write by and large in demotic. The rewards were great. "Any book accepted for teaching purposes," Mrs. Helen Kazantzakis has told us, "was to be retained in use during four consecutive years in all Greek schools throughout Greece, as well as abroad. To the authors chosen, this meant reputation and considerable income."[69]

67. Triantafyllidis, *I glossa mas*, p. 57.
68. Triantafyllidis, *Quo-usque*, p. 136.
69. *Biography*, p. 51.

Kazantzakis now set to work, together with his wife Galateia, and their efforts met with success. A reader called *The Two Princes* was sanctioned for 1914–1918; five additional books won prizes in the following year.[70] All of these bore Galateia's name as author, but Helen Kazantzakis claims that Kazantzakis himself was principally responsible: "Perhaps his wife did help him to a certain extent. But as though he mistrusted the jealousies which even then his name aroused, he begged her to sign these books in her own name alone."[71] That Kazantzakis was at least a collaborator is confirmed by Prevelakis and also by a letter that Kazantzakis wrote in 1914 while relaxing luxuriously at a spa:[72]

"I'm taking the baths because I'm a bit tired, or rather because I can afford 200 drachmas. I can imagine your deadly boredom in Irakleion. Only one cure I know: you should write schoolbooks. . . . I told you so years ago, but my idea will seem less chimerical to you now that 60,000 drachmas have filtered their way into my pocket. . . .

"And what's more, just imagine this: In Constantinople last year, a competition was announced by the Patriarchate for the four grades of the elementary school. Ah well, I submitted two and . . . both were awarded prizes. . . . The other day I got a telegram from the Patriarchate asking me to write two more books (on commission!) because none of the others submitted was worth anything. Within ten days I hope to have finished them here and sent them off. . . . There you have my affairs and my fanfaronade. . . ."

70. Triantafyllidis, *I glossa mas*, p. 61, and bibliographical data in *Deltio*, VI (1916), p. 38. Alexiou, E., pp. 63, 88; *Biography*, p. 51.

71. *Biography*, p. 52.

72. Prevelakis, p. 12: "Kazantzakis had already collaborated with his wife Galateia, in 1914, on the writing of the children's books which bear her name." *Biography*, p. 52.

As I have indicated, the language of books submitted in 1914 and immediately afterward was circumspect, to say the least. Since the governmental position was in itself a no-man's land between demotic and *katharevousa*, it is little wonder that some of the books exhibited a mixed style in which a form like πάπιαι could appear next to another like πεταλοῦδες, and which Triantafyllidis stigmatized afterwards as "linguistic anarchy."[73] Kazantzakis' *The Two Princes* was demotic in diction and syntax, but it shifted accents and added final ν in order to give the semblance of purity:[74]

τοὺς κακομοίρους, χωρὶς νερὸ καὶ λάσπην, τὸ
βασιλόπουλο χαρούμενον. . . .

(Compare demotic κακόμοιρους, λάσπη, χαρούμενο)

This writing was hack work in a sense, a necessity forced upon Kazantzakis and his wife because of their penury; yet Kazantzakis always elevated his hack work into something more. Even the puristic translations, which he was now able to give up, were a part of his campaign to introduce vitalism, pragmatism, and evolutionary theory into Greek thought. The readers of 1913–1915 were obviously part of his campaign to revitalize Greek education; they inaugurated an involvement with the schools that Kazantzakis was to maintain for three decades. It is hardly necessary to say that in working on textbooks, primers, and translations he had the opportunity to do much more than just introduce his type of demotic into the schools; he could help to establish a standard of literary excellence, and could also play his part in introducing Greek pupils to the children's classics of other lands. We should remember that his "hack work" over the years included translations or adaptations of *Oliver Twist, Kari the Elephant, Un-*

73. Triantafyllidis, *I glossa mas*, p. 61.
74. *Ibid.*, p. 82.

cle Tom's Cabin, The Last Days of Pompeii, and practically all of Jules Verne.

DEMOTIC IN THE SCHOOLS, 1917–1920

We must now pursue the fortunes of pedagogical demoticism into Venizelos' second period, 1917–1920, even though Kazantzakis' educational involvement during these years seems to have been minimal. Yet his predicament and his sense of loss after 1920 can be understood only if we know what Venizelos' successors overturned.

The central facts I mentioned when tracing the career of Alexander Delmouzos. In 1917 demotic was sanctioned as the exclusive language in the first four grades and as a partner with *katharevousa* in the fifth and sixth. The original decrees were promulgated in May 1917 by Venizelos' Provisional Government in Thessaloniki.[75] King Constantine was forced to leave Greece in June, and in July the new government in Athens extended the Thessaloniki decrees to the entire land. Within a matter of weeks new texts had been approved for the 1917–1918 school year that began in September. In addition, Parliament created two new posts of overseers charged with studying all matters related to the reform and with training teachers so that "this innovation of supreme significance to the nation" might be applied with success.[76] Delmouzos and Triantafyllidis were appointed to these posts, and Dimitrios Glinos, who in 1916 had been imprisoned by the royalists, became Secretary-General in the Ministry and a member of the Educational Council—all of which meant in effect that the Educational Association was now fully in charge, only seven years after its founding.[77]

75. Triantafyllidis, *Niki*, p. 1.
76. Triantafyllidis, *Niki*, pp. 1, 3; Triantafyllidis, *Quo-usque*, pp. 140–41.
77. Sotiriou, p. 42.

We should not overlook or minimize what this involved in terms of personnel. As seems to be the rule in Greek politics, and especially at this time of the extreme polarization that had resulted in the national schism, a government establishes itself through a general purge. Venizelos placed his followers in key positions in the educational realm as elsewhere, and it was only natural that after his fall the opposition should do the same, restoring those purged by purging the purgers.[78] In imposing demotic in the complete and perhaps even ruthless way they did, the Venizelists made inevitable an equally complete and ruthless reaction; if we overlook this fact, however, we can say with assurance that these were great years for the demoticists and for education as they conceived it. We can surely appreciate their impatience to do all they could, now that they had the chance.

"Today," proclaimed Venizelos, "we have laid the foundations of a great work; let us pray that it may come to a favorable end for the good of the nation."[79] The Educational Association was understandably jubilant, although surprised at the suddenness and completeness of the governmental decision. An important part of the Association's program was now official; the ideals put into practice at Delmouzos' experimental school at Volos could now be extended everywhere.[80] Under the headline "Victory," an editorial in the Association's Bulletin proclaimed: "This victory for demoticism, the victory of the Idea that Psiharis was the first to preach anew in our times and to establish deeply within the national consciousness, we salute as our own victory."[81]

I noted earlier that from the very start the Educational Association had encouraged its members and friends to prepare

78. Glinos, *Paideia*, p. 96.
79. Triantafyllidis, *Quo-usque*, p. 135.
80. *Ibid.*, p. 142.
81. Triantafyllidis, *Niki*, p. 4.

textbooks against the great day that had now suddenly arrived. Because of this long preparation the demoticists were now able to produce an entirely new set of materials for the first and second grades (because of the lack of time, puristic books were allowed in the third and fourth grades for one more year).[82] Writing, judging, sanctioning, printing, and circulating the texts had to be accomplished within the two-and-one-half months between the promulgation of the new law and the opening of school. Although seven years' experience had given the demoticists a clear idea of the language they wished to use, this language had never been actually applied except in the Volos school and in limited samples solicited by the Association. Nor could the 1914–1915 texts be employed, for their language, as we have seen, embodied precisely the kind of artificiality and compromise that the Association had been struggling to overcome. The guidelines accompanying the new laws were entirely clear in this regard:

"Readers intended for the first four grades of elementary school . . . should be written in the *common spoken* (*demotic*) language, free from all archaism or regionalism. . . .

"We believe that by means of this precise statement regarding the language, the limits within which it must operate have been traced in advance with great explicitness, in such a way that being in accord with the pan-hellenic linguistic sense in spoken expression and also with the models which are available in the demotic ballads and the works of the great poets of modern Greece, it may avoid every tendency either toward purification or archaism, or toward what is known as *malliarismos*."[83]

The new texts were thus to be in the idiom stabilized and cultivated over the past decades by poets like Solomos, Valao-

82. Triantafyllidis, *Quo-usque*, p. 142.
83. *Ibid.*, pp. 136–37.

ritis, and Palamas, who had in turn taken the demotic ballads as their own prototypes.[84] While honoring the spoken word and admitting lexical items from all parts of Greece, the authors were to eschew both vulgarity and pugnacious eccentricity. The aim, as in the time of Korais, was for a dignified but comprehensible *ḳoine*, the great difference being that dignity was now recognized in modern Greek civilization itself.

The Ministry was naturally anxious to see what, in practical terms, these guidelines would produce. Thus the new overseers submitted to the Educational Council a memorandum offering "specimens of the linguistic form of the new readers."[85] The first specimen concerns us in particular, since it was taken from a second-grade reader written by Galateia Kazantzaki. We do not know if Nikos Kazantzakis collaborated in this text as he had in previous ones; but we can assume, I believe, that even if there was no joint authorship this time, the previous collaborations had helped to form Galateia's style. Thus we see Kazantzakis playing a role once more, whether directly or indirectly, in the demoticization of Greek education.

Here are some passages from Galateia's book:

Γεννήθηκα σ' ἕνα μικρὸ χωριὸ κοντὰ στὴ θάλασσα. Ὅλη μέρα ἔτρεχα στὸν ἄμμο καὶ ἔπαιζα μὲ τοὺς φίλους μου. . . . Πάντοτε ὁ πατέρας μοῦ κρατοῦσε κάτι. . . . Πάντοτε, ὅ τι καὶ ἂν μοῦ ἔδινε, τὸ μισὸ τὸ φύλαγα τῆς Τασούλας, τῆς ἀδερφούλας μου. . . .

Ἡ μητέρα ἄφηνε τότε τὸ ἐργόχειρό της, φώναζε καὶ τὴν Τασούλα μας καὶ ἄρχιζε: Δῶσε τῆς ἀνέμης νὰ γυρίση, παραμύθι ν' ἀρχινίση, Καλησπέρα σας![86]

84. For striking examples of old and new, plus an account of the demoticists' program, see Glinos, *Oi hoiroi.*
85. Triantafyllidis, *Quo-usque,* pp. 143–44.
86. *Ibid.,* pp. 143–44. The title is "The Three Friends."

Among the other specimens offered by the overseers was a new prose-rendering of the *Odyssey*. This should be compared with the 1905 version that I quoted earlier (pp. 139-40).

". . . Ἐσὺ ὅμως, Ἀχιλλέα, εἶσαι ὁ πιὸ εὐτυχισμένος ἀπ' ὅλους τοὺς ἥρωες, γιατὶ καὶ ζωντανὸς ὅταν ἤσουν σὲ τιμούσαμε ὅλοι σὰ θεό, καὶ τώρα πάλι στὸν Ἅδη εἶσαι βασιλιὰς τῶν πεθαμένων. Γι' αὐτὸ δὲν πρέπει νὰ λυπᾶσαι ποὺ πέθανες."

Ὁ Ἀχιλλέας μοῦ ἀποκρίθηκε: "Μὴ μὲ παρηγορεῖς γιὰ τὸ θάνατό μου, Ὀδυσσέα. Προτιμοῦσα νὰ δουλεύω σὲ φτωχὸ ἄνθρωπο καὶ νὰ βλέπω τὸ φῶς τοῦ ἥλιου παρὰ νὰ εἶμαι ἐδῶ στὸν Ἅδη βασιλιὰς τῶν πεθαμένων. Ἂς ἀφήσωμε ὅμως αὐτὰ κι ἔλα πές μου, ζῆ ὁ πατέρας μου ἢ πέθανε; Καὶ γιὰ τὸ παιδί μου τί ξέρεις; ἦρθε στὸν πόλεμο; Πολέμησε σὰν ἀληθινὸ παιδί μου." . . .

" Ἔλα, παιδί μου, ἔλα μέσα, νὰ χαρῆ ἡ καρδιά μου, ποὺ ἦρθες, στὴν καλύβα μου μόλις γύρισες ἀπὸ τὸ ταξίδι σου." . . .

Ὁ Τηλέμαχος ἀποκρίθηκε: "Καλέ μου Εὔμαιε, ἐγὼ πάντα σὲ θυμοῦμαι. Καὶ τώρα ἐπίτηδες ἦρθα ἐδῶ, γιὰ νὰ σὲ ἰδῶ καὶ γιὰ νὰ μάθω τί κάνει ἡ μητέρα μου."[87]

The new educational program continued to be systematically applied in 1918 and 1919, although the original schedule for demoticization in the upper grades had to be somewhat modified.[88] Kazantzakis' involvement must have been minimal, since he lived abroad in Switzerland during the 1917-1918 academic year, isolating himself in villages or monasteries whenever he could in 1919 and 1920 in order to finish his

87. *Ibid.*, p. 145. Citations are from Book xi, 482-93, and Book xvi, 25-26, 30-33.
88. *Ibid.*, pp. 139, 141.

verse-drama *Herakles,* and devoting his major energies during these years to his work for the Ministry of Welfare. Though temporarily occupied in affairs not primarily educational, he was obviously in touch with everything happening in the schools and assuredly would have contributed in a normal and untraumatic way to their increasing demoticization in the succeeding years had the Venizelist regime been able to sustain itself.[89]

As events conspired, however, the entire experiment was overturned in 1920, with the result that Kazantzakis' continuing efforts on behalf of the schools, and his demoticism in general, involved him consistently in traumas.

Frustration, 1920–1940, and the "Odyssey"

THE ANTI-DEMOTICISM

FOLLOWING VENIZELOS' FALL

I have indicated the crucial effect upon Kazantzakis of Venizelos' fall in November 1920, following so soon upon the murder of Dragoumis, and have stressed the role played by these events in shaking him loose from his nationalism though not from his allegiance to demotic. His position was extremely difficult now, not solely because the opposite party was in power, but because the deposition of Venizelos by the royalists in November had been in effect a vote against demotic—indeed, as the opposition put it, against the demoticist clique that, with the protection of the Venizelist "tyranny," had inserted the spoken tongue into the schools by force.[90]

Though the linguistic and political divisions did not always

89. An indication of this was his interest in a special school and home for abandoned children, an institution regulated by the Ministry of Welfare. In the spring of 1920 he convinced his sister-in-law to go and teach there. Alexiou, E., p. 111.

90. Glinos, *I Krisi,* p. 3.

coincide with precision—a group of anti-Venizelist demoticists issued a manifesto opposing their party's linguistic purism— the new government now proceeded systematically to undo everything that the previous regime had accomplished. I have already indicated that this meant the purging of Venizelos' key officials and their replacement in large measure by those who had been purged in 1917. Delmouzos and Triantafyllidis resigned as Overseers, Glinos as Secretary-General in the Ministry.[91] There were the expected dismissals of top personnel in the university, and the equally expected "leniency" shown to lesser personnel in the schools, who were simply transferred wholesale to less desirable posts. Hardly any individual school was left unaffected. Demotic as a medium of instruction was forbidden and the demotic textbooks were prohibited, with the Faculty of Philosophy at the university seeking to have them publicly burned.[92] In addition, the arguments employed against demoticism at the Nauplion trial were reinvoked. In the name of religion, fatherland, and morality, attempts were made to strengthen the sanctioning of *katharevousa* in the 1911 Constitution by means of an amendment that would specifically prohibit the use of demotic in the schools and would grant the government the right to dissolve organizations (like the Educational Association) whose aims were "contrary to the official language stipulated in the Constitution."[93]

KAZANTZAKIS ATTEMPTS TO LIVE ABROAD

This was the situation soon to prevail in Greece when Kazantzakis prudently departed for Paris after Venizelos' defeat. He did not remain abroad for long. After his return to Athens in 1921 he worked on his play *Christos* and toured Greece with

91. Glinos, *Paideia*, p. 94.
92. Glinos, *I Krisi*, p. 3; Delmouzos.
93. Glinos, *I Krisi*, p. 4.

Sikelianos, all the while seeking some means whereby he could afford to live abroad and pursue his career (at least for the time being) outside Greece. An opening came early in 1922 when he signed a contract with the publisher Dimitrakos for a series of history textbooks for elementary schools, for which he was to receive an advance in the form of a regular stipend.[94] (The language was demotic, which meant that both author and publisher were proceeding on the hope of some change in official linguistic policy in the future.) With the assurance of a regular income, Kazantzakis left Greece again in May 1922, determined this time to remain abroad, though forced for the present to draw his income from as many Greek sources as he could find.

The remarkable fact is that even under these circumstances Kazantzakis never wavered in his demoticism, which, though developing originally along with his nationalism, was now sufficiently autonomous to continue on its own, or to be linked with his growing allegiance to international communism. The problem was not his zeal, but how to apply it. Far from wavering in his faithfulness to demotic, he became increasingly pugnacious on its behalf, which was perhaps a predictable response to his removal from a natural context for his linguistic crusade. As an example of this increasing pugnaciousness and perhaps even fanaticism, we have a letter to Galateia in which he stated his conditions for accepting the post of foreign correspondent on an Athenian newspaper, a post offered him through the intervention of George Papandreou and that tempted him with a generous and regular income.[95] Yet in his conditions he was adamant: "(1) complete demotic, without compromises, (2) complete communist ideology, without compromises." After which he himself added: "I have become

94. Prevelakis, p. 12; *Epistoles*, pp. 20, 166.
95. Vrettakos, p. 77.

intransigent."[96] I stress this intransigence because I believe it to be a remote but determining factor in that fanaticism's most crucial manifestation: the language of the *Odyssey*, the work which he always considered his *magnum opus*.[97] In reviewing Kazantzakis' efforts to apply his demoticism in the years 1922–1936, we ought therefore to keep the *Odyssey* in mind. We shall see that almost all of his other outlets during this period brought him complete or partial frustration. This is one of the chief reasons, I believe, determining him to make the *Odyssey* a demotic dictionary as well as a work of art. I shall treat the consequences in their proper place.

DIFFICULTIES, 1922–1928

For the present, we find Kazantzakis in Vienna, developing his links with communist groups there, working on a poetic drama about Buddha, and attempting to combine Buddhism and political activism in the synthesis that he was to formulate soon afterward in his *Saviors of God*. His income, as we have seen, depended upon the arrangement with Dimitrakos for the history textbooks. Beyond this, Kazantzakis had been negotiating for the general editorship of a series of translations of European novels and philosophical works bearing on Greece. In addition, he and Galateia had been "writing, translating, or adapting a whole series of tales" for the same publisher, "most of which circulated without any indication of the author or translator."

The hope that these endeavors might bear fruit in Greece was increased somewhat in the autumn of 1922, immediately after the catastrophe in Asia Minor, when the military under Colonel Plastiras gained control in a bloodless coup. Kazantzakis wrote at once to his wife Galateia, who was still in Greece: "I hope that now, with the political change, it will be

96. *Epistoles*, p. 198.   97. *Biography*, pp. 457, 468.

easier to work. Perhaps some of our books will be accepted."
Soon he was sending her lists of suitable novels for the collection of works bearing on Greece, and was corresponding
about translators. His one inflexible condition continued to
concern the language to be used: "When Dimitrakos delivers
to you the French books he ordered, give them out to be translated wherever you think best. The fee is 50 drachmas the
sheet. Free translation, in demotic. (I'll write you the details
later.)"[98]

Conditions did improve somewhat as far as demotic was
concerned. (Glinos returned to the Ministry; the 1918 readers
were sanctioned again for use in elementary school.)[99] But
for one reason or another, Kazantzakis' efforts were accompanied by the traumas I referred to earlier. His own history
texts for each of the elementary grades, for example, form a
little history of their own. He composed the first-grade text
in Vienna at the height of his illness: the famous episode of
the facial eczema. Then, one of the manuscripts vanished in the
mails when he dispatched it to Greece. The thought of rewrit-
ing it from scratch filled him with dismay, yet he did rewrite
it a year later, in Italy: "The other day I sent [Dimitrakos]
the history text. I have to admire myself. I didn't have any
aids, any source books, yet I wrote out the whole thing from
memory in a very few days."[100] Ironically, all this work for
Dimitrakos, the purpose of which was to bring in a monthly

98. *Epistoles*, pp. 20, 65, 95, 103, 166, 283.
99. Sotiriou, pp. 47–48. As time went on, however, Glinos' educational plans were sabotaged by the opposition, and no essential
progress in demoticization was made. After the Pangalos coup
(June 1925) demotic was partially removed again from the schools,
and Glinos was dismissed. In 1934 it was limited to the first four
grades and in 1935 to the first three. Full details and documentation are in Triantafyllidis, *Eisagogi*, pp. 585–93.
100. *Epistoles*, pp. 156, 243.

stipend and thus enable Kazantzakis to live abroad (he was now in Germany), proved financially useless because of inflation. At one point he stated to his wife that he was not even asking Dimitrakos to send money any longer because "the way the drachma has fallen, for the work I do for him I re-receive one pound a month!"

As if sickness, postal mishaps, political upheaval, and inflation were not enough, Kazantzakis was experiencing difficulties with his former allies on the periodical *Noumas*. They found his spelling too radical. Sending his wife a piece he had written and asking her to place it in this periodical, he added: "The one thing I request of you, if you submit it, is that the orthography be retained exactly as it is. It is based on a carefully researched system, and I don't want a single change."[101] In 1928, just before Venizelos was returned to power, Kazantzakis was still apprehensive about inroads against his "carefully researched system." "I'm sending you the *Saviors of God*," he wrote from Moscow to Prevelakis, who had agreed to arrange for the work's publication in Athens. And then he added: "Do what you can to have our spelling used." (It wasn't.)[102]

CONTINUED DIFFICULTIES EVEN AFTER VENIZELOS
RESUMES POWER

In view of the political climate not only from 1920 to 1922, but from 1922 until Venizelos' return, it would have been remarkable had Kazantzakis not been frustrated in his activities as a demoticist. But the frustration continued even in the period 1928–1932, when conditions became extremely favorable. Not only was Venizelos back in power, but Kazantzakis' friend George Papandreou served as Minister of Education for the

101. *Ibid.*, p. 168, 199.   102. Prevelakis, p. 92.

latter two years.[103] Education was given great priority under the Venizelist regime, which instituted an ambitious program of school construction, deemphasized the classics in favor of practical training in agriculture and the various trades, and reinstated demotic in the primary schools, with considerable support from the teachers involved.[104] Perhaps it could be said that the suppression of demotic in 1920 had served a useful purpose, for many teachers who had resisted the vernacular in 1917 now—having experienced their pupils' apathy when *katharevousa* was reinstated—tended to change sides, and many even demanded that the spoken language be sanctioned for all grades of the elementary school, not just for the first four. This indeed happened; demotic made inroads, moreover, into the secondary school curriculum as well when it was sanctioned in 1931 to accompany *katharevousa* in the first two grades of the gymnasium.[105]

This comparatively favorable climate, which lasted even beyond Venizelos until the advent of Metaxas in 1936, naturally stimulated Kazantzakis to a new explosion of activity, with the double aim of aiding demotic and securing himself an income. In particular, he attempted to take advantage of a law promulgated in 1929 that permitted the classics to be taught in translation (at first only in girls' academies—we remember Delmouzos' *parthenagogeion!*—but later more universally). Kazantzakis sought to convince Papandreou to award him the commission to do Plato. But circumstances were once more against him. "I don't have much hope now that I've read the law," he wrote to his friend Prevelakis. "The selection of the translator depends on the Academy; conse-

103. Prevelakis, p. 175.
104. Campbell and Sherrard, p. 146.
105. Delmouzos.

quently it is impossible for us to be chosen. And Papandreou will never be willing to put his foot down."[106]

In general, harassment, frustration, and trauma continued to plague him, just as it had from 1920 to 1928. His own publishers, for example, resisted his extreme demotic. In 1930, after sending the manuscript of the first volume of his *History of Russian Literature* to Eleftheroudakis, he confessed his fear "that he will reproach me for my language. Good god, how shameful not to be free!"[107]

Kazantzakis was also in increasing trouble with Dimitrakos, who had commissioned him to prepare adaptations of Jules Verne but considered the results objectionably *malliari*. These same adaptations later involved Kazantzakis in an extended and petty lawsuit, occasioned, among other things, by a dispute over word-count. In addition, since nothing came of the hope to do Plato, he contracted with Dimitrakos for a French-Greek dictionary which—as we might have predicted—was never published.

This ill-fated dictionary forms a small, sad story in itself. The earliest reference comes in a letter to Prevelakis dated May 1, 1930. Apparently Prevelakis proposed to the publisher that he and Kazantzakis collaborate, and that the work include both *katharevousa* and demotic. Kazantzakis was immediately enthusiastic: "I wrote to Dimitrakos at once and asked him to give us a definite answer, now that I'm in Paris and have many source-books here. I told him that we had both planned out this work and had already compiled our own word-lists in demotic. Please go and see him; maybe we'll succeed in getting this job, which interests me very much. I would never undertake it alone. Together, we'll determine how we shall collaborate so that the work will be done quickly

106. Prevelakis, pp. 178, 193, 195, 200; *Biography*, p. 231.
107. Prevelakis, p. 201.

and completely." Eventually they decided, simply, that Kazantzakis would do the first half of the alphabet and Prevelakis the second.[108]

The contract was soon signed. It stipulated that Kazantzakis and Prevelakis were to take every entry in the *Nouveau Petit Larousse Illustré* and place after it "all the corresponding Greek words in both the learned and the demotic languages, using for this all the sourcebooks which store up words from the treasure of both the learned and demotic Greek languages." With this written guarantee, Kazantzakis, providing himself with 40,000 file-cards, immediately commenced his part.[109]

From the very start, however, he saw that he could not do justice to the demotic aspect, and he began thinking of a subsequent collaboration with Prevelakis on a French-demotic dictionary: "I awake in the middle of the night and begin work. . . . I'm now at B. Absorbing and passionate work. I labor more than fifteen hours a day, but progress is slow. This entire job can really be nothing more than a preparation for our future dictionary. Otherwise, if I had to stop at every word in order to find the demotic equivalent, etc., not even three years would be enough. I record as many terms as I have ready-to-hand. I'm doing fine with the plants because I have Gennadios [Φυτολογικὸν λεξικόν, 1914] and with the nautical terms with Palaskas [Γαλλοελληνικὸν λεξικὸν τῶν ναυτικῶν ὅρων, 1898]. Having troubles with the birds and fish. I'm doing the text in *katharevousa,* and suggest we leave the demotic text for our own dictionary."[110] After three months of "tireless, persistent labor," he announced that his part was finished. "I've reread all of it. Naturally, a host of demotic words es-

108. *Ibid.*, pp. 193, 235–236, 242, 247, 259, 265, 296.
109. *Ibid.*, p. 210. *Biography*, p. 239.
110. Prevelakis, p. 237.

caped me. I added quite a few in the rereading, but scores are still missing. We must press the issue, however. This dictionary will be of use only as the basis for our own, to which we shall devote a good deal of time, calmly, in the future."[111]

Unfortunately, neither the future dictionary nor the present one for Dimitrakos ever became a reality. Prevelakis was unable to find time to do the second half, the publisher reneged on the contract, litigation followed, and all Kazantzakis' labors went for naught.[112] Years later, in 1951, André Mirambel suggested to Kazantzakis that they collaborate on a dictionary, and for a moment it seemed that Kazantzakis' 40,000 entries might see the light.[113] "We're thinking of finishing it in two years," Kazantzakis wrote in a letter. "A tremendous job and a very difficult one. But Mirambel is so learned, and I love demotic so much, that I hope we will create a good and very useful work." But nothing came of this effort either. It should be evident that the lexicographical work undertaken in the 1930's by Kazantzakis and certain others (for example, Petros Vlastos) was pioneering as far as demotic was concerned. There was, and indeed there still is, no completely adequate, comprehensive dictionary of the spoken language written in that same language.

In the years that followed, Kazantzakis did not embark on any new grandiose labor for demotic. Yet the harassment caused him by the language question continued. In 1933, still trying desperately to earn his living, he experimented with a scheme whereby he would translate the best Spanish poets and write articles about Spain's cultural life. These articles would be submitted to Greek newspapers, but he would be paid by the Spanish government. He thus offered the articles free to the Greek press. As usual, he asked Prevelakis to act as his

111. *Ibid.*, p. 247.
112. *Ibid.*, pp. 348, 350, 365, 366, 368; *Biography*, pp. 247, 254.
113. *Biography*, pp. 504–05; Prevelakis, pp. 634, 638.

agent in Greece: "The terms are splendid: I don't want pay-
ment, I don't even ask that my objectionable name be printed;
thus they won't even have any trouble in 'correcting' my language as much as they please." Later, after a publisher had accepted, insisting, however, that Kazantzakis' name be used:
"This bothers me, because he'll doubtlessly alter the language.
I'll write him to accept a pseudonym if he refuses to publish
unadulterated demotic." In other words, Kazantzakis insisted
on preserving the integrity of his name in its relation to demotic, though his financial need forced him to allow his articles to be "corrected."[114]

The newspapers were one thing; what hurt much more
was criticism from supposed friends, or from the new generation of youths who ought to have been on his side. In 1933
Kazantzakis complained to Prevelakis about a group of young
authors who were preparing a manifesto "against all those who
write genuine demotic" ("genuine" was Kazantzakis' own
term) and whose chief whipping boy was himself.[115] "Miser-
able fallen generation!" he commented. As for friends, he
was greatly embittered in the same year when Lefteris Alexiou,
his former brother-in-law, sharply attacked his translation of
the *Divine Comedy* because of its *malliari* idiom. "I don't understand anything," Kazantzakis objected. "What does *malliari* mean? Rich? Where does he find the *malliarosini*—that
is the forged, far-fetched, unintelligible word? I shudder when

114. Prevelakis, pp. 356, 359. Kazantzakis' predicament was
evidently shared by others, if we can judge from a lecture by
Glinos delivered in December 1922. Here he complained about the
increasing number of demoticist poets and novelists who were
using *katharevousa* or a mixed idiom in their journalism—among
them "the scimitar of demoticism," Palamas himself (under the
pseudonym of "W") and "the Cerberus of Psiharism in Greece,"
Tankopoulos. See Glinos, *I Krisi*, pp. 15–17.

115. Prevelakis, p. 398.

I see how impossible comprehension is in even such a simple, simplistic matter. What can we say then to other people, or about other matters?"[116] Alexiou dragged the controversy on for years; Kazantzakis finally defended himself in a long letter published in 1937, part of which I cited near the beginning of this essay.

In 1934 and 1935 Kazantzakis was still having trouble with his schoolbooks, though probably just as much because of his politics, now, as his language. His solution was to have them, and also the three or four dozen children's poems he had written, published under the name of Eleni Samiou.[117]

Finally, he continued to be harassed by the newspapers. In 1935, when he was publishing a series of travel articles about Japan, he begged Prevelakis, who was again acting as his agent, to insist that the papers stop "correcting" his language. "Today they had τῆς χωνεύσεως, which is disgusting. We had agreed that they were to keep hands off."[118]

Considering all this, it is no wonder that Kazantzakis allowed himself to vent a little self-pity when the occasion presented itself in these articles. The pretext was his interview with a Chinese purist, who cried: "How is it possible . . . for educated men to write the way the people talk? . . . It is as if someone came out in your country and supported the idea that you must write not in the language of Plato but in the language that the peasants and fishermen speak. What would you do to him?"

To this, Kazantzakis replied with a bitter laugh, obviously thinking of himself: "What would we do to him? We would send him in exile far away from Greece; we would insult him and call him 'bought' and 'traitor' and we would never allow

116. *Ibid.*, p. 366.
117. Prevelakis, p. 413; *Biography*, pp. 295, 299, 322, 324, 330.
118. Prevelakis, p. 448.

him to set his foot in the Academy. And we would do whatever we could to make him die of starvation!"[119]

Later, when Kazantzakis met the fervent Chinese demoticist Hu Shih, he thought of the "epic struggle" of Greece's demotic movement; invoked the names of Psiharis, Pallis, Palamas, Eftaliotis, Filintas, and Vlastos; and then described himself and Hu Shih as two soldiers "who have lived abroad for a long time, fellow fighters in the same struggle."[120]

RELATION BETWEEN HARASSMENT AND THE "ODYSSEY"

I trust that I have given sufficient examples to show the difficulties experienced by Kazantzakis in the decade following 1922 when he was hoping to establish himself abroad, and then continuing after his return to Greece in 1933. The only instances in which he managed to publish "uncorrected" demotic were in his translations of Spanish poetry and of Dante, and in the collected travel articles brought out in book form.[121] Under the Metaxas regime, which established itself in 1936, conditions became much more difficult for the linguistic reformers even though the dictator himself had demoticist tendencies and thought very highly of Kazantzakis' translation of Dante.[122] Officially, *katharevousa* reasserted itself to such a degree that a high-school teacher, for example, was forced to apologize publicly for lecturing on Solomos "in a language contrary to the linguistic policy of the government."[123]

119. Kazantzakis, *Japan-China*, p. 223.
120. *Ibid.*, p. 227.
121. Kazantzakis, *Synchroni* . . . ; Kazantzakis, *Dante*; Kazantzakis, *Taxidevondas*.
122. Helen Kazantzakis, in a letter to the author, October 1970.
123. Delmouzos, p. 1,469. Even under the completely favorable conditions of 1946, a critic objected to certain *malliara* locutions in Kazantzakis' play *Kapodistrias*. See Thrylos, *To Theatro*.

Having reviewed the frustrations that Kazantzakis experienced during this period, we should remember that this was precisely when he was composing his *Odyssey*. The first draft was begun in 1925 and completed in 1927. But the poem as we presently know it started to take shape with the second draft in 1929, which is also when Kazantzakis began systematically and consciously to make the epic a receptacle for his demotic zeal. The subsequent drafts were undertaken in 1931, 1933, 1935, 1937, and 1938. When the poem was published at the very end of 1938, after having passed the Metaxas censorship, Kazantzakis was still trying to eke out an income from second-grade readers whose language would naturally be subject to "correction."[124]

What I am suggesting, in short, is that the harassment and frustration from 1920 to 1938 were both too various and too unrelenting to leave Kazantzakis unaffected. He was getting nowhere in his battle for "genuine" (i.e., extreme, pan-hellenic) demotic; or at least the returns were completely incommensurate with the effort. But he was not affected as one might expect: he did not give in or compromise. Rather, quite the reverse: he became even more intransigent. If he could not succeed in public ways—journalism, textbooks, dictionaries —he would succeed in a "private" way: poetry.[125] (We are reminded of the similar reaction after the theatrical frustration of 1910, when he retreated from public to private drama.) He would make his *magnum opus*, the *Odyssey*, a textbook of demotic, a thesaurus, a dictionary. Like Dante after his exile from Florence, Kazantzakis would have his revenge, not,

124. *Biography*, p. 355.
125. Even in the newspapers, poetry was exempt from correction. *Kathimerini*, which had tampered with the language in the travel articles, published Kazantzakis' translation of *Faust* as he wished it; this was in 1937, during the Metaxas era.

however, by placing his enemies in appropriate circles of hell, but by composing the great Greek epic in a language repugnant to the hated intellectuals of Athens and perhaps incomprehensible to them as well.

I do not suggest that Kazantzakis consciously went about his work in this way, any more than he consciously made the epic a justification for his own inability to act effectively in the "real world" of politics. But I do believe that the linguistic extremism seen in the *Odyssey* was not only a continuation of Kazantzakis' genuine and wholly admirable love of the Greek language; it was also a compensation for his previous frustration, personal in motivation rather than artistic, and therefore all too often mechanical rather than aesthetic in its application.

I do not deny that Kazantzakis' demoticism resulted in certain improvements of individual lines in the poem, especially in the early drafts. I shall give examples of changes that at the very least replaced trite and bookish tropes with living ones very demotic in flavor. Yet this should not blind us to the overall arbitrariness of the proceedings. By the time Kazantzakis had completed the *Odyssey* and poured into it all the words (not to mention the spelling) that he could not use elsewhere, he still had not solved the problem of where and how to apply his linguistic zeal. He still had not found the proper literary vehicle for his demoticism. This vehicle, if it came at all, came later, after 1940, in the translation of the *Iliad* and in the novels.

Let us look more closely, now, at the demoticism of Kazantzakis' *Odyssey*, and then at the controversies that followed the epic's publication.

The *Odyssey, Iliad,* and Other Writings

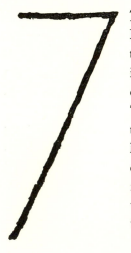

The Odyssey *as Demotic Repository*
I have perhaps given the impression that Kazantzakis' major energies during the period 1920–1938 went into dictionaries, journalism, and textbooks. This is far from true; I merely wished to indicate the frustrations plaguing his manifold attempts to witness for demotic. The period is rich politically, religiously, and artistically, for in it we see Kazantzakis' flaring attraction to Russia (followed by partial disillu-

sion), his Buddhism, *The Saviors of God,* the novels *Toda Raba* and *Le Jardin des Rochers* (both written in French), and translations of the *Divine Comedy* and Part One of *Faust.*

But from 1925 onward, everything took second place to the *Odyssey.* The epic became Kazantzakis' repository not only for demotic, but for all the political and religious experience of the decade during which it was composed. It gave him the scope he needed, for without worrying about publishers' requirements or deadlines, he could simply accrete experience —and words—until he was satisfied. As far as his demoticism was concerned, for the first time he could compose freely, unharassed by the reproaches of publishers, and liberated from the need to adhere to original texts, as was the case in his translations of Dante and Goethe. The *Odyssey* became a bottomless well into which he could pour all his linguistic zeal.

Especially in the decade 1927–1937, Kazantzakis' demoticism and the writing of the *Odyssey* were synonymous. In 1927 he was already collecting nautical terms for the second draft of his sea-epic.[1] The collecting continued throughout the years that he was composing the subsequent drafts, and in the later stages he went through his lists systematically, to be sure that every item of this lexical treasure had indeed been enshrined and hopefully preserved in the poem.[2] We have ample information about all this, because his major source for words was Prevelakis, who also served Kazantzakis as confidant, friend, literary critic, and agent. The letters written to Prevelakis while Kazantzakis was preparing the second draft, for instance, attest to his linguistic industriousness and enthusiasm; they also indicate his broader aims and criteria, and give ex-

1. Prevelakis, pp. 37, 39.
2. Prevelakis in an interview with the author, April 1967.

amples, otherwise very rare, of some of the specific revisions he made.

The first thoughts about a second draft come from Russia in February 1929: "I'm returning through Siberia and will get off at several cities I missed on the way out. But my mind is already turned toward the *Odyssey*. I therefore have to ask you again for certain things for the *Odyssey*: (1) Words. Write me whatever new words you have found. (2) They said that the first volume of the Demotic Dictionary [i.e., the Academy's dictionary] would be printed. Is this true? (3) Send me . . . Daskalakis' *Kynego* [hunting terms], Drosinis' *Psarema* [fishing terms] . . . and anything else on Greek animals and birds; maybe, if it's available, the book by Granitsas [Τὰ Ἄγρια καὶ τὰ ἤμερα τοῦ βουνοῦ καὶ τοῦ λόγγου, 1921]. . . . Love for demotic has again overcome me. Please, send whatever you think will be good for me."[3]

Subsequent letters are variations on this theme:[4]

"I have leafed through all the Bulletins [he is speaking of the Λεξικογραφικὸν ἀρχεῖον τῆς μέσης καὶ νέας Ἑλληνικῆς] and have taken a good deal. Send me whatever linguistic material you have ready. . . . This draft of the *Odyssey* will be only the second; thus I have time. Perhaps I'll be in Greece during the third or fourth drafts, and then I'll resume my linguistic investigations. Maybe we can take a long trip together then, to the islands, Epirus, the Mani, Roumeli—and pillage."

"Don't forget me regarding linguistic material. Before beginning the *Odyssey* again I must have a new crop of words."

"Do me a favor: Look through *Laographia* and find me

3. Prevelakis, pp. 113–14.
4. *Ibid.*, pp. 121–22; 130, 149, 162, 318.

some exorcisms and some interesting curses. Especially exorcisms against malaria."

"One more favor: Can you find out the demotic names for the enclosed list of birds? It's difficult, but I need them so much!"

"Thanks for ζερβοδεξοχέρης. I used it immediately."

In all fairness to Kazantzakis, and in spite of the reservations I expressed earlier, there did seem to be some congruence between his linguistic program and the *Odyssey*'s needs as a work of art. This was especially true at the stage of the second draft, when he was primarily trying to improve the verse, the later drafts being devoted to accretions of new material. Certain broader aims and criteria emerge, showing that Kazantzakis was not merely an arbitrary "collector."

He liked words, so he claimed, not simply because they were rare, or hitherto unused in the written language, but because they were alive on the lips of the people, with all the nuances that only spoken words can develop.[5] Thus, in criticizing the translation that Prevelakis was undertaking of *Toda Raba*, Kazantzakis said he would prefer the form Μόσκοβος to Μοσκοβίτης, because the former carried with it all the associations of the popular ballads about Daskaloyannis' promise: Τὸ Μόσκοβο θὰ φέρω. Instead of the international term γκέτο [ghetto] he would use Ὀβριακή, because that is what the Jewish quarter was actually called in Irakleion. Instead of πονεῖ, ἀντίκρυ, χάμω, he would prefer πονάει, ἀντίκρα, χάμου. He claimed that this was just a personal idiosyncrasy, but he obviously preferred these forms because they reproduced the actual speech of the Greek peasant.

The stress on living terms, and especially terms that had

5. *Ibid.*, p. 148.

found their way into the popular ballads, was part of Kazantzakis' general attitude toward his verse, for he said that his
aim was to achieve the "elasticity and naivete of the demotic
ballads." His poem "must not be read, but be declaimed by
a rhapsode day and night near the edge of the sea, at a great
festival. In this way it will acquire a heartfelt warmth, a *sans
façon*, something of spontaneity, and will depart from learned
works of the lamp. Simplicity is what is still needed, working
and reworking of the abstract ideas until they become legend,
picture, and act."[6]

It is to Kazantzakis' credit that he was opposed to all
"non-living" words; that is, not only to the hated *katharevousa*, but also to terms manufactured by the demoticists,
even by Psiharis himself, who had used the word σαρκοανάφτρα (literally: she who ignites the flesh) as the title for
one of his stories. Kazantzakis' reaction was clear: "I don't
like the word σαρκοανάφτρα (good god, what ugly words of
the lamp—this way of inventing words!)" Kazantzakis was
extremely touchy on the subject of coinages, for people continually accused him of manufacturing his own words "in the
office." He protested that in the whole of the *Odyssey* at this
stage (second draft, 1929) he had no more than ten coinages.
We shall see presently that by the time the epic reached its
definitive form he had reduced the number, so he claimed,
to five.[7]

The aim of naivete, of distance from "learned works of the
lamp," may seem extremely remote from the actual poem
Kazantzakis eventually produced; yet his store of living demotic expressions did enable him to transmute many of his
abstractions into pictures or at least into concretions. A good
example is the revision of the opening lines of Book I, which

6. *Ibid.*, p. 145; *Biography*, p. 224. Prevelakis, pp. 187–88.
7. Prevelakis, pp. 148–49, 164.

read as follows in the first draft: Σὰ σκότωσε τοὺς ἄνομους μνηστῆρες στὸ παλάτι . . . . Kazantzakis replaced the abstract σκότωσε (killed) with the pictorial θέρισε (reaped, mowed down); the frequently used, colorless abstraction ἄνομους (unlawful) with a rare demotic term, abstract still, but more precise as an epithet for the suitors, γαύρους (haughty); the classical term μνηστῆρες (suitors) with the demotic "corruption" of νέους (youths), νιούς; and the noun παλάτι (palace) with a pictorial equivalent, φαρδιὲς αὐλές (wide courtyards). The line now reads: Σὰ θέρισε τοὺς γαύρους νιοὺς μὲς στὶς φαρδιὲς αὐλές του. . . .[8]

Similar revisions can be seen in three early versions of lines 4 to 6 of the Prologue, fortunately preserved for us in Kazantzakis' letters. The second draft reads:[9]

Καλή 'ναι ἐτούτη ἡ γῆς, ἀρέσει μας, σὰν τὸ φιλντίσι
    λάμπει·
τί νὰ σκαλίσουμεν ἀπάνου της, πρὶ νὰ μᾶς πάρει ὁ Χάρος;

The figure here—"the earth shines like ivory, what shall we carve upon it before Charon takes us?"—is trite and certainly not very indigenously Greek; it is hardly a figure that lives on the lips of the people. Thus Kazantzakis abandoned it in his first attempt at a third draft, and substituted a much more indigenous, and audacious, trope:[10]

Καλή 'ναι ἐτούτη ἡ γῆς, ἀρέσει μας, σὰν τὸ σγουρὸ σταφύλι
στὸν μπλάβο ἀγέρα, Θέ μου, κρέμεται, στὸν ἄνεμο κουνιέται
κι ἀργάζεται μὲς στὴν ἑρμιάν, ἀργά, τὴν ἀγουρίδα μέλι.

The earth is now a curly cluster of grapes hanging in the air, swaying in the wind, and slowly "working" the individual

---

8. *Ibid*., pp. 145, 165. Korais would have approved the use of γαῦρος, because it is a demotic word with an ancient pedigree.
9. *Ibid*., p. 182.   10. *Ibid*., p. 248.

unripe grapes into honeyed ripeness. A year and a half later, as he was strolling down the Paseo del Prado in Madrid on a bright, sunny day, he decided to change the colorless abstraction ἄνεμος (wind) to the rare, concrete δρόλαπας, a specific term for a violent, icy wind with rain, or perhaps to καταχνιά (mist). The concluding figure, that of working unripe grapes into honey, he abandoned completely, but in the process he introduced the demotic and specific τσιμπολογοῦν (peck at, nip) in place of the abstraction ἀργάζεται. This version reads:[11]

Καλή 'ναι ἐτούτη ἡ γῆς, ἀρέσει μας, σὰν τὸ σγουρὸ σταφύλι
στὸν μπλάβο ἀγέρα, Θέ μου, κρέμεται, στὸ δρόλαπα (ἢ
καταχνιά;) κουνιέται
καὶ τὴν τσιμπολογοῦν τὰ πνέματα καὶ τὰ πουλιὰ τοῦ
ἀνέμου.

The definitive version is identical, retaining δρόλαπας, a word that was incomprehensible to most of his readers, instead of the familiar καταχνιά.

These examples afford only a very cursory view of the *Odyssey* as demotic repository. But they will give some sense, I hope, of the systematic way in which Kazantzakis introduced concretions, rare words, and outlandish metaphors into the poem, sometimes to its benefit but in the sum total, I believe, to its detriment. (Some further examples will be seen when I speak of the Glossary and then of the controversy that followed the epic's publication.)

PUBLICATION, GLOSSARY, SPELLING

The *Odyssey* was brought out in December 1938 in an edition of 300 copies printed in a huge and imposing format, at the

11. *Ibid.*, p. 360.

enormous price of 1,000 drachmas.[12] Kazantzakis had produced something that all readers found challenging and some incomprehensible. To aid the latter, he quickly had printed a glossary of about 2,000 difficult words, assuring skeptics in a headnote that the terms were "taken from all regions of Greece and inserted after a lengthy and difficult process of selection." Anticipating the charge that he had made them all up himself—a charge predictably hurled at all *malliari* demoticists from Psiharis onward—Kazantzakis certified that in the whole of the *Odyssey*'s 33,333 verses there were only five coinages, specifically: ἀστροπόταμος, βορράστρι, βοδάλαφο, νεροβούβαλος, χεραγκαλιά, meaning Milky Way, north star, elk, hippopotamus, and arm-in-arm, respectively. (Elsewhere, he explained the origin of two of these. For *elk* he coined βοδάλαφο by joining the Greek words for *ox* and *deer*, because "a missionary told me in Irkutsk that the Chinese word for elk is a composite of the three words donkey-deer-ox, since the elk resembles all three." Βορράστρι for *north star* he coined an analogy with the normal word for *morning star*: μεράστρι, commenting: "Βορράστρι seems so correct and good that it may actually exist.")[13]

Here are some representative entries from the Glossary:

αγνια—το πρώτο γάλα της μάνας μετα τον τοκετο.
ακρασόβρεχτος—νεκρος που δεν τον έπλυναν με κρασι
    απο τη βιάση.
αλάνης—αλήτης
αλαφροαίματος, αλαφροήσκιστος, αλαφροστοίχιστος, αλα-
    φροφάνταχτος—νεραδοπαρμένος που βλέπει ξωτικα,
    ξωπαρμένος.

12. Zografou, p. 229; *Biography*, pp. 352–360; Vrettakos, p. 211.
13. Prevelakis, p. 164.

αλετροπόδα—αστερισμος της Μεγάλης Ἀρκτου· λέγ. και:
αμάξι, καράβι, εφτα αδέρφια, εφτάστρι.
γαβάθα—βαθι ξύλινο ή πήλινο πιάτο.
γαβαθάρης, γαβαθας—κρασοπιοτης, φαγας.
γενι—υνι· λέγ. και σιδεραλέτρι.
γεράνι—το ξύλο σε πηγάδι που έχει μιαν πέτρα στη μιαν
άκρα και τον κουβα στην άλη κι ανασέρνουν νερο.
γουλίζω—χτυπω το χταπόδι να μαλακόσει· λέγ. και
σγουραίνω.
διάφορο—τόκος, κέρδος.
ζάβα—τουσλούκι, περικνημίδα.
θαλασόφρυδο—ουρανοθάλασο, ορίζοντας.
καμπανίζω—αιωρούμαι.
κοχέβω—κοιτάζω με την κόχη του ματιου· σημαδέβω,
ρήχνω.
κοψοβούλης—που κόβει, ανατρέπει τη βούληση του άλον.
κρουφογκαστρομένη—γκ. χωρις νόμιμο γάμο.
κωλοτριβιδίζω—κουνω τα πισινα.
λιγολαΐζει—λιγοστέβει ο πληθυσμος.
μούρτζουφλος—με χοντρα φρύδια.
μπάκακας—βάτραχος.
μπαμπακιάζω—ασπρίζω σαν μπαμπάκι.
μπρόστια, τα—είσοδος.
μως—άμα ως.
πιζέβλια—ξύλο πάνω απο το ζυγο του βοδιου.
πυκνοπαιδούσα—που κάνει συχνα παιδια.
ρεπιδιάζω—ανοίγω σα ρεπίδι.
σαστικος—αραβωνιαστικος.
σιδερόχορτο—μαγικο βοτάνι που ανοίγει κάθε πόρτα.
σιμοχνοτω—σμίγω το χνότομου, ζυγόνω στόμα με στόμα.
τρυγονοσούρτης—το πουλι που οδηγάει τα τρυγόνια· αρχη-
γος, οδηγος.
φωτογόνι—τζάκι.

χελιος—χρώμα ζώου (γίδας, γαϊδάρου κλτ.): στη ράχη
μαβροπο, στην κοιλια και λαιμο άσπρο.
ψιλόπονο—οι πρώτοι πόνοι του τοκετου.

From these entries it can be seen that many of the "difficult" words were self-explanatory, even though unfamiliar. It can also be seen how colorful, evocative, and pictorial demotic expressions tend to be, and how rooted in the sensual experience of everyday Greece—characteristics that, as I shall argue, perhaps made them inappropriate for the poem in which they appeared, although wonderfully appropriate for the novels of Kazantzakis' final period.

We should pause here to consider the peculiarities of Kazantzakis' spelling.[14] These are in evidence in the above entries from the Glossary in contrast to my earlier citations from the *Odyssey*, all of which were in a spelling "corrected" by Prevelakis.[15] In advocating a simplified and phonetic orthography, Kazantzakis was following in the footsteps of Psiharis, Pallis, and Vlastos; in other words, his "carefully researched system" was not entirely his own.[16] He eliminated both breathings and two of the three accents, retaining only the acute (Psiharis had kept both circumflex and grave for certain usages). As he explained in the headnote to the Glossary, the acute goes on the accented syllable, but if the word is accented on the final syllable, no mark is placed there. "Several monosyllabic words take an accent to distinguish them from their homonymns: νά, τί; πού; πώς; ώς (έως) γιά (ή) μά (in oaths), etc. Also several polysyllabic words: γιατί; ωχού, αχού, αλοί, καταπού, etc. Spelling has been simplified a little; double

14. The whole question of a revised orthography for demotic is discussed at length in Triantafyllidis, *Apanta*, vii, 3–391. See also Kordatos, *Istoria*, pp. 186–92.

15. Prevelakis, p. πζ´.

16. For Psiharis' system, see *To Taxidi mou*, p. 6.

consonants have been abandoned, with the exception of the two gammas since they are needed to indicate pronunciation: αγγίζω, φαλάγγι, etc." In addition, Kazantzakis replaced diphthongs with their phonetic equivalents: αφτος instead of αὐτός. Finally, he tended to join enclitics to the word proceeding: Ποτε ο Αγγελος δεν είταν τόσο κοντάμου, τόσο μέσαμου, όσο όλες ετούτες τις μέρες.[17] The program for spelling reform in Greece has made no more headway than has George Bernard Shaw's program in England, and indeed this aspect of demoticist theory and practice was abandoned even by the most radical proponents, including Kazantzakis, who eventually allowed his books to be printed in normal orthography although he retained his system in his private letters, notes, and manuscripts. The full, uncompromising system, however, was employed in the first edition of the *Odyssey*, no doubt adding to the discomfort of those readers who required everything to be familiar.

Here are the verses I cited earlier, as they were originally printed:[18]

Σαν πια ποθέρισε τους γάβρους νιους μεσ' στις φαρδιες
αβλέςτου, . . .

Καλη 'ναι τούτη η γης, αρέσειμας, σαν το σγουρο σταφύλι
στον μπλάβο αγέρα, Θέμου, κρέμεται, στο δρόλαπα
κουνιέται
και την τσιμπολογουν τα πνέματα και τα πουλια του ανέμου

CRITICAL RESPONSE, AND KAZANTZAKIS' REACTION

Let us turn now to the controversy that followed the *Odyssey*'s publication. Language was not the only problem; critics naturally reacted to other aspects, the Marxists for example finding Kazantzakis' nihilism repulsive. But, as might have been ex-

17. The citation is from Prevelakis, no. 37 of the photographs.
18. Kazantzakis, *Odysseia*, Bk. I, 1; Prologue, 4–6.

pected, the bulk of the comment in the early stages concerned language, perhaps because to treat content you had to read the entire poem.

Of the linguistic and stylistic discussion, much dealt with Kazantzakis' daring use of the seventeen-syllable line in defiance of the normal fifteen syllables common to the popular ballads. However, since this is not directly relevant to his crusading demoticism, I shall pass on to comments about the specifically lexical elements—especially tropes and diction.

There was considerable praise for the daring, fanciful metaphors and similes, coupled however with the feeling that many of these were merely decorative, little curlicues in the clutter of an oriental rug, without true artistic relevance or internal necessity.[19] But in the best instances, Kazantzakis had done what any good writer must do: he had freshened words by using them in new or unfamiliar contexts. Laourdas, probably the fairest and most perceptive of all the critics involved, singled out the trope we have already encountered: $\theta \epsilon \rho i \zeta \epsilon \iota$ applied to the suitors; also the adjective $\pi \iota \kappa \rho \acute{o} s$ (bitter, sad) applied to the seashore.[20] These usages typify, respectively, demotic's concreteness and its tendency to endow the inanimate world with a living soul. Laourdas also liked the way Kazantzakis exploited the nuances that words have gained in the spoken language. $\Theta \epsilon o \beta \acute{a} \delta \iota \sigma \tau o \nu$ means "trodden or frequented by God." In normal spoken usage, however, it is an epithet applied specifically to Sinai and Mount Athos. When Kazantzakis then used this term as an epithet for Mount Olympus, he did not communicate solely a literal significance; he also transferred to Olympus all the nuances—the reverence, sense of something "wholly other" and at the same time familiar and all-too-human—that the word had gained through its associa-

19. Lambridi, p. 10; Laourdas, *Odysseia,* pp. 9–10.
20. Laourdas, *Odysseia,* p. 8 ff.

tion with the holy mountains. Finally, Laourdas praised some of the synthetic adjectives employed by Kazantzakis—e.g., φεγγαρόστρωτος—and even certain complete coinages that were excitingly fresh and evocative because composed on analogy with existing words that they immediately suggested, for example, the demotic term λιανοτούφεκο, meaning sporadic rifle-fire, skirmish, ἀψιμαχία. Odysseus did not have a musket (τουφέκι), he had a bow (δοξάρι). Thus the lovely coinage λιανοδόξαρο: a skirmish with bows and arrows.

The attitude of the favorably disposed critics was also expressed in the comments by Elli Lambridi, a philosopher and demoticist who wrote by far the most extensive and penetrating critique of the poem's metaphysic. She praised the idea of making the epic a repository for the entire demotic language, seeing that this language was so threatened by *katharevousa*, yet demurred when it came to the actual result.[21] She argued that all too often the rare words were inserted for their own sake, as though Kazantzakis was writing a dictionary instead of a poem. Moreover, these words made the reading of the poem so difficult and cumbersome that "although I had the glossary next to me, I neglected many times to open it, with the certainty that I would not lose much if I lacked the name of a certain kind of buffalo. . . ."

Other critics went much further than this, and questioned the entire undertaking.[22] Markos Avyeris (a Marxist, formerly part of Kazantzakis' circle, and the man who supplanted him as Galateia's husband) attacked the poem as poem, quite aside from the nihilistic ideology. As far as the rare words were concerned, they derived, he claimed, from the "lamp," the notebook, and not from living speech; thus they were just as dead as the hated *katharevousa*. According to this view, Kazantzakis was paradoxically accomplishing precisely the op-

21. Lambridi, p. 11.   22. Avyeris, p. 1,346.

posite of what he intended. We may discount Avyeris' critique somewhat because of the author's personal antipathy to Kazantzakis. But we must acknowledge that the same charge was made afterward by Vrettakos, who remained favorably disposed toward Kazantzakis in general and who in 1957 wrote what is by far the best book on his work. Vrettakos disputed the analogy with Dante and Tuscan. "The case of a language that is spoken but not written is one thing; that of a language that requires a special . . . glossary in order to be comprehended, is quite another thing."[23]

More specific objection was raised, as usual, to Kazantzakis' extreme disregard of accepted forms: to his conversion of neuter nouns into masculine, ὁ μήλιγγος, ὁ δέντρος, ὁ μυαλός; to his suppression of syllables, μώς (μόλις), στρηνιάει (στρηνιάζει), ἀνιοῦν (ἀνοίγουν).[24] Kleon Paraschos, who agreed in theory with Kazantzakis' desire to include rare words, nevertheless took exception to the length of many of the syntheses: χρουσοδαχτυλιδόστομος, ἀστρογιαλοχορεύω, διπλοτετρακάγκελος. He also censured cacophonous lines such as τυλιγαδίζοντας τὰ πόδια του καὶ τσεβδοβαταλάλαε.[25] Lambridi elaborated a long list of cacophonies; and Avyeris accused Kazantzakis of going backward to the harsh idiom employed by the first demoticists.[26]

It is significant that this type of adverse opinion has persisted, as we have seen, for example, in the comments of Vrettakos, written in the late 1950's. We will recall that in defending his translation of Dante, Kazantzakis wrote: "In the *Divine Comedy,* all the demotic words that seemed rare and unknown became commonplace and well-worn in time, losing the striking nuance of rareness that they possessed when they

23. Vrettakos, p. 546.
24. Paraschos, p. 1,230; Vrettakos, p. 533.
25. *Odyssey,* v, 54.   26. Avyeris, p. 1,251.

were first written. I hope that the same will one day happen in our demotic, and that all the words and expressions in my translation that now provoke astonishment will have by then become pan-hellenic, and that only a minimum will remain rare."[27] Perhaps two or three decades are not enough in which to judge, but certainly, in the thirty years that have elapsed since the *Odyssey* appeared, Kazantzakis' hopes have not come true. Educated Greeks with a fondness for hyperbole are still known to claim that they find the epic easier to read in Kimon Friar's English translation than in the original.[28]

Kazantzakis was obviously terribly hurt by these reservations concerning the work that had served as receptacle for an entire decade's creative energy, metaphysical yearning, and linguistic zeal. At first he received the news stoically. From England, in 1939, he wrote: "I've read the critiques by Avyeris and Para-schos calmly, guilelessly, almost happily—since the supreme recompense is to have no recompense."[29] To Lambridi he replied snidely since she was only a woman.[30] But when Laourdas changed his opinion about the poem and published in 1943 a monograph explaining his about-face, Kazantzakis was moved to a full-scale, dispassionate, yet embittered rebuttal.[31]

On the specific problem of his diction, he answered Laourdas in his accustomed way, invoking Dante, Rabelais, and Luther, and reaffirming his duty to save the words that were in danger of dying out because of "the intellectuals' laziness and dearth of linguistic education, and the linguistic corruption of the people by schools and newspapers." Then, switching his position, he said that there is no reason why the language of poetry

27. See pp. 30–31, above.
28. For example, the poet Vafopoulos in a conversation with the author, May 1967.
29. Prevelakis, p. 491.
30. Kazantzakis, *Ena anoichto*; Kazantzakis, *Meta tin kritiki*.
31. Kazantzakis, *Ena scholio.*

should be exactly that of everyday speech; indeed it ought to be "higher." It is always an image of its creator: Dante's *pexa et hirsuta* language has all the severe traits of Dante himself; as for Kazantzakis, his plethora of adjectives derives from his need to express his emotion "spherically, from all sides." In answer to the charge that he employed Cretan dialect, he swore that there were only some thirty exclusively Cretan words in the entire poem, and that these were used only because no pan-hellenic equivalent existed. For example: ψυχανε-μίζουμαι, to have a presentiment; σεισηλίζω, vibrating of heated air as it rises from bare sun-drenched rocks; μανοκυ-ρουδάτο, a child whose mother and father are both alive.

Mrs. Helen Kazantzakis offers further defense that attempts to show Kazantzakis' kinship with the original humanists who tried to purify the language:[32] "The Athenian intellectuals were not all against Nikos for his extremely rich language of the people. But they assuredly did not understand this language for the most part and they believe even today that Nikos himself formed new words or made exclusive use of Cretan words. The truth is that among the various words available Nikos chose those which according to him were the purest, the closest to ancient Greek, and the most harmonious. For example, in place of καρδάρα [milk-bucket], he employed the word ἀρμε-γός [from ἀρμέγω, to milk]; in place of γλίτσα [shepherd's crook] he employed βοσκοράβδι [from βοσκός, shepherd, and ραβδί, stick]."

Mrs. Kazantzakis also insists that the poem was and is incomprehensible only to those Athenian intellectuals who have become isolated from their village roots; it is easily intelligible to peasants and also to intellectuals whose Greek has not been circumscribed by the fashionable Athenian patois: "Dr. Patrikios, director of Evangelismos Hospital, bought the *Odyssey*

32. Letter from Eleni Kazantzaki to the author, Jan. 29, 1960.

after returning from a long stay in France. All his friends made fun of him and refused to believe him when he told them that he understood it without a dictionary. Dr. Patrikios himself has told me that he then took the *Odyssey*, went off to his native island, Kefalonia, and read it to his sister, a simple peasant. And his sister understood the poem and liked it. The same thing happened to Mr. Friar. He took the *Odyssey* and gave it to his mother, who was from Asia Minor. She read it and understood it."

I cite all these rebuttals with the hope that the reader will immediately recognize how contradictory they are. Kazantzakis first invokes the great battlers for the vernacular idiom, then says that poetic language ought to be "higher" than the language of everyday speech. His wife insists that peasants can understand him, but then describes how he suppresses words such as γλίτσα, that the peasants would know and use, in order to choose terms nearer the ancient Greek, though based on roots still alive in the modern language. As clashing as all these assertions are, each one describes, in part, what Kazantzakis was doing, for his linguistic program consisted of many contradictory aspects. He was not simply recording the diction, grammar, and tropes of the spoken language, despite what he himself says. Actually, he comes nearest the truth when he notes that poetic language is always an image of its creator— in other words, not something that can be precisely classified and described by linguists, but something as furtive, complex, and contradictory as personality itself.

LANGUAGE IN RELATION TO SUBJECT MATTER

In the entire controversy, no one, so far as I know, emphasized what ought to have been most important: the fact that language cannot be discussed apart from subject matter. It is on this ground, I believe, that the *Odyssey* is a linguistic failure.

Certainly a poet has the right to use difficult, even incomprehensible, words of whatever origin he wishes; certainly poetry is not common speech, even when it aspires to the quality and diction of common speech. What matters is not the type of words or grammar used, but how these elements relate to the content of the poem or novel, and how skillfully the artist has fused together expression and content so that one is unthinkable without the other. Furthermore, the very genre of the poetic epic, as opposed to the novel, puts major emphasis on the linguistic surface as opposed to characterization and "philosophizing." The poetry must carry us; its rhythms and euphonies must achieve an incantatory autonomy, floating us effortlessly over any shoals of unreality, dryness, or gaucherie. But when the poem at the same time becomes a treasurehouse of words that might otherwise be lost, and beyond this a huge propaganda medium for spelling reform, the reader is not carried so comfortably over the various shoals, especially when the voyage lasts 33,333 verses.

Kazantzakis' linguistic program, taken in a vacuum, was admirable; the fault lay in the context, despite the fact that past epics had been used to "establish" vernacular Italian or French. One might object that Joyce, in *Ulysses*, employed vocabulary, syntax, and punctuation that hinder the reader's comprehension. But Joyce (whether he failed or succeeded is beside the point) attempted rigorously and imaginatively to match language to content, to observe the rule of congruity. There are many places in his novel where linguistic elements are introduced fully as arbitrarily as are Kazantzakis' demotic words, yet they represent lapses from an otherwise artistically justified procedure, whereas Kazantzakis' procedure, in its essence, was an imposition of educational zeal upon art.

The poet Cavafy is another example of this congruence between expression and content. His language is the most bizarre and arbitrary mixture of *katharevousa*, demotic, byzantine, and ancient Greek; he places ancient words and syntactical constructions next to the most illiterate demotic in what seems a completely random way, as though drawing from a lottery. Yet this linguistic hodgepodge is precisely equivalent to what he is trying to say. His point is that any particular era of Greek history is the correspondent or repetition of any other. What better way of conveying this than by jumbling all stages of the Greek language together in a box and then drawing at random?

Such congruence does not exist, or exists only minimally, in the *Odyssey*. The language is rich in metaphors drawn from nature, from the most basic experiences of the Greek peasantry. Yet at least half the poem is about Odysseus' rejection of the soil, flight from the rootedness implied in peasant life, and final belief that nothing is real except the imaginings of the mind. Abstractions are made concrete, linguistically, yet the poem treats a man who always looks beyond the concrete person or event to the abstract and metaphysical. The epic's content is generally philosophical and intellectual—not bad in itself, but bad when expressed in a language that is out-of-keeping; when a high tone (the author's utterly serious, Biblically urgent attitude toward his characters and material) clashes against a low diction; when supreme sophistication and immense learning aspire to express themselves with the "naivete of the demotic ballads."[33] Lastly and most comprehensively, the language, though meant to be true to the spirit of the Greek people, to express what is best in them, is employed in a poem that has nothing essentially to do with Greece or the Greek people, but is indeed completely contrary to the spirit of Greece, and was written by a man who, by his own confession, did not at that period "see, hear, or taste

33. Prevelakis, p. 145.

the world" as a Greek does.[34] As Kazantzakis himself later realized, how can a Greek, especially a Cretan, be at the same time a nihilistic Buddhist?[35]

A completely responsible critique of the poem would have to supplement these linguistic comments with more general considerations about style, characterization, etc., and would also have to describe what the epic is really about, and place it in its proper literary tradition. Because our concern now is chiefly linguistic and because I have attempted a more comprehensive critique elsewhere, I shall not do this.[36] Here, we are interested in the peculiar ways in which a bilingual situation led and perhaps misled a man with extraordinary linguistic capabilities. Though judgments of poetic quality are ultimately subjective (and in any case particularly rash for people like myself not born to the language), I can only repeat that in the relationship between language and subject matter we have one criterion for judgment, and that in this case we discover an incongruity that erodes the aesthetic unity found in fully realized poems.

Reconciliation with Greece, 1940 and After, Leading to New Literary Modes

Still, it was good that Kazantzakis wrote the *Odyssey*. Obviously, he had to write it, had to get it out of his system, and, as he would say, exorcise certain demons. His failure seems to have been a *felix culpa,* for something decisive happened after 1940. Perhaps the stimulus was the rigor of the German

34. Kazantzakis, *Ena scholio,* p. 1,029.
35. Jouvenel, *En Souvenir,* p. 104. Speaking of his "stage" at Berlin, Kazantzakis told Jouvenel: "Je ne pouvais décidemment pas être boudhiste! J'avais, un instant, oublié qu'on ne peut être Crétois et boudhiste!" (See pp. 1,581–82 of *Nea Estia* reprint.)
36. Bien.

occupation (April 1941 to October 1944), during which good and evil were not the phantasmagoria of nothingness Kazantzakis had made them in the *Odyssey*, but all too real. It is interesting that in the final canto of the epic he had introduced two Greeks and made them formulate the distinctively hellenic view of life as opposed to the Buddhistic. For a Greek, they announced:[37]

Καλὸ κι ἀληθινό 'ναι τὸ ψωμὶ καὶ τὸ νερὸ κι ὁ ἀγέρας,
μπαίνουν βαθιὰ στὰ σωθικὰ τοῦ ἀντροῦς καὶ τὸν
    κορμοψυχώνουν·
κι ἀργά, μὲ τὸν πολὺν ἀγώνα μας, γίνεται ὁ γίσκιος κρέας.

"Black bread, clear water, and blue air are good and real;
they sink deep in man's entrails, give him flesh and soul,
till slowly with great strife all shadows turn to meat."

But this had been just a debate, one theory opposed to another—and in any case, the Buddhism had prevailed. Now, however, owing in all likelihood to the rigors of the war, Kazantzakis' own words seemed to turn to meat inside him and become real. He grew increasingly reconciled not only to the visible, palpable world, but to his own nation, for the Greek people's suffering and resistance during this period gave them a unity and dignity that had been lacking in the years following the Asia Minor catastrophe. These events caused not only Kazantzakis but many other Greek writers to change their styles and themes, to deepen their national consciousness, to reacquire knowledge of the peasant culture and thus find their own roots.[38]

Whatever the precise reason, Kazantzakis reimmersed himself lovingly in the hellenic and neo-hellenic world. By reim-

37. *Odyssey*, xxiv, 977–79.
38. Theotokas, *Neoelliniko*, p. 7.

mersion I mean not just something outward and superficial
—such as the use of Greek characters and history in his plots—
but also a deep change in attitude: final acceptance of the natural world as both real and good, a return to earth after several
decades' sojourn in the clouds of metaphysical pessimism.
Most important, with this new attitude Kazantzakis was willing to use subject matter completely congruent with the concrete, pictorial, earthy demotic that he had been championing
for so many years.

The choice open to Kazantzakis—that of continuing in his
old mode or beginning something new—was perhaps conveyed most dramatically by an appeal directed to the "solitary
of Aegina" by Laourdas, who had been one of the *Odyssey*'s
most articulate admirers when the epic first appeared, but had
then changed his mind.[39] The appeal came in 1943, after Kazantzakis had already embarked on his new mode, as evi-
denced in the novel *Zorba*, begun in 1941; it would be wrong,
therefore, to say that Laourdas influenced Kazantzakis. Nevertheless, this former disciple's words are a convenient expression
of a problem felt strongly by many Greeks at this time:[40]

"I would like to tell you . . . : love our land. That and that
alone is our salvation. To transform Western decadence into
imaginative literature is neither needed by us nor appropriate
for you, who are worthy of much more substantial and permanent creativity. Before you, around you, inside you lies
another need: to make literature out of neo-hellenism. This
need is deeper and more substantial, more worthy of your
talents. Your *Odyssey* is a great mistake, in and of itself. But
if you so desire, it can become the first step toward immortal-
ity. The second will be another epic, one that fictionalizes the
struggle of neo-hellenism."

39. Zografou, p. 263.
40. Laourdas, *Scholio*, p. 1,341. Reprinted in Zografou, p. 270.

PERSISTENCE OF OLD MODES

As events turned out, the second, neo-hellenic "epic" was attempted in prose, in the form of a series of novels. In these Kazantzakis came closer to achieving the fusion of sublimity and naivete that he admired in the folk ballads; in these, and also in his translation of Homer's *Iliad*, he found more appropriate contexts for his beloved language, and outlets for his educational zeal—more appropriate because that zeal could now be ruled, yet not compromised, by aesthetic considerations. The old modes remained to some degree. Indeed it took Kazantzakis another decade before he could stop denigrating the artistic and personal redirections that commenced after 1940, and consciously admit to himself that perhaps they were indeed an advance.

For many years, at the same time that in his novels he was establishing the new attitude, he was persisting in the old in certain completed works and in others that were projected but never undertaken. The completed works to which I refer are the plays *Kouros* (written 1949) and, to a lesser degree, *Sodom and Gomorrah* (1948) and *Christopher Columbus* (1949). *Kouros* in particular continues the elevated style, remoteness, and artificiality of Kazantzakis' previous mode. All three plays employ a rhythmic prose that could more accurately be called "verse paragraphs." The projected works were a pair of ambitious epics, *Faust*, Part III, and *Akritas*. Beginning in 1950, Kazantzakis persisted in believing that the "Third Faust" should be his last utterance, his swan song, and he even claimed at one point that he was working so furiously at the novels simply because he did not feel ready yet to undertake the new epic, which he hoped would mark out "the limits of [his] powers."[41] The allegorical artificiality and metaphysical obsession of this epic as Kazantzakis planned it are evident from

41. Prevelakis, pp. 641; 633.

his remarks to Prevelakis and from the plot-outline that was discovered among his papers.[42] Prevelakis reproduces this for us in the *Four Hundred Letters*, commenting that in this sketch Kazantzakis "rediscovers his old world-view of the *Saviors of God* and the *Odyssey.*"

The *Akritas*, projected from 1939 onward, is similar. Though meant to fictionize medieval and modern Hellenism, and to exploit the folk epics and popular ballads, in attitude it lay just as far from the Greek acceptance of reality as did the *Odyssey*, since the hero was meant to start from where Odysseus left off, from the summit of Nada, and from there, "beyond place and time . . . enjoy times and places and his own *jet jaillissant* like a dream." "What I'd like," Kazantzakis wrote to his friend Prevelakis, ". . . is to climb to the highest level, beyond fleshly reality. . . . I shall play, free from the bonds of reason; I shall dance without feet." He was aspiring to what he considered Shakespeare's achievement in the final plays, to a poetry that—in the words of Taine which Kazantzakis invokes in his sketchbook for *Akritas*—"aboutit au fantastique. . . . Rejetant la logique ordinaire, [cette poésie] en crée une nouvelle . . . ; elle ouvre le pays de rêve."[43] In sum, Kazantzakis aspired in the *Akritas* to the sublime "reality beyond reality" that is indeed the achievement of Shakespeare and the greatest of poets but that lay beyond Kazantzakis' powers and most assuredly was incongruent with his demoticism. It seems to me fortunate that he did not pursue this chimera, but instead learned to dance with feet on real, not dream, ground, in prose, and in the pedestrian setting of the novel.

PROSE (THE NOVELS) AND VERSE (THE "ILIAD")

But despite the plays and the planned works such as *Faust*, Part III, and *Akritas*, Kazantzakis was undeniably establishing

42. *Ibid.*, p. 622, 625–626.   43. *Ibid.*, pp. 486, 483, 489.

his new mode. Perhaps what we should invoke here is D. H. Lawrence's dictum, "Never trust the artist. Trust the tale," and thus judge from the novels themselves, not from Kazantzakis' statements or plans. The initial document was *The Life and Times of Alexis Zorba*, begun in 1941. This constituted Kazantzakis' *mea culpa*, his acceptance of the charges that were to receive formulation in Laourdas' appeal two years later. But *Freedom and Death, Christ Recrucified* (called *The Greek Passion* in America), and *The Last Temptation* are equally relevant, even though they do not deal as bluntly as does *Zorba* with the conflict between a (non-Greek) obsession with metaphysics and a (Greek) love of the small details of everyday life. They are relevant because they all derive their artistic power from Kazantzakis' obvious love of the details of Greek reality, a love completely congruent with his other love for the concrete, pictorial Greek language which that reality produced.

It is interesting that Kazantzakis could function in the new mode only when writing prose narrative; as soon as he composed in verse or even in the "verse paragraphs" he employed in his dramas, he reverted to a stiff and rather self-conscious sublimity out of keeping with the demotic language he was using. Yet Kazantzakis, like Greek writers in general, always considered verse the highest form of expression and prose the vehicle for journalism, travel books, and similar ephemerae— an attitude deriving from Greek literary tradition, which is so rich in poetry and so comparatively meager in the novel. This attitude was deep enough to make him persist in considering his novels ephemeral, as we shall see below, and also to make him persist in the delusion that his full powers could be tested only by the kind of projected epics we have just been discussing. We are left here with an impasse in which we see Kazantzakis condemned to work against himself: pushing himself to write in precisely the way that contradicted and nullified his linguistic gifts.

But, at one point at least, Kazantzakis found a way out of this impasse, a way in which he could apply his beloved demotic to the full, and in verse, yet avoid the troubles to which verse seemed otherwise to lead him. This was in his translation of Homer's *Iliad*. Here was a means whereby he could fulfill his continuing need to write poetry, perform a patriotic act at a time when Greece was again enslaved (Kazantzakis, unlike Sikelianos, did not display his patriotism in open defiance of the Germans), make splendid and legitimate use of his pan-hellenic demotic vocabulary, and follow in the tradition of the early demotic revolutionaries, especially Pallis.

The story of Kazantzakis and demotic has a happy ending because he finally discovered how and where to apply his linguistic zeal. It was in these two fruits of the new mode—the translation of the *Iliad*, and the novels—that Kazantzakis finally provided his fervor with a proper artistic context, and thus vindicated his linguistic program. His aesthetic success in each case, however, must be analyzed separately, for in each case language was made to serve the particular needs of the genre. In the novel, which thrives on realism and especially on realistic dialogue, he was able to take his peasant language and put it where it belonged: in the mouths of peasants. He was also able to match demotic to the concreteness, the detailed examination of everyday life, which is the novel's particular forte as a genre. In the two Homeric translations (he also completed a first draft of the *Odyssey* before his death) he was stimulated to ransack demotic's variety and concreteness for the purpose of expressing the visual and auditory concreteness of Homer. His legitimate problem was to find a living correspondent for every word, compound epithet, and turn of speech that Homer had employed, in order to make a truly neo-hellenic equivalent.

Compared with his own *Odyssey*, the translation gave him a greater latitude and freedom, for every Greek is so familiar with the plot and details of Homer's epics that it did not matter so much if some of Kazantzakis' rare words or daring compounds were not immediately intelligible. Though perhaps incomprehensible in a vacuum, they showed forth their meaning in context. In his own *Odyssey* the ideas were difficult and strange, and the meaning was all; thus unintelligible words became a great annoyance to the attentive reader. In Homer, Kazantzakis was more at liberty to play with language, the reader more willing to surrender to the incantatory autonomy of the verse and be carried along by its rhythm, euphony, and inventive brilliance. In addition, Homer gave Kazantzakis historical and aesthetic justification for using a truly pan-hellenic vocabulary, since the original itself contained elements from more than one of the ancient dialects.[44] Thus the nature of the task afforded Kazantzakis legitimate latitude in various ways. At the same time, however, he was held in check because he collaborated in this project with the distinguished Homeric scholar I. Th. Kakridis, who shared Kazantzakis' love of demotic but not his pugnaciousness.[45] He was also held in check by the fact of translation itself. He could not impose lexicography upon art by using six adjectives where Homer

44. Stavrou, p. 124.

45. When the work was finally completed and ready for publication, Kakridis wrote a prologue that approached the linguistic element tactfully. Kazantzakis complained to him: "In the prologue it should be made apparent that if the reader stumbles over a word, it is because he doesn't know it . . . and does not know the richness of the demotic language. The way you've put it, it sounds as though we are asking forgiveness for having used a strange term. . . ." *Biography*, p. 539.

had used only one. Lastly, he was checked by the nature of the poem. The linguistic crusader had pledged fealty to an original that, as Kakridis has written, is "not primitive, but classical. . . . Kazantzakis' language softened in the service of Homer. The lion became tame for a while. . . . Kazantzakis temporarily denied his characteristic refusal to accept anything from classical measure or restraint."[46] Because both Homer and Kakridis acted as moderators, Kazantzakis was able to fuse his linguistic zeal with aesthetic good taste.

In sum, I would say that the *Iliad* was the most naturally appropriate poetic vehicle that Kazantzakis found for his demotic crusade. He was not inhibited by the fiercely tight rhyme-scheme of the terzina, as he had been in his Dante translation; he was not dealing with highly philosophical and abstract concepts, as in his plays and much of the *Odyssey*. Able to strike a balance between freedom and decorum, stimulated to use all his word-lists and all his ingenuity, yet always constrained to simplicity and humbleness by the Homeric original, he produced in this translation some of the best verse of his career.

KAZANTZAKIS' COLLABORATION WITH
PROFESSOR KAKRIDIS

I should like now to present various details of the *Iliad* translation, before returning again to the novels. Fortunately, Professor Kakridis has written a chronicle of his collaboration, and much of what he records is of great relevance to our study of Kazantzakis' demoticism.

We must begin with a few words about Kakridis himself. Although by profession a teacher of ancient Greek literature and a specialist in Homer, Kakridis will most likely be re-

46. Kakridis, *Chroniko*, p. 119.

membered as a fighter for the demoticization of scholarship
and the universities. In the early 1940's, because he published
a book in which accents were omitted, he became the center
of the renowned "war of the accents," was accused by his pro-
fessorial colleagues of (among other things) following "an
orthographical system entirely removed from the Greek language," was tried, and relieved of his job.[47] But he took his
demoticism with him to the University of Salonika, where the
spoken language became an accepted medium of instruction
in the faculty of philosophy. Kakridis eventually became rector
at Salonika, and head of the commission appointed by George
Papandreou to reorganize Greek education at all levels.

The collaboration between Kazantzakis and Kakridis was
initiated by a chance encounter in January 1942.[48] Kazantzakis
had come to Athens from Aegina to ask Papandreou's opinion
of his plan to translate the *Iliad*; Kakridis had come to see
Papandreou about the court proceedings that were then
plaguing him. Thus the two men met. Kazantzakis asked
the famous Homeric scholar to lend him some appropriate
books on Homer's language, epoch, and the Homeric question.
A few months later, after having read Kakridis' essays, Kazantzakis suggested that they collaborate: "For years I've
longed to translate the *Iliad* but I haven't dared. With your
help, I'm ready."

Kazantzakis convinced the Germans to allow Kakridis to
visit him in Aegina for a few days. "We rose at six in the
morning and worked until nightfall in order to lay the foundations," writes Kakridis. "We discussed the meter we would
choose for our translation, the archaic coloring we would give

47. See *Biography*, p. 418; Triantafyllidis, *Katathesi*; Kordatos,
Istoria, pp. 221–24.
48. Kakridis, *Chroniko*; *Biography*, pp. 405–06. Also see Kakridis, *Metaphrase*; Kakridis, *N.K.*

it, the high tone we were to maintain; we talked about the proper names, the compound epithets, about the question of whether, and to what degree, we would replace the elements of Homeric culture with those of modern Greek culture. We read excerpts from Polylas, Pallis, Eftaliotis, and naturally from Homer himself."

The agreement was that Kazantzakis would compose a first draft, independently, whereupon Kakridis would then list the places where he differed or objected—a list that was eventually to fill 2,000 pages. Kazantzakis worked furiously on the draft, as was his custom, finishing in three and a half months. The work of revision took twelve years. "The linguistic material of the *Iliad* was reexamined in its every detail; a host of Homeric studies prodded the translators' imaginations to resurrect the world of the epic. At the same time, neo-hellenism's expressive treasure had to be examined. The Academy's Neohellenic Lexicon, and Vlastos, were leafed through continually. We read and catalogued glossaries from various regions of Greece, wherever we found them printed. We studied folk ballads and tales, popular texts, proverbs, enigmas. I record here the books studied just by Kazantzakis during the initial period: literary investigations by Wilamowitz, Helbig, Rothe, Bérard, Bethe, Scheffer, Nilsson, Schadewaldt, Severyns. Open in front of him at all times he kept the translations of Voss, Polylas, Pallis, Zervos, Eftaliotis, Scheffer, Mazon. Medieval, and modern Greek texts: Χρονικὸ τοῦ Μωρέως, Ἀκρίτας, Μαχαιρᾶς, Πτωχοπρόδρομος, Legrand's Μεσαιωνικά, Μακρυγιάννης, Κολοκοτρώνης, Τερτσέτης. Once he asked me to send him all the volumes of the year book of the Society of Byzantine Studies, so that he could catalogue their linguistic material.

"None of this effort was wasted. On the contrary, a host of expressive means—phrases, words, especially compounds—

were added to the horde retained in Kazantzakis' vigilant memory." For the Homeric λευκώλενος Ἥρη the translators found κρουσταλλοβραχιονάτε μου from a popular ballad. A medieval poem gave them οἱ κυράδες οἱ μακρομαντούσες, which they used to translate Homer's τρωάδες ἑλκεσίπεπλοι. Another popular ballad provided them with a living equivalent for δυωκαιεικοσίπηχυ ξυστόν—they simply increased the ballad's τετραπήχινο σπαθὶ to εἰκοσαπήχινο, not at all concerned that they had cut two πήχες off Homer's sword. Another ballad gave them the epithet μακρολαιμονδάτα, applied to water-jugs in the original, but just as appropriate for Homer's swans: οἱ δουλιχόδειροι κύκνοι.

Here are some further equivalents:[49]

ἀσημοκαρφοπλούμιστος	ἀργυρόηλος
ἀστρομάτης	ἑλίκωψ
ἀχνογελόχαρη	φιλομμειδής
δρεπανόγυρτη	ἀμφιέλισσα
λαμπροφωτούσα	φαεσίμβροτος
μακροβίγλης	εὐρύοπα
ὀμορφοστεφανούσα	εὐστέφανος
πικρολεβεντομάνα	δυσαριστοτόκεια
ροδομάγουλη	καλλιπάρηος
στριφτοζάλης	εἰλίπους
συφεροντονούσης	κερδαλεόφρων
φουντομάλλης	ἀκρόκομος

Only infrequently was a Homeric compound replaced by a periphrastic locution, for example ἠχήεσσα θάλασσα by θάλασσα ὅλο λάλο. But the famous "well-greaved Achaeans" taxed Kazantzakis' ingenuity to no avail. Even though metallic greaves do not exist in modern warfare, he found certain equivalents. "I know only four words for κνημίδες," he wrote to

49. Stavrou, p. 124.

Kakridis at one point. A few months later the list was expanded to seven: ζάβες, τουσλούκια, χολέβα, σκουφούνια, καλτσούνια, γκέτες, τυλοχτάρια. But with none could he make a compound that suited him aesthetically. "I can't sleep because of εὐκνήμιδες. . . . Couldn't you ask someone? Or perhaps we should advertise in *Nea Estia*. We've got to find something."[50] In the end he gave up. The Achaeans became simply καλαντρειωμένοι.

IMPROVING ON PALLIS

Kazantzakis did not give up easily, or often. We should remember that one of the challenges he set himself in attempting something that had already been done so well by Pallis was precisely to discover solutions to problems that Pallis had found too formidable. I have already spoken of the way in which Pallis served as a link in a chain of transmission, carrying forth the work of Korais, Vernardakis, and Psiharis, and being carried forth in his own turn by Kazantzakis, whose *Iliad* is dedicated to Pallis' memory. I have also noted that discipleship for Kazantzakis meant the effort to honor one's master by surpassing him. Thus the translators of the new *Iliad* aspired consciously to exploit (a) the greater knowledge of Homeric life and language and (b) the greater knowledge of demotic's resources available to them in 1942, compared to what was available to Pallis in 1904.[51]

But there were additional reasons for a new translation.[52] Pallis, as we have seen, subscribed to Psiharis' view of the Homeric question; accordingly he omitted more than 3,000 verses on the ground that they had been composed at a later date by rhapsodes. These verses were restored by Kazantzakis

50. Kakridis, *Chroniko*, p. 117.
51. Homer, *Iliad*, prologue, p. 12.
52. *Ibid.*

and Kakridis. More importantly, the ideas of Psiharis had led
Pallis to strive in his translation for the flavor of the demotic
ballads. We have seen how he accordingly changed the proper
names to modern equivalents and dressed the ancient heroes
in the clothes, speech, and atmosphere of 1821. Kazantzakis
and Kakridis felt that this had been a mistake. Like Pallis,
they saw their translation as a challenge to "deepen . . . the
expressive powers of the modern Greek language," as they
claim in their introduction. But this did not mean that they
had to distort the original by demoticizing its every aspect. On
the contrary, they chose to preserve the details of Homeric culture as far as possible, and to approximate the grandeur and
high tone of Homer, departing from the familiarity affected by
Pallis.[53] Thus, for example, they did not continue Pallis' alteration of the proper names; Λενιώ became Ἑλένη once again.[54]
Nor did they choose, like Pallis, to employ the 15-syllable line
of the popular ballads, but rather the 17-syllable verse that
Kazantzakis had used in his own *Odyssey*. This gave the poem the slightly unfamiliar and dignified quality they wanted.

The difference between the two versions can be felt clearly
in the following passages selected for comparison by the critic
Petros Haris:[55]

(Pallis)

Κι' ἔμειναν μόνοι οἱ Δαναοὶ νὰ πολεμᾶν κι' οἱ Τρῶες
κι' ὥρα ξανάσμιγαν δεξὰ ὥρα ζερβὰ στὸν κάμπο,
κι' ἔρηχναν ἕνας τ' ἀλλουνοῦ τὰ φράξινα κοντάρια
ἀνάμεσα ἀπ' τὰ ρέματα τοῦ Ξάνθου καὶ Σιμόη.

53. Stavrou, p. 122.
54. There were some exceptions. Homer's Ate became Typhla
(Phrenia in Pallis). Stavrou, *Omirou*, p. 123; Kakridis, *Chroniko*,
p. 118.
55. Haris, P., pp. 129–30. The lines are Book vi, 1–4.

(Kazantzakis-Kakridis)

Ἔτσι ἀπομεῖναν πιὰ στὸν πόλεμο μονάχοι οἱ Τρῶες κι᾽
οἱ Ἀργίτες,
κι᾽ ἅπλωσε ἡ μάχη ἀκόμα πιότερο μιὰ δῶθε καὶ μιὰ κεῖθε
στὸν κάμπο, ἀνάμεσα στοῦ Σκάμαντρου καὶ στοῦ Σιμόη
τὸ ρέμα,
ὁ ἕνας στὸν ἄλλο ἀπάνω ὡς ἔριχναν μὲ τὰ χαλκὰ κοντάρια.

The reader may also like to compare Kazantzakis' rendition
of the opening lines with the rendering by Pallis cited earlier
(p. 109). The new version reads:

Τὴ μάνητα, θεά, τραγούδα μας τοῦ ξακουστοῦ Ἀχιλλέα,
ἀνάθεμά τη, πίκρες πού 'δωκε στοὺς Ἀχαιοὺς περίσσιες
και πλῆθος ἀντρειωμένες ἔστειλε ψυχὲς στὸν Ἅδη κάτω
παλικαριῶν . . .

Regarding these lines, Kakridis has explained how he and
Kazantzakis struggled with the patronymic Πηληιάδεω, "son
of Peleus," and finally gave up.[56] After rejecting awkward
verses such as

Τραγούδα, θεά, τὸ θυμὸ τοῦ Ἀχιλλέα, τοῦ γιοῦ τοῦ
Πηλέα . . .
Θεά, τοῦ γιοῦ τραγούδα, τοῦ Πηλιὰ τὴ μάνητα Ἀχιλλέα

they retained Pallis' ξακουστοῦ Ἀχιλλέα.

Lastly, the reader may find it interesting to compare the text
Kazantzakis finally published with an early draft. In Kakridis'
"Chronicle," as in the prologue to the finished version, we read
of the immense labor that both men expended on their translation, the diligence with which they cast and recast every line,
discussed and solved every crux, striving to find precisely the

56. Kakridis, *Chroniko*, pp. 117–18.

right demotic word. We do not have the complete early drafts, but Kakridis has published a few lines as Kazantzakis first conceived them:[57]

Μα τότε ο φτεροπόδαρος θεϊκος αντιγνωμάει Αχιλλέας:
—Ατρείδη ξακουσμένε, που όλουςμας σε αχορταγια
περνάςμας,
αρχοντομερτικό πώς άλο θές οι Αργίτες να σου δώσουν;
Αμοίραστα δεν ξέρω πουθενα πολλα να μένουν κούρσα·
κι όσα, πατώντας κάστρα, αρπάξαμε, τα μοιραστήκαμε όλα,
κ' είναι ντροπη να τα μαζέψουμε πίσω ξανα απ' τ' ασκέρι.
Μα τόρα εσυ για χάρη του θεου την κόρη δώσ', κ' οι Αργίτες
τρίδιπλα, ναι, θα σ' τα πλερώσουμε, τετράδιπλα, αν ο Δίας
δώσειμας πιά να διαγουμίσουμε την πυργοστήθα Τροία.

These were composed in 1942. Thirteen years later, in the definitive version, they appeared as follows:

Τότε ὁ 'Αχιλλέας ὁ γοργοπόδαρος τοῦ ἀπηλογήθη κι εἶπε:
'''Υγιὲ τοῦ 'Ατρέα τρανὲ κι ἀπ' ὅλους μας ὁ πιὸ συφερτολόγος,
καὶ πῶς οἱ 'Αργίτες οἱ τρανόψυχοι νὰ βροῦν ἀρχοντομοίρι
νὰ σοῦ τὸ δώσουν; Βιὸς ἀμοίραστο δὲν ἔχουμε, ὅσο ξέρω·
τὶ ὅσα ἀπ' τὰ κάστρα διαγουμίσαμε, τὰ μοιραστήκαμε ὅλα,
κι οὔτε θὰ ταίριαζε τὸ ἀσκέρι μας νὰ τὰ μαζέψει πάλε.
Μὰ τώρα τούτη ἐσὺ λευτέρωσε γιὰ τοῦ θεοῦ τὴ χάρη,
κι ἐμεῖς διπλὰ νὰ σὲ ξοφλήσουμε καὶ τρίδιπλα, ἂν μιὰ μέρα
μᾶς δώσει ὁ Δίας ἡ καλοτείχιστη νὰ γίνει Τροία δική μας.''

THE "ILIAD" AS CULMINATION

All that I have said, and the examples I have given, should convey Kazantzakis' intense and prolonged involvement in this project. What place his *Iliad* will occupy in Greek cultural

57. *Ibid.*, p. 116. The lines are from Book 1, 121 ff.

life in the long run is difficult to predict. So far, the translation has never been officially adopted for use in schools, and has not affected the general esteem for Pallis' pioneering version. Despite what I said earlier, it may remain a literary curiosity because of its strange combination of ultra-demotic with a meter very foreign to the demotic poetic sensibility. The 15-syllable line of the ballads is to Modern Greek what the iambic pentameter is to English; thus Pallis' translation, despite its liberties and omissions, sits more easily on the ear and is likely to continue to be favored, especially by those who cannot read Homer in the original. But only time, of course, will deliver the final verdict. If we think, however, of Kazantzakis himself and his repeated efforts to body forth his passion for demotic, we must see the *Iliad* translation as a culmination, the fruition of cultural and linguistic hopes that had previously been frustrated. It is no surprise that in an interview given in 1957, shortly before his death, although citing the *Odyssey* as his most basic work, Kazantzakis placed the *Iliad* translation second.[58] But it is in his letters that the full impact of the translation is conveyed most unmistakably. Here we see his growing euphoria as the reality of publication came closer and closer:[59]

(*September 9, 1952, to Börje Knös*) "On returning home, I found the manuscript of the *Iliad* translation. . . . A great temptation; I plunged at once into the Homeric verses as I might into the cool sea on a sweltering day. I am looking at the translation freshly now, correcting it, and am overjoyed at seeing the wealth, harmony, and plasticity of our demotic

58. Evelpidis.
59. The cost of publication was underwritten by the translators, since no Greek publisher would accept the book! Prevelakis, pp. 538, 628. Quotations from *Biography*, pp. 514, 519, 539–40.

language. I don't think that I've ever felt a greater sensual pleasure. What a language, what sweetness and power!"

(*June 12, 1953, to Börje Knös*) "I hope by the end of the month to return to Antibes. There I'll await Kakridis, so that we can harness ourselves to the great work. I persist in thinking that this work is a . . . literary monument that will give glory to our demotic tongue."

(*September 12, 1955, to Kakridis*) "Dear Fellow-Combatant: How wonderful to see the *Iliad* published . . . bless you! The other day I had a dream. I was laughing . . . and saying to you: 'Ah, when will the second edition come out, so that we can correct that *kalognomos?*' (You see, this term won't leave me in peace.) In the morning I looked it up in the big Dimitrakos dictionary and I found. . . . Enough of that! I shan't say a word until the second edition."

(*November 9, 1955, to Kakridis*) "Well-beloved, victorious Fellow-Combatant: I believe that this day has been one of the happiest of my life. Eleni came up to my desk, leaping up the steps four at a time, hiding her hands behind her. 'Close your eyes!' she called to me. And I understood at once. The *Iliad*!

"I closed my eyes, took it into my hands, kissed it, and opened my eyes. Well, how marvelous it is to struggle for years and years while the fruit of your struggle is slowly taking shape, and for you to hold it in your hands! . . . Now, let's tuck up our sleeves. The *Odyssey* comes next! . . ."

The Novels

PROSE VS. VERSE

These letters may give the impression that the *Iliad* was the whole of Kazantzakis' life. But this man of extraordinary energy and enthusiasms had the capacity to struggle on many fronts at once; a single culminating experience at a time did not satisfy him. As we can see from the dates, even before the fruit of his labors with Kakridis had ripened, Kazantzakis had completed all the major novels. Indeed, the bulk of his efforts after 1940 went into prose, and I think it fair to say that it was even more in the novels than in the *Iliad* translation that he finally vindicated his linguistic program.

Much of the difficulty arose simply from the unsuitability of verse—that of the *Iliad* excepted—to Kazantzakis' literary personality, quite aside from the question of his perhaps limited talent as a poet.[60] If nothing else, verse thrives on concision, whereas Kazantzakis' temperament, and his lexicographical ambitions, pushed him toward the expansive, the comprehensive. His mind was an accretive one in all things; he needed the freedom to describe, to narrate, to spin out threads in all directions involving dozens of characters, to relate anecdotes, indulge in digressions—in short, to encompass the reader in a complete and huge fictional world, to mesmerize him. What he failed so long to realize is that in our day, when the eye has replaced the ear as our literary receptor, this mesmerization is accomplished not so much by the euphony and rhythm of verse as by plot, theme, characterization, and style; in short, it is accomplished superlatively by the novel. Joyce had moved from verse to prose early in his career, after realizing where his talents lay; so had Faulkner. Neither tried to delude himself about the reasons for the change. Faulkner once confessed: "I'm a failed poet. Maybe every novelist wants to write poetry first, finds he can't and then tries the short story, which is the most demanding form after poetry. And failing at that, only then does he take up novel writing."[61] But in this matter as

60. Vrettakos, the most perceptive of Kazantzakis' critics, agrees that Kazantzakis' talents lay in prose, not in verse. Vrettakos, p. 611.

61. Meriwether, p. 238.

in others, Kazantzakis' extraordinary, and otherwise admirable, persistency became his own worst enemy. "Never trust the artist. Trust the tale."

To the very end, despite the increasing number of occasions when he lowered the mask and admitted the truth to himself, Kazantzakis persisted in asserting that the prose works were ephemeral, the poetic "basic."[62] Because of his own literary education and the Greek traditions that formed him, he linked poetry with so-called permanent themes and concerns: the soul, the great questions of whence we have come and whither we shall go—namely, abstractions, metaphysics. Conversely, he linked the novel with the physical and concrete, thus for him the passing and—alas—unimportant. Or at least this denigration of the concrete, and along with it, of prose, was a mask he donned to hide from himself his own very great attraction to "the world," to muffle the diabolical voice that kept telling him that the ephemeral and concrete are willy-nilly the only things of value, even, paradoxically, of eternal value. As late as 1948, when he was ready to publish *Christ Recrucified* and had planned a whole "series of similar novels," he nevertheless wrote a preface called "Hazain Pirouit" in which he defensively justified his new genre as a kind of lark, a drunken spree in which his mind "turns its back on the abyss [i.e. metaphysical truth], gazes at the verdant upper world with its embroideries—men, trees, insects, empires—and rolls on the green grass, like a donkey in springtime."[63] But he promised that he would return afterward to his duty, which was to gaze bravely in the other direction, at the abyss, and—this is unstated but implicit—to write poetry not prose. (We have already seen his plans for the epics *Akritas* and *Faust*, Part III.)

62. Evelpidis.
63. Prevelakis, pp. 596, 597–98; *Biography*, pp. 385–86; Prevelakis, *O Poiitis*, p. 318.

All this may have been simply a cushion for Kazantzakis lest his novel prove a failure, but I think it was closer to an honest self-deception, something he really could not help, than to a premeditated tactical move in order to forestall adverse criticism. In any case, Prevelakis dissuaded him from employing this introduction, and it never reached print.[64]

But in spite of himself and in spite of such pronouncements, Kazantzakis did increasingly come to accept the novel as a genre. This meant a corresponding acceptance of the "embroideries of this verdant upper world" as the appropriately prosaic subject matter he would now "temporarily" treat. Kazantzakis knew much of the world with some intimacy—Berlin, Russia, France—but as he saw Greece again under foreign domination, and then, in exile, as he grew older and more nostalgic, his natural subject matter became his own country and its people, whom he came to regard now with a much more mature, mellowed admiration than in his early nationalistic period, before 1920.

It seems obvious to us, who know Kazantzakis almost exclusively through the late novels, that the modern Greeks were his proper, inevitable subject matter, and thus it is difficult for us to realize that in the thirty-three-year period between *The Masterbuilder* (1908) and *Zorba* (begun 1941), there was not a single page of his published imaginative writing—that is, of completed, published fiction or poetry or drama—that treated modern Greece directly or in which an actual modern Greek was allowed to speak the demotic tongue that Kazantzakis had worshipped so continuously. His heroes and settings had been either non-Greek, or drawn exclusively from ancient Greek mythology or from Byzantium, though he insisted that he always wrote about contemporary problems, symbolically. Kazantzakis' acceptances in later life were thus twofold: a

64. Zografou, p. 274 ff.; Prevelakis, *O Poiitis*, p. 318.

new prosaic genre involving prose, and a new prosaic, earthy subject matter, the Greek people. The genre and material matched in his mind at first for negative reasons, because both were ephemeral, secondary and also because the novel lent itself to the expansive, digressive, anecdotal nature of the new material. It was only gradually that he began to value the novel for positive reasons, and to rejoice that the very medium he had now chosen had forced him to treat his materials, modern or not, in a new and refreshing way.

FRENCH VS. GREEK

It was only gradually, as well, that Kazantzakis began to see the vital connection between the demotic language he had so long espoused, and the new type of peasant, agrarian material he was using. One of the strangest twists in Kazantzakis' literary development was that although he sensed, even before 1940, the need to write about the concrete ephemerae of modern Greece, and the appropriateness of prose for such writings, he believed he could succeed by writing in French. This "twist" in his career is something we must now consider, for it is part of the background to Kazantzakis' eventual emergence as a novelist writing in demotic.

Kazantzakis employed French for reasons primarily financial and political, as well as because of the difficulties he found in having his type of demotic printed in Greece without "corrections." But, to some degree at least, this use of French confirms what we have seen before: his refusal for so many years to be bothered about probably the most elementary ingredient of literary craftsmanship, the congruity between language and material. In the *Odyssey*, we remember, he maintained an elevated tone, an attitude of absolute seriousness toward his material, yet he tried to achieve this with the slapdash diction of fishermen and shepherds. He lacked the aesthetic tact of

John Milton, who resembles Kazantzakis in so many other ways, but who deliberately matched language to theme, employing an idiom more formal, sonorous, and archaic than the normal speech of his time in order to achieve aesthetic congruity with the elevated subject matter and moral seriousness of *Paradise Lost*. Nor did Kazantzakis go the other way, as did Joyce in *Ulysses*, and compose a mock epic in the middle or low style, something more appropriate to "genuine" demotic. Instead, he coupled together by violence the racy, fancifully daring speech of the people with a wholly inappropriate elevation and seriousness, to beget a work that is an aesthetic hybrid.

The first attempts to treat the Greek people novelistically exemplify this same aesthetic insensitivity about the relation between language and material. Yet in every other way they were encouraging moments when Kazantzakis lowered his metaphysical mask, when he deigned to turn his back on the abyss and to roll a little in the concrete wonders and miseries of everyday ephemeral life—which, after all, is what every artist must do sooner or later. These attempts predate 1940, showing that the decisive change that occurred during the German occupation was not so much a plunge into something entirely new as a liberation of something previously suppressed. The mask first came down in 1929, at the very time Kazantzakis was embarking on the huge metaphysical journey of the *Odyssey*. He planned a novel to be set in Crete just prior to 1900, with his peasant grandfather, warrior father, and decadent intellectual self as chief figures. As usual, he asked Prevelakis to send him aids—a collection of Cretan ballads, a description of marriage customs, and anything else that might be useful: anecdotes, tragic stories, details of funerals, wine festivals, monks, warriors, farmers.[65] "I shall try," he said,

65. Prevelakis, p. 142.

"to make this book simple, epic, of peasant character [χωριά-
τικο]." But then, in the same breath, he announced that he
planned to write it in French. Moreover, he would finish it in
a month at most; at present he allowed himself to think about
it only in the afternoons, because his best hours were devoted
to reading source material for the *Odyssey*. Poetry obviously
came before prose. The book, called *Kapetan Elia*, was indeed
completed in a month. Kazantzakis characteristically denigrated it, along with *Toda Raba*, as a "tiny offhand job." He
set the manuscript aside, and eventually tore it up.[66]

But the need to return to Cretan subjects continued, despite
himself. In 1933, he wrote to Eleni: "I feel I am now ripe to
leave a work solidly founded in the Greek, i.e., the Cretan
earth."[67] Late in 1935, he projected a new version of the material of *Kapetan Elia*, under the title *Mon Père*.[68] It would
seem that he was being prodded to turn to Cretan subjects by
Eleni, just as he was most definitely prodded by her to write
Zorba in 1941 and *Christ Recrucified* in 1948.[69] "I'm working
on the *Odyssey*," he informed her. "I'll write *Mon Père* whenever the need drives me to it. But I'll be sure to write it, for
your sake."[70] He completed a first draft on this book in 1936,
then let the manuscript sit, worked on it again in 1940, and
finally rejected it.[71]

By this time Kazantzakis was definitely aware that the
Cretan subject matter and the vehicle, French, were mis-
matched. As far back as 1934, Kazantzakis had begun to have
doubts about writing in French, although his reason seemed
primarily commercial. The silence that greeted the publication

66. *Ibid.*, pp. 146, 722.
67. *Biography*, p. 281.   68. *Ibid.*, p. 325.
69. *Ibid.*, p. 395; Jouvenel, p. 95 (*Nea Estia*, p. 1,577).
70. *Biography*, p. 325.
71. Prevelakis, p. 458; *Biography*, pp. 326, 327, 390, 395.

in Paris of *Toda Raba* would liberate him, he asserted, from "the temptation to write in French again."[72] On the other hand, two years later he composed *Le Jardin des Rochers* directly in French (in six weeks!), renewed his hopes that he might find a European audience by means of this novel, and projected "a series of books that I intend to write in French and in which I shall make use of the vision I have of life."[73] He also began *Mon Père* at this time, as we have seen. But *Le Jardin des Rochers* did not win him a European audience, and by 1940 he was much more definite and embittered about the way in which "marketing" had constrained him. "Yesterday," he complained to a friend, "I finished my novel on Crete, about 500 pages, but written in French. This is where I've ended up:—I, the fanatic lover of our language, am forced to write in a foreign tongue. In Greece, I have not a single publisher, and elsewhere I have three."[74]

The use of French was perfectly understandable, given Kazantzakis' continued financial difficulties and his hopes to make a career outside of Greece. He wished desperately to be successful; French was a major language; therefore he would employ it even though he had always tended to despise French civilization as rationalistic, superficial, and degenerate. (He once confessed that the very thought that *Kapetan Elia* would be published in France acted as a damper on his enthusiasm for writing it.)[75] But as always he worked against himself, submitting unpolished, off-hand books like *Toda Raba* and *Le Jardin des Rochers* to his European publishers while he continued to devote his heart and soul to the *Odyssey* and to demotic. The allegiance to Greek in the poetic works, "the ones that mattered," was inevitable and admirable; yet we are discouraged by Kazantzakis' inability to see that the beloved

72. *Biography*, p. 299.
74. *Biography*, p. 390.

73. Prevelakis, pp. 457, 456.
75. Prevelakis, p. 145.

demotic belonged even more imperatively with the books like *Mon Père* that "did not matter." It is clear that nothing further could happen until he ceased to denigrate the novel and began to change his attitude toward contemporary material.

GRADUAL ACCEPTANCE OF PROSE IN GREEK

As I pointed out earlier, this decisive change in attitude began coming to the surface only after 1940 under the influence of the occupation, which had forced Kazantzakis into contact with his fellow Greeks and given him new experiences that demanded new forms of expression.[76] Even now the change was gradual and full of hesitations. At first he felt responsibility not toward a literary form per se but simply toward characters who had to be preserved, memorialized. (We remember that there was no appreciable novelistic tradition in Greece, and that Kazantzakis therefore never sensed the need to equal or surpass his predecessors, as he had in the epic, drama, and translations.) Prodded by his wife, and still protesting that he was a born playwright, he began *Zorba* in 1941. He did not think of it as a novel; it was simply a memorial to a friend. Furthermore, he continued to express his renewed, mellowed patriotism in verse: in the *Iliad* translation, as we have seen, and in the verse dramas *Kapodistrias* (1944) and *Konstantinos Palaiologos* (1944), both of which deal strongly and obviously with the contemporary Greek plight, though the latter uses a Byzantine setting.

It was not until after Kazantzakis commenced his final self-exile from Greece that he began consciously to value the novel, to realize that the very medium he had now chosen forced him to treat his materials—modern or not—in a completely different, refreshing way. At this time also he finally saw the

76. *Ibid.*, p. οδ΄.

vital connection between the demotic language he had so long espoused, and the new type of peasant, agrarian material he was using. *Zorba* was now behind him; he had begun *Christ Recrucified*, the first of the novels written in exile. Knowing that his chances of returning to Greece were small, he once again faced the problem of earning a living abroad. His decision not to write the final novels in French was a crucial one. Regarding this decision, it would be nice to say that he was motivated entirely by aesthetic, self-critical insight, but this is probably not the case. An external factor played a role, namely the good fortune of *Zorba*, which by this time had been translated into Swedish and had paradoxically enabled Kazantzakis to capture the European market (a French version had already been published, and an English firm was asking for rights).[77] In Kazantzakis' decision to let the novel join forces with demotic rather than French, this external factor was surely just as important as any sudden insights regarding the congruence between language and material. Yet this was hardly the first time an artist had partially stumbled or been pushed into what was aesthetically right for him, and it does not diminish the value or correctness of the result.

In any case, the letters of this period reveal Kazantzakis' conscious valuation of the novel, and imply his conviction that demotic was the only suitable medium for his efforts in this genre, as it had been for his earlier efforts in epic and drama. In 1947 he was able to announce grandly to his Swedish translator Börje Knös: "I love the modern Greek language with such a passion that I didn't want to sign a contract for a series of books with a large Paris publishing firm which proposed that I write directly in French five books like my novel *Toda Raba*. My post is in Greek literature. The evolution of our lan-

77. *Ibid.*, p. 586.

guage is passing a decisive, creative moment and I do not want at any cost to desert my post."[78] Most important here is what is implicit but unstated: that he will serve demotic by means of prose.

In a second letter, written in 1948 as he was completing *Christ Recrucified*, he showed a fully conscious awareness of the importance for him of the new genre, and also seemed to be implying—again without actually saying it—that demotic was the only possible vehicle for his new subject matter: "These days I've been finishing the novel I started. . . . It is contemporary, taking place in a village in Asia Minor. . . . Naturally I don't know if it is any good, but I'm writing it with great gusto. The novel-form offers me an outlet where I can make use of certain 'human' qualities I possess, qualities which do not find their way into poetry or drama, at least not in this manner. Good spirits, humor, ordinary 'human' everyday talk, laughter, jokes with plenty of salt, difficult concepts formulated with peasant simplicity—all these were in me, and it's only in the novel that I've been able to deposit them and find relief. These things were a part of myself which had to be given expression. . . ."[79]

Once more I must stress that we are not dealing here with a sudden, or even a complete, conversion. At the same time that Kazantzakis expressed the above sentiments, he also wrote the suppressed preface to *Christ Recrucified*, cited earlier, in which he denigrated the novel as a form and promised to turn once more to the abyss. And in 1950, in the same breath in which

---

78. *Biography*, p. 463. Actually, Kazantzakis is remembering something that happened in 1932, when he withdrew *Toda Raba* from the Rieder publishing house despite the offer of a contract for additional books, and offered his novel instead to Renaud de Jouvenel. For the reasons, see Prevelakis, pp. 307, 309.

79. Prevelakis, p. 592.

he hailed the new genre as a rejuvenation and gave notice of forthcoming novels, he made clear that he wished eventually to tackle the "Third Faust." He was a man always caught between clashing antitheses.[80]

Yet, something was happening. Though implication is all we have, Kazantzakis seems finally to have come round to the early demoticists' insistence that it is unthinkable to treat the Greek people and their customs naturalistically unless you employ the words the people actually speak. When Kazantzakis says "formulated with peasant simplicity" he means: conveyed in a way that preserves not just the events and facts, but the flavor, of Greek life. His novels do convey this flavor; that is what distinguishes them. I wish to stress my conviction that this result could not have been accomplished without his own special type of demotic.

THE FLAVOR IMPARTED BY DEMOTIC

It is one of the ironies of literary history, defying all common-sense expectation, that Kazantzakis should have produced novels that "worked" when he wrote them in demotic and then had them translated into other tongues, whereas when he composed directly in French, the magical flavor failed to appear. Despite his consummate knowledge of French, Kazantzakis' ear was so specifically and finely tuned to demotic that in order to bring peasant speech to life, he had to record it exactly as he heard it.

This can be seen if we take characteristic bits of dialogue or narration from the final novels, even in translation, and compare them with a passage from *Toda Raba*, which is in the same mode of the fanciful, the naive, the tall tale, and which —if we consider only the subject matter—indeed might very convincingly appear word for word in any of the later works.

80. Prevelakis, p. 627; *Biography*, p. 548.

The demotic passages sparkle, creating the illusion of actual, genuine speech, and making us warm to the people who are speaking; the French passage from *Toda Raba* is flat, lacking the effervescence that Kazantzakis was able to achieve only when he wrote directly in his own language. Here is the passage in question:[81]

... vers le soir, je m'étends sur un rocher, auprès d'un vieux pêcheur accroupi, qui avait jeté sa ligne et attendait le poisson. Nous parlons. De la mer, des guerres, de la misère des hommes, des figues... Tout à coup il se tourne et me dévisage:

— Tu m'as l'air instruit. Pourrais-tu me dire comment Christ a gagné le premier disciple?

"Je lui répète ce que racontent les Écritures, il secoue la tête et sourit:

— Moi seul le sais. Comment s'appelait-il?

— André.

—C'est ça, André. La tempête était déchaînée, le vent faisait rage; les pêcheurs rentraient désespérés, les filets vides. Tout à coup, un feu qui flambe sur la rive et auprès du feu une ombre d'homme. "Celui-là dînera," pense l'un des pêcheurs affamés, et il court vers le feu, au bord de la mer.

— Ce n'était pas la mer, c'était un lac.

— Eh! qu'importe! Voilà ce qui vous perd, vous autres lettrés. Il court vers le feu, il trouve la braise à moitié consumée et des restes de poisson. Mais l'homme avait disparu. Il appelle; âme qui vive!

"Le lendemain la tempête était plus forte. De nouveau les pêcheurs désespérés rentraient les filets vides; et de nouveau, voici le feu sur la rive et l'ombre d'homme! Le

81. Kazantzakis, *Toda Raba*, Plon edition, p. 195 ff. (English translation, p. 162 ff.)

pêcheur de la veille court, il atteint l'homme qui grillait des poissons enfilés sur un roseau. L'homme est jeune, d'une trentaine d'années, tanné par le soleil comme un pêcheur. Il a les pieds nus.

— Que fais-tu là?

— Tu le vois, je fais cuire du poisson.

— Comment as-tu fait par cette mer démontée? Nous autres nous n'avons pas mangé depuis deux jours.

—Vous ne savez pas jeter les filets. Je vous apprendrai. Le pêcheur qui était André, tu l'as sans doute deviné, tombe aux pieds de l'homme:

— Maître, je ne te quitterai plus!

"Le soir, André dit à son frère:

— J'ai trouvé un homme qui sait prendre des poissons par le plus gros temps.

"Le frère le dit à ses amis et c'est ainsi que, peu à peu, Christ—car c'était lui—recruta ses disciples. Au commencement, il leur enseigna la manière de prendre le poisson; petit à petit, avec le temps, de pêche en pêche, il en fit des apôtres!"

CONGRUENCE BETWEEN LANGUAGE AND MATERIAL

How can we explain what I have called the "effervescence" of the novels written directly in demotic? Why do these novels make us warm to the people in them, and why do they create the illusion of reality even though they are so obviously unrealistic in so many ways? Why do they preserve not just the events and trappings, but the flavor, of Greek life as that life was apprehended by Kazantzakis?

As answers to these elusive questions I have offered Kazantzakis' reconciliation with the concrete reality of everyday experience, his acceptance of prose as the best means for conveying this reality, and his eventual realization that if he were going to write prose, he must do so in Greek and not in French.

But all these answers are obviously just formulas that, while summarizing certain demonstrable changes in Kazantzakis' outlook and procedure, do not by any means guarantee the results that I have characterized as effervescent, warming, and the like. To get at the cause of these qualities (which are admittedly subjective) we must perhaps be synthetic and impressionistic, saying that novels like *Zorba, Christ Recrucified*, and *The Last Temptation* succeed all-in-all because in them we feel a unified and consistent flavor that in turn comes from a successful marriage of language to content. The realism is not by any means a congruence between Kazantzakis' characters and events and what we ourselves know of the world; it is rather a congruence between the author's vision and his means of expression, a congruence so successful that it puts forth its own authenticity, making us apprehend the characters and events as real even though they are not.

These novels *are* the language in which they were written. In them, Kazantzakis' special type of demotic forms a natural partnership with characterization, narration, and description. The qualities we sense in the above-mentioned works are basically linguistic, the fruits of Kazantzakis' long cultivation of demotic. I refer to the specificity and earthiness of these gambols in the verdant grass of the concrete, earthy, world; the metaphorical richness; the wealth of anecdote and fable, so natural and inevitable in the context of the novels—that is, of the people who have naturally produced the anecdotes and fables Kazantzakis employs; the gift of straightforward storytelling, a gift that he had suppressed for so many years or had relegated only to the "unimportant" travel books; the plenitude of detail, and especially the extraordinary sensitivity to the details of the natural environment; the almost animistic attitude toward sea, sun, stars; the combination of impassioned rhetoric with cracker-barrel pithiness; the effortless evocation of a Biblical ambiance.

In all these qualities, the specifically linguistic component cannot be separated from the vision, the attitude toward life, that Kazantzakis always possessed. If his language was unpredictable, inconsistent, unregulated, this was—looked at positively—a reflection of his cult of fluidity, his hatred of anything fixed. His style, like the characters he presented as heroes, was inventive, "irresponsible," devilish, always tugging at the leash with which grammarians wished to confine its freedom. If his language was naughty, this reflected his hatred of bourgeois respectability. If it was pan-hellenic, this reflected his generalized eclecticism, and his desire to fuse disparates into a workable—yet always dynamic—synthesis. If he tampered with vowels, genders, even the normal prose-rhythms of spoken Greek, all this was once again related to his material, or at least to his vision of that material. As his wife has stated:

Kazantzakis knew French "well enough to write in it on any subject at all, except on Crete. For Crete, he needed the ancestral tool—that broad-breathing language with the guttural sounds in the cradling rhythm of the African waves; the language of this strange people who felt constrained in the tongue of their own race, impelled by the need to expand it and add resonant vowels to certain words or change their gender to make them more 'virile.' "[82]

Kazantzakis' artistic vision led him to exaggerate the physical and spiritual power of his characters without at the same time making these characters essentially different from the human norm. His language reflects this; the normal words are distorted by means of demotic's power of augmentation, yet the normality still penetrates. Thus his men are ἀντρα-

82. *Biography,* p. 387.

κλαράδες, their hands are χερούκλες. Even ordinary actions have an intensity for which accustomed locutions are too pale; Kazantzakis' people δρασκελίζουν their thresholds instead of simply entering the house; μοχτοῦν or μάχουνται instead of simply trying; σηκοχτυποῦν κάποιον κάτω instead of thrashing him; ταυροκοιτάζονται instead of leering; καβαλλικεύονται ἀπὸ θυμὸ instead of getting angry. Abstractions or faded concretions are scrapped in favor of vivid concretions most often drawn from village life: χαρτοπόντικας (writer), μπροσταρόκριος (leader), οὐρανοθάλασσα (horizon). An indecisive person has desires that καμπανίζουν; a secretive one has something hidden κάτω ἀπὸ τὴν καταπαχτὴ τοῦ στήθους του; rainy weather is ἀνακλαημένος; an adolescent is a χνουδομάγουλος υἱός; fratricides are ἀδερφοφάδες; and so forth. All these unusual locutions (and these are obviously just the barest sampling) give Kazantzakis' novels a freshness and intensity that would be unthinkable if they had been deprived of the flexibility, variety, and inventiveness available in demotic Greek.[83]

The language in itself, I must repeat, does nothing. The novels succeed because their language is joined to vision and is therefore no longer arbitrarily imposed in order to counteract the linguistic narrowness of newspapers, schoolmasters, or professors. Nor is it coupled by violence with high poetic style or with abstract philosophical concerns, as it was in the *Odyssey*. In the poetry, the particular eccentricities of demotic tend to be merely decorative; they are felt as embellishments, as consciously "artistic" baubles on the bare dress of plot and characterization. In the novels, because we now have characters, scenes, incidents—in sum, a vision—in keeping with the language used, the linguistic eccentricities are fused into the overall substance so that they are no longer decorative, but

83. See Andriotis.

organic. None of this means that Kazantzakis' style will be pleasing to everyone. It is obviously too lush for the taste of many Anglo-Saxons in particular, but Greeks as well have found it repulsive. The influential critic Karandonis, for example, says that every page of Kazantzakis' writing exhibits the identical tone of "epic bombast," and he characterizes the language as containing "a vocabulary of immeasurable richness, a daring and fluent . . . inventiveness that surpasses every measure of good or bad taste."[84]

What I have been attempting to stress is that since language is so organically related to vision in the novels, we no longer have the right to consider it as something separate. When we complain about Kazantzakis' style, we must realize that we are complaining about his entire way of viewing the world. To suggest that the novels would have been better if written in a different way is meaningless, since a change in style would also have changed the works themselves in their essence, depriving them of their virtues at the same time that it relieved them of their faults. To suggest conversely that the language is so extraordinarily vivid that it atones for artificialities in characterization or plot is equally meaningless. The organism must be praised or condemned in its wholeness.

Again, I am not suggesting that everyone will find this wholeness to his liking. I do believe, however, that even those temperamentally at odds with Kazantzakis should recognize the novels as an aesthetically appropriate expression of their author's way of viewing life. If we are willing to grant each man his vision, even if it differs from our own, then we must see the best of the novels (*Freedom or Death*, *Saint Francis*, and especially *The Fratricides* are flawed by comparison with *Zorba*, *Christ Recrucified*, and *The Last Temptation*) as artistically genuine, as having an authenticity lacking in the works

84. Karandonis, *Periptosi*, p. 265.

where Kazantzakis was not so true to his own vision and where expression and content were not so successfully wedded.

INFUSION OF POETRY INTO THE NOVEL

To those like myself, however, who do not find Kazantzakis' vision repugnant, the novels may have an importance in other ways as well. Perhaps we can see this most clearly if we refer to another writer who is similar to Kazantzakis in his closeness to a surviving agrarian tradition and in his use of an exuberant, rhetorical demotic. The following remarks about William Faulkner also apply to Kazantzakis:[85] "Faulkner is at the moment the only writer who offers a genuine threat to the so-called common style, who is undisturbed by the ban on adjectives, who is willing to employ rhetoric and restore it to its old dignity. One often wishes that he offered a more formidable threat than he does, instead of so frequently making himself an exhibit for the defense, but even when his . . . language becomes literary rather than truly rhetorical, he has a way of suffusing an entire novel with at least the spirit of poetry."

Faulkner's "spirit of poetry" does not come in spite of the language, but because of it, excesses and all. My feeling is that Kazantzakis also suffuses his novels with this spirit. Ironically, he achieved his most convincingly poetic effects only when he abandoned verse for prose, when his deliberate cultivation of the sublime gave way to earthiness. We remember his plan for the *Akritas*, where he desired to "climb to the highest level, beyond fleshly reality,"[86] to obliterate time and place, to enjoy the real world as though it were a dream—all in an effort to duplicate the poetic achievement of Shakespeare in the final plays, and to enter the sublime "reality beyond reality." Fortunately, as I said earlier, he did not pursue this

85. Rovere, p. xi.   86. Prevelakis, p. 483.

chimera, which was so beyond his powers and incongruent with his demoticism. Instead, he reached the poetic and spiritual by indirection, through the prosaic and earthy.

The word "poetic" is a very slippery one, but if by poetic we mean some added dimension beyond the prosaic, something beyond the ordinary verifiable facts of everyday life, if this dimension can be created by unchained imagination, or by fantasy, or the intense moral urgency that E. M. Forster calls "prophecy,"[87] or even by the exaggerations found in tall tales, then I would submit that Kazantzakis' novels are indeed suffused with the spirit of poetry, and therefore worthy of our attention and respect. Carrying this still further, I would say that Kazantzakis, along with certain other novelists, has solved one of the great literary problems of his period: how to graft poetry (in the above sense) onto the realistic genre of the novel and produce a successful symbiosis in which neither the realism nor the added dimension kills off its opposite.

In large measure this problem has been one of language: how to employ in the novel the verbal richness, exuberance, and flexibility that has always been natural to poetry. The novel has tended to resist this. It grew up as a reaction against the irrelevance of much poetry to the everyday life of the middle classes, and, aspiring from the very start to a realistic portrayal of manners, morals, behavior, and speech, found itself condemned to a language that was functional and drab rather than fanciful, which obediently provided information instead of puffing itself "irresponsibly" into the operatic bravura we find in poetic drama, both Shakespearian and classical, and in lyric poetry. In short, highly imaginative, figurative language—that which we generally call poetic—drifted away from the novel, which nevertheless kept gaining ground as the dominant literary expression of the modern age.

87. In *Aspects of the Novel.*

The problem has been how to introduce poetic language into the novel, while at the same time retaining the latter's realistic orientation and making such language artistically necessary—organic—rather than merely an arbitrary imposition. Those who have solved the problem to greater or lesser degree—Joyce, Proust, Mann, Lawrence, Conrad, Faulkner—have become the supreme novelists of their period. It is obvious from the list that the solutions have been various: Joyce's expressive form; Proust's reverie; Lawrence's attempt to match in lyrical prose the ecstasy and frenzy, the very rhythms, of his embraced lovers; Conrad's sonorous sea-voice; Mann's irony. Kazantzakis' solution is closest to Faulkner's—agrarian demotic, flavored with rhetoric. Both had the advantage of writing about simple, often barely literate people whose speech and minds are effortlessly fanciful. Kazantzakis' situation was also very much that of the Irish writers at the turn of the century. For Yeats, great literature arose when individual cultivated intelligence married "the image that is born from the people."[88] J. M. Synge invoked Ireland's "popular imagination that is fiery and magnificent and tender," concluding that "those of us who wish to write, start with a chance that is not given to writers in places where the springtime of local life has been forgotten . . . and the straw has been turned into bricks."[89]

To solve the difficult artistic problem of yoking poetry to the realistic novel, Kazantzakis merely had to write "realistically" about the Greek people, employing the fanciful, poetic speech that is their endowment. At the end of his career he attested to what he had done for demotic, but perhaps did not think sufficiently of what demotic had done for him. For Psiharis' beloved *romaiika* gave to the novels the special flavor

88. This is from a conversation Yeats had with Joyce. Ellmann, pp. 87–88 (chapter 5).
89. In the Introduction to *Playboy of the Western World*.

that distinguishes them. After a decade of crusading demoticism, and another two decades of frustrations that drove him to impose his linguistic zeal upon the unreceptive subject matter of the *Odyssey*, Kazantzakis finally succeeded in wedding language to material in an aesthetically justifiable way and thus in producing the most genuine works of his career. In the translation of the *Iliad* and at least three of the novels his demoticism at long last found a proper artistic embodiment; Kazantzakis and demotic became fellow-workers, each adding stature to the other.

Epilogue

I have offered a necessarily subjective—and perhaps arbitrary
—appraisal of Kazantzakis' career in its relation to the language question. Whether his unbending demoticist extremism
was admirable or just obstinate, whether the various works
were affected for ill or for gain, are judgments depending
ultimately on individual taste. Perhaps, when all is said and
done, we must assign Kazantzakis' language to what Seferis
calls "a purism of the left" and recognize that it displays some
of the "plethora of sound, the rigidity of expression . . . , the
endless multicompounded conjured-up adjectives" that the poet deems characteristic of that demoticist purism.[1] I myself—

1. Seferis, "Elliniki Glossa," in *Dokimes*, pp. 32, 394.

always with the hesitation appropriate to any foreign speaker —believe that Kazantzakis' language, even given these characteristics, is artistically proper at least for the novels, and I hope that I have presented my case convincingly.

But we have also been dealing in this study with matters that are much less subjective. It should be clear that the extraordinary literary renaissance in Greece—something in which Kazantzakis' career played only one small part—cannot be even imagined aside from the crusade to employ the living language instead of *katharevousa*. This is not a subjective judgment or a question of taste; it is a fact. It should be clear, furthermore, that the linguistic consciousness of Greek writers, because of the language question, developed in ways not duplicated in other countries in the period under consideration. One and all, these writers were drawn into the controversy, not only in its purely linguistic form, but in the broader areas of politics and culture. The effort was—and is—to fuse some kind of viable national identity out of the classical-Byzantine past and the occidental-oriental present, out of Greek paganism and Greek Christianity, out of village and city, peasant and burgher. The one thing that has continued throughout the nation's history, and that cuts across all the contradictions, is language, and thus the crucial need to keep this too from being split and contradictory.

Kazantzakis was one among many helping to bring this ideal closer, and therefore to amalgamate the traditional with the contemporary in a meaningful way. He saw the whole of the Greek language as a single resource, the whole of Greek culture as alive and relevant for today. Naturally, he did not do everything superlatively. In his attempts to link present with past he may be much less important than Palamas, Seferis, Cavafy, or Sikelianos. His unique contribution was more the linkage of (a) pagan with Christian, (b) village solidity with his own very urban uprootedness.

What of the future? Kazantzakis' particular response to the language question—the intransigence about every inflectional detail, the obsession with preserving words at all cost—is outdated, probably even self-defeating, since extremism in Greece always seems to provoke extreme reversals. Though necessary and indeed noble at a time when demotic was establishing itself, it does not appear relevant to the present situation in which the spoken language, much more stabilized, thanks to the work of Triantafyllidis and the other stalwarts of the Educational Association, enjoys a momentum stronger than the edicts of governmental regimes.

Thus Kazantzakis' books will most likely not be taken as models for correct style in the future; his importance will be more historical—as one of many who helped to cultivate the language and prove its versatility. For he was born in the crucial period when men-of-letters in Greece had the extraordinary challenge of taking the third *koine* in Greek history and making it, unlike the spoken *koines* of hellenistic or of Byzantine times, the medium of sophisticated writing. As I have said, he was one of the lesser figures in this endeavor, and moreover one who may not be very relevant to the future evolution of demotic. In the long run, the significance of his demoticism will most likely appear to be more private than public, more artistic than cultural—namely, the way in which it expressed the excessive and intransigent soul of a man whom fate had thrown right into the eye of an extraordinary linguistic storm. Kazantzakis' continuing importance for the development of the Greek language may perhaps be questioned; the importance of the Greek language for the development of Kazantzakis may not.

Bibliography

Books are listed alphabetically, according to the abbreviations employed in the footnotes. For books in Greek, Athens is the place of publication, unless another place is given. Items included in G. K. Katsimbalis' Bibliography of Kazantzakis are so indicated by a K followed by their number in the Bibliography.

Alexiou, E.: Ἀλεξίου, Ἕλλης. Γιὰ νὰ γίνει μεγάλος. 1966.

Alexiou, L.: Ἀλεξίου, Λευτέρη. "Δάντη, Ἡ Θεία Κωμωδία, στὰ ἑλληνικὰ ἀπὸ τὸ Ν. Καζαντζάκη." Τὸ Κάστρο, Ἡρακλείου, Ἰούν. 1937, σελ. 11–50. (K 923)

Andriotis: Ἀνδριώτη, Ν. Π. "Ἡ γλώσσα τοῦ Καζαντζάκη." Νέα Ἑστία, Χριστούγεννα, 1959, σελ. 90–95.

Apology: [Τριανταφυλλίδη, Μ.] "Ἀπολογία τῆς δημοτικῆς." Δελτίο τοῦ Ἐκπαιδευτικοῦ Ὁμίλου, τόμ. Δ´ (1914), 46–196.

Arharios: Ἀρχαρίου Δημοτικιστή. "Κόλπα καὶ πολιτική." Νουμᾶς, 12 Δεκ. 1910, σελ. 269. (Κ 801).

Asteriotis: Astériotis, Démétrius. Lettres neo-Grecque. *Mercure de France*, 15 Dec. 1928, p. 723.

Atkinson: Atkinson, B. F. C. *The Greek Language*. London 1933.

Avyeris: Αὐγέρη, Μ. " Ἡ νέα Ὀδύσσεια." Νέα Ἑστία, 15 Σεπτ. καὶ 1 Ὀκτ. 1939, σελ. 1247–56, 1344–49. (Κ 942).

Bachtin: Bachtin, Nicholas. *Introduction to the Study of Modern Greek*. Cambridge 1935.

Bien: Bien, Peter. *Nikos Kazantzakis*. N.Y. & London 1972. (Columbia Essays on Modern Writers.)

Biography: Kazantzakis, Helen. *Nikos Kazantzakis: A Biography*. N.Y. 1968.

Browning: Browning, R. *Medieval and Modern Greek*. London 1969.

Campbell and Sherrard: Campbell, John and Philip Sherrard. *Modern Greece*. London 1968.

Castiglione: Castiglione, B. *The Book of the Courtier*, tr. George Bull. Penguin Books, 1967.

Chaconas: Chaconas, Stephen George. *Adamantios Korais, A Study in Greek Nationalism*. N.Y. 1942.

Chronicle of the Morea: *Chronicle of the Morea*, τὸ Χρονικὸν τοῦ Μορέως . . . ed. John Schmitt. London 1904. (Byzantine Texts, ed. J. B. Bury.)

Clogg, Bible Society: Clogg, Richard. "The Correspondence of Adhamantios Korais with the British and Foreign Bible Society." *Greek Orthodox Theological Review* (Brookline, Massachusetts), XIV (1969), 65–84. (Spring 1969)

Clogg, Burgess: Clogg, Richard. "The Correspondence of Adhamantios Korais with Thomas Burgess 1789–1792." *Anzeiger der phil.-hist. Klasse der Österreichischen Akademie der Wissenschaften*, 106 (1969), So. 3, pp. 40–72.

Costas: Costas, P. S. *An Outline of the History of the Greek Language*, with particular emphasis on the *koine* and the subsequent periods. Chicago 1936.

Delmouzos: Δελμούζου, Α. Π. " Ὁ δημοτικισμὸς καὶ ἡ ἐπίδρασή του στὴν ἑλληνικὴ παιδεία." Νέα Ἑστία, 1 Νοεμ. 1939, σελ. 1463–71.

Delmouzos, To protypon: ———. "Τὸ πρότυπον δημοτικὸν σχολεῖον καὶ οἱ ἐπικριταί του." Δελτίο τοῦ Ἐκπαιδευτικοῦ Ὁμίλου, τόμ. Α′ (1911), 14–52.

Deltio: Δελτίο τοῦ Ἐκπαιδευτικοῦ Ὁμίλου.

Digenis Akritas: Les Exploits de Digénis Akritas, épopée byzantine du dixième siècle, publiée pour la première fois d'après le manuscrit unique de Trébizonde, par C. Sathas et E. Legrand. Paris 1875.

　　Digenes Akrites. Edited with an introduction, translation and commentary by John Mavrogordato. Oxford 1956.

Dimaras: Δημαρᾶ, Κ. Θ. Ἱστορία τῆς νεοελληνικῆς λογοτεχνίας, τρίτη ἔκδοση. 1964.

Dimos Irakleiou: Δῆμος Ἡρακλείου Κρήτης. Ἀναμνηστικὸ λεύκωμα Νίκου Καζαντζάκη. 1961.

Dragoumis: Δραγούμη, Ι. Ἑλληνικὸς πολιτισμός. 1913.

———. Μαρτύρων καὶ ἡρώων αἷμα. 1907.

———. Ὅσοι ζωντανοί. 1911.

———. Σαμοθράκη. 1909.

Dragoumis, Megali Idea: ———. [Ἴδα]. "Ἡ Μεγάλη Ἰδέα." Νουμᾶς, 11 Ὀκτ. 1909, σελ. 6.

Dreux: Dreux, Bathilde, "Panorama de la littérature grecque." Les Nouvelles Littéraires, 4 janvier 1930, p. 6.

Duckworth: Duckworth, H. T. F. Notes on Alexander Pallis' Romaic Version of the New Testament. Cambridge 1906.

Ellmann: Ellmann, R. The Identity of Yeats. London 1964.

Episima: Ἐπίσημα Πρακτικὰ Ἐφημερίδος Συζητήσεων τῆς Βουλῆς (1911).

Evelpidis: Εὐελπίδη, Χρύσου. "Ὁ Καζαντζάκης γιὰ τὸ ἔργο του καὶ γιὰ τὴν ἑλληνικὴ λογοτεχνία." Κρητικὴ Πρωτοχρονιά, 1962, 192–94.

Fanourakis: Φανουράκη, Γεωργίου Α. "Ἑρμηνευτικὲς παρατηρήσεις στὸν Καπετὰν Μιχάλη." Καινούρια Ἐποχή Φθιν. 1958, σελ. 184–99.

Fauriel: Fauriel, C. Chants populaires de la Grèce moderne, 2 vol. Paris 1824–25.

Ferguson: Ferguson, Charles, "Diglossia," Word, xv (1959), 325–40.

Fotiadis: Φωτιάδη, Φώτη. Τὸ γλωσσικὸ ζήτημα καὶ ἡ ἐκπαιδευτική μας ἀναγέννησις. 1902.

Geanakoplos: Geanakoplos, Deno J. *Greek Scholars in Venice*. Cambridge, Mass., 1962.

Ghavriilidis, Lakonika: [Γαβριηλίδη, Β.] "Λακωνικά. Ὁ νέος συγγραφεύς." Ἀκρόπολις, 8 Μαΐου 1907. Ξανατ. στὴ Νέα Ἑστία, 15 Μαΐου 1958, σελ. 751. (Κ 749)

Glinos, Enas Ataphos: Γληνοῦ, Δ. "Ἕνας ἄταφος νεκρός: μελέτες γιὰ τὸ ἐκπαιδευτικό μας σύστημα. 1925.

Glinos, Ethnos: ———. "Ἔθνος καὶ γλώσσα. Δελτίο τοῦ Ἐκπαιδευτικοῦ Ὁμίλου, τόμ. 5 (1916), 47–62, τόμ. 10 (1922), 47–93.

Glinos, I Krisi: ———. "Ἡ κρίση τοῦ δημοτικισμοῦ." Δελτίο τοῦ Ἐκπαιδευτικοῦ Ὁμίλου τόμ. 11 (1923–24), 3–45.

Glinos, Oi hoiroi: ———. [Γαβριὴλ, Ἀντ.] Οἱ χοῖροι ὑΐζουσιν, τὰ χοιρίδια κοΐζουσιν, οἱ ὄφεις ἰΰζουσιν. 1921.

Glinos, Paideia: ———. [Δ. Φ.] "Παιδεία καὶ πολιτική." Δελτίο τοῦ Ἐκπ. Ὁμ. τόμ. 9 (1921) 94–98.

Hadzidakis: Χατζιδάκη, Γ. Μελέτη ἐπὶ τῆς Νέας Ἑλληνικῆς ἢ Βάσανος τοῦ ἐλέγχου τοῦ ψευδαττικισμοῦ. 1884.

Haris, M.: Χάρη, Μάνου. "Ἡ σχέση Καζαντζάκη καὶ νέων." Δῆμος Ἡρακλείου Κρήτης, Ἀναμνηστικὸ λεύκωμα Νίκου Καζαντζάκη. 1961.

Haris, P.: Χάρη, Πέτρου. "Τὸ τραγούδι τῶν Ἑλλήνων." Νέα Ἑστία, Χριστούγεννα 1959, σελ. 129–30.

Homer, Iliad: Ὁμήρου. Ἰλιάδα, μετάφραση Ν. Καζαντζάκη-Ι. Θ. Κακριδῆ. 1955.

Hortatsis: Χορτάτση, Γ. Ἐρωφίλη. Κριτικὴ ἔκδοση Σ. Ξανθουδίδη. 1928.

Hourmouzios: Χουρμουζίου, Αἰμ. "Δημοτικισμὸς καὶ πεζὸς λόγος." Νέα Ἑστία, 1 Νοεμ. 1939, σελ. 1440–52.

Householder: Householder, F. W. "Greek Diglossia," *Georgetown University Monograph Series on Languages and Linguistics*, no. 15 (1962), 109–29.

Jouvenel, En Souvenir: Jouvenel, Renaud de. "En Souvenir de Kazantzaki." *Europe*, Juin 1958, pp. 85–105. Reprinted in *Nea Estia*, 1 Nov. 1962, pp. 1570–84.

Kakridis: Κακριδῆ, Ι. Θ. "Τὸ χρονικὸ μιᾶς συνεργασίας." Νέα Ἑστία, Χριστούγεννα 1959, σελ. 115–20.

———, metaphrase: ———. Ἡ μετάφραση τῆς Ἰλιάδας. Καινούρια Ἐποχή, Χειμώνας 1956, σελ. 17–64.

——, N. K.: ——. Νίκος Καζαντζάκης. Καινούρια Ἐποχή, Φθινόπωρο 1959, σελ. 17-27.

Kalligas: Καλλιγâ, Παύλου. Θάνος Βλέκας. 1923.

Kaloyeropoulos: [Καλογεροπούλου, Δ. Ι.] " Ὄφις καὶ Κρίνο."
Πινακοθήκη, Φεβρ. 1906, σελ. 228-29. Ξανατ. στὴ Νέα
Ἑστία, 1 Μαΐου 1958, σελ. 689-90. (Κ 737)

Kaltchas: Kaltchas, N. Introduction to the Constitutional History of Modern Greece. N.Y. 1940.

Karandonis: Καραντώνη, Ἀντρέα. Εἰσαγωγὴ στὴ νεώτερη
ποίηση. 1958.

Karandonis, Periptosi: ——. " Ἡ περίπτωση Καζαντζάκη."
Καινούρια Ἐποχή, Φθινόπωρο 1958, σελ. 265-67.

Katsimbalis—Κατσίμπαλη, Γ. Κ. Βιβλιογραφία Ν. Καζαντζάκη, Α΄ 1906-1948. 1958.

Katsimbalis, O agnostos Kazantzakis: ——. " Ὁ ἄγνωστος
Καζαντζάκης." Νέα Ἑστία, τόμ. 63-64 (1958).

Kazantzaki, Galateia: Καζαντζάκη, Γαλάτειας. Ἄνθρωποι καὶ
Ὑπεράνθρωποι. 1957.

Kazantzakis, Dante: Καζαντζάκη, Νίκου. Δάντη. Ἡ Θεία
Κωμωδία, στὰ Ἑλληνικὰ ἀπὸ τὸν Ν. Καζαντζάκη. 1934.
(Κ 39)

——, [defense of Spasmenes . . .]: ——. "Σπασμένες Ψυχὲς" [ἄρθρο ἐπεξηγηματικὸ]. Νουμᾶς, 27 Σεπτ. 1909,
σελ. 2-4. Ξανατ. στὴ Νέα Ἑστία, 1 Ὀκτ. 1958, σελ. 1498-
1501. (Κ 143)

——, Ellinika poiimata: ——. "Φιλολογικαὶ Ἐπιστολαί.
Ἑλληνικὰ ποιήματα." Νέον Ἄστυ, 16 Φεβρ. 1909. Ξανατ.
στὴ Νέα Ἑστία, 1 Σεπτ. 1958, σελ. 1288-90. (Κ 232)

——, Ena anoichto: ——. " Ἕνα ἀνοιχτὸ γράμμα γιὰ
τὴν Κα Ἕλλη Λαμπρίδη." Νεοελληνικὰ Γράμματα, 25
Μαρτ. 1939, σελ. 13. (Κ 191)

——, Ena scholio: ——. " Ἕνα σχόλιο στὴν ʼ Ὀδύσεια'." Νέα Ἑστία, 15 Αὐγ. 1943, σελ. 1028-34. (Κ 197)

——, England: ——. England. N.Y. 1965.

——, Epistoles: ——. Ἐπιστολὲς πρὸς τὴ Γαλάτεια. 1958.

——, Faust: ——. Γκαῖτε: "Φάουστ". Καθημερινή, 7
Σεπτ. 1936 . . . 5 Ἰουλ. 1937. (Κ 725, 727)

——, glossary: ——. Λεξιλόγιο τῆς Ὀδύσειας.

——, Hairetismos ston Iona Dragoumi: ——. "Χαιρετισμὸς στὸν Ἴωνα Δραγούμη." Νέα Ἑστία, 15 Μαρτ. 1941, σελ. 223. (Κ 87)

——, H. Bergson: ——. "H. Bergson" (Ἀνατύπωμα ἀπὸ τὸ Δελτίο τοῦ Ἐκπαιδευτικοῦ Ὁμίλου, Ὀκτ. 1912). 1912. (Κ 6, 160)

——, I ekti epeteios: ——. " Ἡ ἕκτη ἐπέτειος. Ἴων Δραγούμης." Ἐλεύθερος Τύπος, 1 Αὐγ. 1926. Ξανατ. στὴ Νέα Ἑστία, τόμ. 68, σελ. 978–80. (Κ 170)

——, Japan-China: ——. *Japan-China*. N.Y. 1963.

——, Journey to the Morea: ——. *Journey to the Morea*. N.Y. 1965.

——, Kritika meletimata: ——. "Κριτικὰ μελετήματα. Γιὰ τοὺς νέους μας." Νέα Ζωή, Ἀλεξανδρείας, Φεβρ.-Ἀπρ. 1910, σελ. 232–39. (Κ 149)

——, La littérature grecque contemporaine: ——. "La littérature grecque contemporaine." *Monde*, 16 Mars 1929, p. 5.

——, [letters to his father]: ——. "Δέκα ἀνέκδοτες ἐπιστολὲς τοῦ Καζαντζάκη." Νέα Ἑστία, Χριστούγεννα 1959, σελ. 203–10.

——, Letter to Lefteris Alexiou: ——. " Ἀπάντηση σὲ κριτικὴ τοῦ Λ. Ἀλεξίου γιὰ τὴ μετάφρασή του τῆς Θείας Κωμωδίας' τοῦ Δάντη." Τὸ Κάστρο, Ἡρακλείου, Ἰούν. 1937, σελ. 3–10. (Κ 187)

——, Masterbuilder: ——. Πέτρου Ψηλορείτη. Ὁ Πρωτομάστορας. 1910. (Κ 11)

——, Meta tin kritiki: ——. "Μετὰ τὴν κριτικὴ τῆς κ. Λαμπρίδη γιὰ τὴν ' Ὀδύσεια'." Νεοελληνικὰ Γράμματα, 22 Ἀπρ. 1939, σελ. 2. (Κ 192)

——, Odysseia: ——. Ὀδύσεια. 1938. (Κ 27)

——, Oi Ellines spoudastai: ——. " Ἐπισολαὶ ἀπὸ τὸ Παρίσι. Οἱ Ἕλληνες σπουδασταί." Νέον Ἄστυ, 8 Μαρτ. 1908. Ξανατ. στὴ Νέα Ἑστία, 1 Σεπτ. 1958, σελ. 1284–85. (Κ 230)

——, Ophis kai Krino: ——. Κάρμα Νιρβαμῆ. Ὄφις καὶ Κρίνο. 1906. (Κ 1)

——, Ragiades: ——. "Οἱ Ραγιάδες." Ἀκρόπολις, 21 Ἰουν. 1910. Ξανατ. στὴ Νέα Ἑστία, 15 Ὀκτ. 1958, σελ. 1563–64. (Κ 153)

———, Report to Greco: ———. *Report to Greco*. N.Y. 1965.

———, Spain: ———. *Spain*. N.Y. 1963.

———, Spasmenes: ———. "Σπασμένες Ψυχές." Νουμᾶς, ἀπὸ 30 Αὐγ. 1909 μέχρι 7 Φεβρ. 1910. (Κ 91)

———, Syllogos: ———. "Σύλλογος Δημοτικιστῶν Ἡρακλείου Κρήτης ' Ὁ Σολωμός'." Νουμᾶς, 7 Ἰουν. 1909, σελ. 9–12. (Κ 140)

———, Synchroni: ———. Σύγχρονη Ἰσπανικὴ λυρικὴ ποίηση. Κύκλος Β' (1933–34) 41–57, 98–105, 142–56, 233–60, 409–28. (Κ 718–722)

———, Taxidevondas: ———. Ταξιδεύοντας: Ἰσπανία, Ἰταλία, Αἴγυπτος, Σινᾶ. Ἀλεξάνδρεια 1927. (Κ 19)

———, Tertzines: ———. Τερτσίνες. 1960.

———, Toda Raba: ———. *Toda Raba*. Paris 1962; N.Y. 1964.

———, To glossikon mas zitima: ———. "Τὸ γλωσσικόν μας ζήτημα." Ἀκρόπολις, 31 Μαΐου, 1907. (Κ 135)

———, Zorba: ———. *Zorba the Greek*. N.Y. 1953.

[Additional material by Kazantzakis may be found under the headings: Biography, Homer, Prevelakis.]

Kontos: Κόντου, Κωνσταντίνου Σ. Γλωσσικαὶ Παρατηρήσεις. 1882.

Korais, Atakta: Κοραῆ, Λ. Ἄτακτα, τόμ. Α'-Ε'. Παρίσι, 1828–1835.

———, Epistoli: ———. "Τὰ εἰς τὴν ἔκδοσιν (1804) τῶν Αἰθιοπικῶν τοῦ Ἡλιοδώρου προλεγόμενα. Ἐπιστολὴ πρὸς Ἀλέξανδρον Βασιλείου. Περὶ . . . τῆς κατὰ μικρὸν βαρβαρωθείσης Ἑλληνικῆς, καὶ τῆς ἐξ αὐτῆς γεννηθείσης τῶν Γραικῶν γλώσσης." Συλλογὴ τῶν εἰς τὴν Ἑλληνικὴν Βιβλιοθήκην, καὶ τὰ πάρεργα προλεγομένων, καὶ τινῶν συγγραμματίων τοῦ Ἀδαμαντίου Κοραῆ. Παρίσι, 1833.

———, Syllogi: ———. Συλλογὴ τῶν . . . συγγραμματίων τοῦ Ἀδαμαντίου Κοραῆ. Παρίσι, 1833.

———, Ton meta: ———. Τῶν μετὰ θάνατον εὑρεθέντων συγγραμάτων, τόμ. στ'. Ἐπιμέλεια Ν. Μ. Δαμαλᾶ. 1888.

Kordatos: Κορδάτου, Ἰω. Ἡ κοινωνικὴ σημασία τῆς Ἑλληνικῆς ἐπαναστάσεως τοῦ 1821. Δ' ἔκ., 1946.

Kordatos, Istoria: ———. Ἱστορία τοῦ γλωσσικοῦ μας ζητήματος. 1943.

Kornaros: Κορνάρου, Β. Ἐρωτόκριτος. Κριτικὴ ἔκδοση Σ. Ξανθουδίδη. Ἡράκλειον 1915, Ἀθήνα 1952, 1967.
———: *The Erotokritos of Vincenzo Kornaros*: A Greek romantic epic, 1645. Ed. John Mavrogordato. London 1929.
Krumbacher: Krumbacher, K. Τὸ πρόβλημα τῆς νεωτέρας γραφομένης Ἑλληνικῆς . . . καὶ ἀπάντησις εἰς αὐτόν. Ὑπὸ Γεωργίου Ν. Χατζιδάκι. 1905.
———: ———. *Geschichte der byzantinischen Litteratur von Justinian bis zum Ende des Oströmischen Reiches*, 527–1453. Munich, 1891, 1897.
———: ———. Ἱστορία τῆς Βυζαντινῆς λογοτεχνίας. Μεταφ. Γεωργίου Σωτηριάδη. 3 τόμ. 1897–1900 (1901).
Lambridi: Λαμπρίδη, Ἕλλης. " Ἡ ' Ὀδύσσεια' τοῦ Ν. Καζαντζάκη. III. Ἡ μορφή της." Νεοελληνικὰ Γράμματα, 15 Ἀπρ. 1939, σελ. 10–11. (K 937)
Laourdas, Odysseia: Λαούρδα, Β. Ἡ " Ὀδύσσεια" τοῦ Καζαντζάκη. 1943. (K 960)
Laourdas, Scholio: ———. "Σχόλιο σ' ἕνα κριτικὸ δοκίμιο." Νέα Ἑστία, 15 Νοεμ. 1943, σελ. 1336–41. Ξανατ. εἰς Ζωγράφου, σελ. 270. (K 967)
———, Trisevyene: ———. Ἡ ἐποχὴ τῆς "Τρισεύγενης". Θεσσαλονίκη 1964. (Κρατικὸν Θέατρον Βορείου Ἑλλάδος, σειρὰ διαλέξεων περιόδου 1963–1964, 2.)
Lawrence: Lawrence, D. H. *Studies in Classic American Literature*, N.Y. 1964.
Layton: Layton, Evro. "Nikodemos Metaxas, the First Greek Printer in the Eastern World." *Harvard Library Bulletin*, v. 15, no. 2 (1967), 140–68.
Legrand: Legrand, E. *Bibliothèque Grecque Vulgaire*. Paris 1880–1913.
Machairas: Machairas, Leontios. *Recital concerning the sweet land of Cyprus entitled 'Chronicle'*. Edited with a translation and notes by R. M. Dawkins. 2 vols. Oxford 1932.
Markakis: Μαρκάκη, Πέτρου. " Ἀνέκδοτα γράμματα τοῦ Νίκου Καζαντζάκη. Τὸ περιοδικὸ 'Πινακοθήκη' κι ὁ Δημ. Καλογερόπουλος." Καινούρια Ἐποχή, Φθινόπωρο 1959, σελ. 30–38.
Marshall: Marshall, F. H. *Three Cretan Plays*: The Sacrifice of Abraham, Erophile and Gyparis, also the Cretan pas-

toral poem The Fair Shepherdess, translated from the Greek, Oxford-London 1929.

Maximus of Gallipoli: Ἡ Καινὴ Διαθήκη τοῦ Κυρίου ἡμῶν Ἰησοῦ Χριστοῦ, Δίγλωττος. Ἐν ᾗ ἀντιπροσώπως τότε θεῖον πρωτότυπον καὶ ἡ ἀπαραλλάκτως ἐξ ἐκείνου εἰς ἁπλὴν διάλεκτον, ὅλα τοῦ μακαρίτου κυρίου Μαξίμου τοῦ Καλλιουπολίτου γινομένη μετάφρασις ... [Γενεύη] 1638.

Megas: Μέγα, Α. Ε. Ἱστορία τοῦ γλωσσικοῦ ζητήματος. 2 τόμ. 1925-27.

Meriwether: Meriwether, James B. & Michael Millgate. *Lion in the Garden*: Interviews with Wm. Faulkner, 1926-1962. N.Y. 1968.

Mihailidis: Μιχαηλίδη, Κ. Μ. Ὁ Βερναρδάκης καὶ τὸ γλωσσικό. Νέα Γράμματα Α΄ (1935), 192-204.

Mirambel: Mirambel. A. "La doctrine linguistique de Jean Psichari," *La Nouvelle Clio* 3 (1957), 78-104.

Modern Greek Writers: *Modern Greek Writers*: Solomos, Calvos, Matessis, Palamas, Cavafy, Kazantzakis, Seferis. Princeton 1972. (Proceedings of the Modern Greek Study Association's 1969 Symposium.)

Neoellinas: Νεοέλληνας. "Ὁ ἰδιαίτερος." Νουμᾶς, 21 Φεβρ. 1915, σελ. 88. (Κ 817). Κοίτα καὶ Ἑλλάς, 25 Αὐγ. 1913, ξανατ. στὴ Νέα Ἑστία, 1 Νοεμ. 1958, σελ. 1616-17.

Palamas, K.: Παλαμᾶ, Κωστῆ. Ἅπαντα. 1962-69.

Palamas, K. Trisevyene: Palamas, Kostes. *Royal Blossom*, or Trisevyene, tr. A. E. Phoutrides. New Haven 1923. (Greek text in Apanta IV, 185-292.)

Palamas, K., Ophis: ———. Διαγόρας. Κάρμα Νιρβαμῆ "Ὄφις καὶ Κρίνο". Παναθήναια, 15 Φεβρ. 1906, σελ. 281. Ξανατ. στὴ Νέα Ἑστία, 15 Ἀπρ. 1958, σελ. 615. (Κ 738)

Palamas, L.: Παλαμᾶ, Λεάνδρου. "Ἴων Δραγούμης." Δελτίο τοῦ Ἐκπαιδευτικοῦ Ὁμίλου, τόμ. 9 (1921), 99-108.

Pallis, Iliad: Ὁμήρου Ἰλιάδα. 1904.

Pallis, New Testament: Ἡ Νέα Διαθήκη, κατὰ τὸ Βατικανὸ χερόγραφο. Μεταφρασμένη ἀπὸ τὸν Ἀλέξ. Πάλλη. Liverpool, 1910.

Papandreou, I diki: Παπανδρέου, Γ. "Ἡ δίκη τοῦ Ναυπλίου."

Δελτίο τοῦ Ἐκπαιδευτικοῦ Ὁμίλου, τὸμ. 5 (1915), 194–205.

Papandreou, Ta oria: ———. "Τὰ ὅρια τοῦ δημοτικισμοῦ." Δελτίο τοῦ Ἐκπαιδευτικοῦ Ὁμίλου, τόμ. 4 (1914), 297–300.

Paparrhegopoulos: Παπαρρηγοπούλου, Κ. Ἱστορία τοῦ ἑλληνικοῦ ἔθνους ἀπὸ τῶν ἀρχαιοτάτων χρόνων μέχρι τῆς σήμερον. 5 τόμ. 1860–72.

Paraschos: Παράσχου, Κλέωνος. Ν. Καζαντζάκη " Ὀδύσεια". Νέα Ἑστία, 1 Σεπτ. 1939, σελ. 1225–31. (Κ 941). Ξανατ. στὸ βιβλίο του: Κύκλοι, 1939.

Politis: Πολίτη, Ν. Γ. Ἐκλογαὶ ἀπὸ τὰ τραγούδια τοῦ ἑλληνικοῦ λαοῦ. Ἕκτη ἔκδοση. 1969.

Prevelakis: Τετρακόσια γράμματα τοῦ Καζαντζάκη στόν Πρεβελάκη. 1965.

Prevelakis, O Poiitis: Πρεβελάκη, Π. Ὁ Ποιητὴς καὶ τὸ ποίημα τῆς Ὀδύσσειας. 1958.

Psiharis: Ψυχάρη. Τὸ ταξίδι μου, ἔκδοση Γ΄. 1926.

Psiharis, brief article: ———. "Ψυχολογικὲς σημειωσούλες. (Ἕνα καινούριο ρομάντζο . . .)." Νουμᾶς, 8 καὶ 15 Νοεμ. 1909. (Κ 784)

Rangabé: Rangabé, A. R. *Précis d'une histoire de la littérature néo-hellénique.* Berlin 1877.

Rankavis: See Rangabé.

Rodas: Ροδᾶ, Μ. " Ἡ δημοτικὴ γλώσσα στὸ θέατρο." Νέα Ἑστία, 1 Νοεμ. 1939, σελ. 1453–57.

Rovere: Rovere, Richard. *Introduction to Light in August* by Wm. Faulkner. N.Y., Modern Library, 1950.

Rutherford: Rutherford, W. G. *The New Phrynichus.* London 1881.

Sakellaropoulos: Ἔκθεσις περὶ τοῦ Λασσανείου Δραματικοῦ Διαγωνισμοῦ, ἀναγνωσθεῖσα ἐν τῷ Ἐθνικῷ Πανεπιστημίῳ τῇ 16 Μαΐου 1910 ὑπὸ τοῦ εἰσηγητοῦ Σ. Κ. Σακελλαροπούλου. 1910. (Κ 787). Ξανατ. στὴ Παναθήναια, 31 Μαΐου 1910, σελ. 119–21 (Κ 796) καὶ στὴ Νέα Ἑστία, 15 Ὀκτ. 1958, σελ. 1560–63.

Seferis: Σεφέρη, Γ. Δοκιμές. Β΄ ἔκ. 1962.

Semenov: Semenov, Anatol F. *The Greek Language in its Evolution.* London 1936.

Sherrard: Sherrard, Philip. *The Greek East and the Latin West*. Oxford 1959.

Siapkaras: Siapkaras-Pitsillidès, Thémis. *Le Pétrarquisme en Chypre*: Poèmes d'amour en dialecte chypriote d'après un manuscrit du xvie siècle. Athens 1952.

Sideris: Σιδέρη, Γιάννη. "Τὸ Ξημερώνει, ὁ σκηνοθέτης καὶ ὁ θίασός του." Νέα Ἑστία, 1 Ἰουλίου 1958, σελ. 1030–31.

Siomopoulos: Σιωμοπούλου, Τάκη. 'Αλέξανδρος Πάλλης (κριτικὴ μελέτη). 'Ανάτυπον ἐκ τοῦ περιοδικοῦ " 'Ηπειρωτικὴ Ἑστία", τόμ. Δ'. Ἰωάννινα 1955.

Solomos: Σολωμοῦ, Διονυσίου. Διάλογος. Ἅπαντα. Ἔκδοση Λ. Πολίτη. 1955. Τόμ. Β', σελ. 11–27.

Sotiriou: Σωτηρίου, Κ. Δ. Ὁ Γληνὸς παιδαγωγός. Στὴ Μνήμη Δημητρίου Α. Γληνοῦ: Μελέτες γιὰ τὸ ἔργο του καὶ ἀνέκδοτα κείμενά του. 1946.

Soutsos: Σούτσου, Παναγιώτου. Νέα Σχολὴ τοῦ γραφομένου λόγου. 1853.

Stavrou: Σταύρου, Θρ. " 'Ομήρου Ἰλιάδα." Νέα Ἑστία, Χριστούγεννα 1959, σελ. 120–25.

Synadinou: Συναδινοῦ, Θ. Ν. "Μία συνέντευξη γιὰ τὸ Νίκο Καζαντζάκη." Καινούρια Ἐποχή, Χειμώνας 1957, σελ. 220–26.

Synge: Synge, J. M. *The Playboy of the Western World*.

Tankopoulos, Oi Krites: [Ταγκοπούλου, Δ. Π.] "Παραγραφάκια, Οἱ κριτὲς βραβευτήκανε." Νουμᾶς, 23 Μαΐου 1910, σελ. 5. (Κ 795)

———, Ο Idios: ———. " 'Ο ἴδιος. Ὅ,τι θέλετε." Νουμᾶς, 13 Μαΐου 1907, σελ. 8. (Κ 756)

———, Ο Pantelideios: ———. " 'Ο Παντελίδειος κι' ὁ λόγος τοῦ Λάμπρου." Νουμᾶς, 13 Μαΐου 1907. Ξανατ. στὴ Νέα Ἑστία, 15 Μαΐου 1958, σελ. 755–56. (Κ 755)

———, Paragrafakia: ———. "Παραγραφάκια." Νουμᾶς, 27 Μαΐου 1907, σελ. 5. (Κ 760)

Theatis: Θεατή. "Ξημερώνει". Ἑστία, 8 Ἰουλ. 1907. Ξανατ. στὴ Νέα Ἑστία, 1 Ἰουν. 1958, σελ. 849. (Κ 764)

Theotokas, Dragoumis kai Barrès: Θεοτοκᾶ, Γ. " Ἕνας ἄλλος Δραγούμης: Α', Δραγούμης καὶ Μπαρὲς." 'Αναγέννηση, Μάϊος 1928, σελ. 394–99.

———, Neoelliniko: ———. Νεοελληνικὸ Λαϊκὸ θέατρο. 1965.

———, Ta provlimata: ———. "Τὰ προβλήματα τοῦ αἰώνος."
Τὸ Βῆμα, 21 Σεπτ. 1958.

Thomson: Thomson, G. *The Greek Language*. Cambridge
1960.

———. Ἡ Ἑλληνικὴ Γλῶσσα ἀρχαία καὶ νέα. 1964.

Thrylos: Θρύλου, Ἄλκη. Ὁ Πρωτομάστορας. Νουμᾶς, 30
Ἰαν. 1916, σελ. 16–17. (Κ 818)

Triantafyllidis: Τριανταφυλλίδη, Μ. Ἀπολογία τῆς δημοτικῆς. Δελτίο τοῦ Ἐκπαιδευτικοῦ Ὁμίλου, τόμ. 4 (1914),
σελ. 46–196. (Ἄπαντα, τόμ. 4, σελ. 119–252.)

———, Apanta: ———. Ἄπαντα. Θεσσαλονίκη 1963.

———, Apo ti glossiki: ———. Ἀπὸ τὴ γλωσσική μας ἱστορία: Βερναρδάκης—Κόντος—Χατζιδάκης. Ἄπαντα, τόμ.
5, σελ. 278–307.

———, Eisagogi: ———. Νεοελληνικὴ γραμματική, τόμ. Α΄:
ἱστορικὴ εἰσαγωγή. 1938.

———, I glossa mas: ———. Ἡ γλῶσσα μας στὰ χρόνια 1914–
1916. Ἡ δημοτικὴ στὴν παιδεία. Δελτίο τοῦ Ἐκπαιδευτικοῦ Ὁμίλου, τόμ. 8 (1920), 4–99. (Ἄπαντα, τόμ. 4,
σελ. 380–416.)

———, Katathesi: ———. Κατάθεση στὴ δίκη τοῦ Ι. Θ. Κακριδῆ. Ἄπαντα, τόμ. 5, σελ. 453–82.

———, Neohellenic Grammar: ———. Νεοελληνικὴ γραμ-
ματικὴ (τῆς δημοτικῆς). 1941.

———, Niki: ———. Νίκη. Δελτίο τοῦ Ἐκπαιδευτικοῦ Ὁμίλου, τόμ. 6 (1916), 1–5. (Ἄπαντα, τόμ. 8, σελ. 177–81.)

———, Quo-usque: ———. Quo-usque tandem. Ἡ γλωσσο-
εκπαιδευτικὴ μεταρρύθμιση. Δελτίο τοῦ Ἐκπαιδευτικοῦ
Ὁμίλου, τόμ. 7 (1917–1919), 86–195. (Ἄπαντα, τόμ. 4,
σελ. 491 κ.ἕ.)

———, Stathmoi: ———. Σταθμοὶ τῆς γλωσσικῆς μας ἱστο-
ρίας: Ὁ Ἀττικισμὸς καὶ ἡ ἀρχὴ τῆς διγλωσσίας. Ἡ
Νέα Διαθήκη καὶ ὁ πρῶτος Δημοτικισμός. Ἄπαντα, τόμ.
5, σελ. 308–65.

Tsirimokos: [Τσιριμώκου, Ι.] Ἐκπαιδευτικὰ νομοσχέδια,
γενικὴ εἰσηγητικὴ ἔκθεσις. 1913.

Venezis: Βενέζη, Ἠλία. εἰς Ἀκρόπολις, 24 Μαΐου 1964, σελ.
5.

Vernardakis: [Βερναρδάκη, Δημητρίου]. Ψευαττικισμοῦ

Ἔλεγχος ἤτοι Κ. Σ. Κόντου Γλωσσικῶν Παρατηρήσεων Ἀναφερομένων εἰς τὴν Νέαν Ἑλληνικὴν Γλῶσσαν ἀνασκευή, ὑπὸ * * *. Ἐν Τεργέστῃ, 1884.

Vlastos, Greek bilingualism: Vlasto, Peter. Greek Bilingualism and some parallel cases. Athens 1933.

Vlastos, Kritikes anapodies: [Βλαστοῦ, Πέτρου] " Ἕρμονας. Κριτικὲς ἀναποδιές. Α΄. Ὄφις καὶ Κρίνο. Κάρμα Νιρβαμή." Νουμᾶς, 19 Φεβρ. 1906. Ξανατ. στὴ Νέα Ἑστία, 1 Μαΐου 1958, σελ. 690–91. (Κ 739)

Voskopoula: Ἡ Βοσκοπούλα. Κριτικὴ ἔκδοση Στυλ. Ἀλεξίου. Ἡράκλειον 1963.

Vrettakos: Βρεττάκου, Ν. Νίκος Καζαντζάκης. Ἡ ἀγωνία του καὶ τὸ ἔργο του. 1957.

Weinreich: Weinreich, Uriel. *Languages in Contact.* New York 1953.

Xenopoulos: Ξενοπούλου, Γ. "Σκιαμαχία." Ἀθῆναι, 25 Ἰουν. 1910. Ξανατ. στὴ Νέα Ἑστία, Ὀκτ. 1958, σελ. 1564–65. (Κ 799)

Yialourakis: Γιαλουράκη, Μ. " Ὁ Καζαντζάκης μοῦ εἶπε." Καινούρια Ἐποχή, Φθινόπωρο 1958, σελ. 154–62.

Zografou: Ζωγράφου, Λιλῆς. Νίκος Καζαντζάκης: ἕνας τραγικός. 1960.

Index